MEMORIES OF SILK AND STRAW

KODANSHA INTERNATIONAL
Tokyo, New York, and San Francisco

MEMORIES
OF
SILK AND STRAW

A Self-Portrait of Small-Town Japan

Dr. Junichi Saga

Translated by Garry O. Evans
Illustrated by Dr. Susumu Saga

DS
897
.T8
S34
1987

Publication of this book was assisted by a grant from Dr. Nobuo Otsuka.

Permission to reproduce the photographs on pages 97 and 213 was received from Mainichi Shinbunsha.

Distributed in the United States by Kodansha International/USA Ltd., through Harper & Row, Publishers, Inc., 10 East 53rd Street, New York, New York 10022. Published by Kodansha International Ltd., 2-2, Otowa 1-chome, Bunkyo-ku, Tokyo 112, and Kodansha International/USA Ltd., with offices at 10 East 53rd Street, New York, New York 10022 and The Hearst Building, 5 Third Street, Suite 400, San Francisco, California 94103. Copyright © 1987 by Kodansha International Ltd. All rights reserved. Printed in Japan.

LCC 86-45724
ISBN 0-87011-792-0 (U.S.)
ISBN 4-7700-1292-6 (Japan)

First edition, 1987

CONTENTS

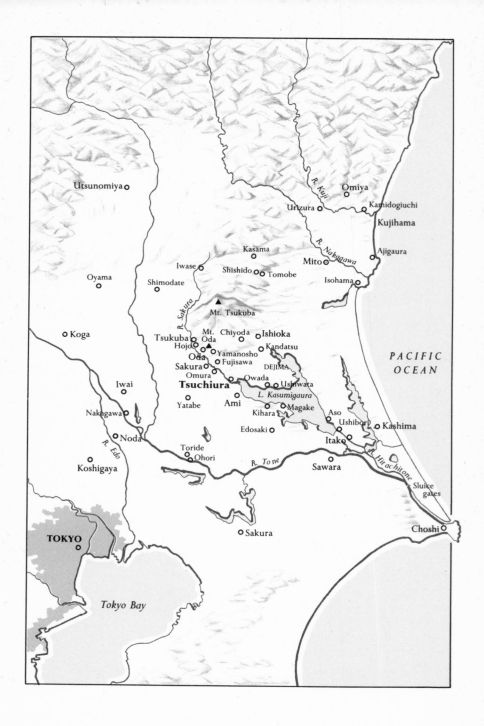

PREFACE

If I had to be ill in Japan, I think I would try to have my illness in Tsuchiura where I could be treated by Dr. Saga. Anyone who inspires in old
people of all walks of life the sort of warmth of rapport that prompted
these reminiscences, anyone with his intensity of curiosity about people,
about the world and its past, must surely be a splendid doctor.

He has certainly produced a splendid book. Its evocation of the Japan
of the first quarter of this century is not rivaled by anything else I have
come across. There are, to be sure, plenty of descriptions of grinding
rural poverty. This was the time—and Dr. Saga's Ibaragi the place—of
Nagatsuka's novel, *The Earth*, which attracted a great deal of attention
when it was serialized in 1910, just about the time when the conscience
of the urban intellectuals was being stirred by their uneasy awareness of
the extremes of riches and poverty that their society contained. But neither in Nagatsuka's somewhat stereotyped characters, nor in the lively
yet still very external pictures given us by foreign observers such as
Isabella Bird or, a generation later, Robertson Scott, do we get, as we get
from the people who sat down to reminisce with Dr. Saga, not only vivid
detail of time and place, not only colorful incident and anecdote, but a
sense of what it must have *felt* like to be growing up on the shores of Lake
Kasumigaura three-quarters of a century ago.

Memories of Silk and Straw invites comparison with Blythe's *Akenfield* or
Hareven and Langenbach's *Amoskeag*. But I suspect, for a young Japanese
reader of today, the world it describes will seem more alien, more completely a vanished world, than the Norfolk or New England of those books
seem to contemporary young British or American readers. The pace of
change has been so rapid, the onset of affluence has been compounded by
so much more intense an influence from foreign values. The lordly Colonel Sempill who came to Tsuchiura to instruct Japan's fledgling fliers
after the First World War, however great his role in the diffusion of
technology, probably had minimal effect as an agent of cultural transmis-
sion, even on Mrs. Okui who nearly went back to England with him. The

occupation by the American army, the vastly increased traffic of students and businessmen, the flood of foreigners among the millions visiting the Science Exhibition at Japan's first great Science City, Tsukuba—above all, the television and the magazines which people can now afford to buy—have vastly widened and internationalized the world in which the modern inhabitants of Ibaragi live.

But it is economic growth and today's level of relative affluence that set the world of silk and straw so much apart from our world of polyester and plastics. Poverty is the dominant, recurring theme of these memories of a rural Japan where even horses and carts were a rarity and most goods were transported to the rivers, and increasingly the railway stations, on the backs of ponies or of men and women. The boys who shuttled back and forth to Tokyo with hundred-pound packs of eggs on their backs, the rice miller's daughter heaving her forty-pound sacks at the age of ten, did so on a diet of which the best that could be said was that most families could afford barley if they couldn't manage rice, and very few were reduced to eating millet. "If you said that someone had 'nothing,' you really meant that they owned not a thing in the world." And the number of people who in this way survived, or failed to survive, on the fringes of society was far from small.

But the majority who did have something and thriftily used everything they had—used every scrap of straw, redyed their clothing, reversed it, patched it—did a lot better than merely survive. There is nostalgia here too—for idle days spent swimming in the lake or messing about in boats, for leisurely New Year festivals, for the days when the friendly blacksmith had time to put iron hoops around a child's much-prized competition top, for the top-of-the-world sense of being the center of attention in a draper's shop, for the excitement of a Sunday expedition across the valley to see the trains go by. And there is a sense of fun. How Dr. Saga's informants enjoy themselves when they describe the foibles of miserly shopkeepers, the vanities of the landlord's agents who drove back from the harvest settlement with their carts deliberately uncovered for maximum display of the gifts they'd received, the incompetent cunning of the poultryman who stuffed his chickens with makeweight sweet potatoes, the innocence—her own innocence—of the geisha at her first Western meal, too timid to protest when the waiter took away her plate before she had finished. And yet one often feels that perhaps it was not always quite so funny at the time. "Decent poverty" in Ibaragi eighty years ago does seem to have had a bit less cakes and ale to it than the decent poverty of rural England as described in *Cider with Rosie* or *Lark Rise to Candleford*. It was a tough world. One of Dr. Saga's old ladies survived to tell him all the technical details of girl infanticide only because the midwife made a botch of dispatching her the first time and was superstitious about having a second go.

Within these stories of hard times one can also find, though, a good many glimpses of what it was that carried Japan from indigence then to affluence now. And I do not mean the coming of the first planes to the naval training base, nor even the coming of the trains, so much as the level of ingenuity and skill and power of organization with which Japanese society around the turn of the century utilized to the full the natural and human resources that were available to it. At the beginning of the 1920s there were already government agencies organizing the stocking of Lake Kasumigaura with red dace. Small fishing companies could book railway transport to the other end of Japan with enough precision to have the train met and their fish redoused with cold water at points on the way. The exacting level of skill required of the seamstresses; the minute complexity of the knowledge fishermen had of their fish, of the way to catch them, and of the manifold techniques used for turning them into marketable commodities; the single-minded self-discipline of the farmers, fitting annual cycles of consumption to seasonal cycles of production; the determination, however reluctant, to send off to school the child whose pair of hands was desperately needed at home—these are the characteristics, recycled into quality circles on production lines and in software houses, that lie behind the fifty-billion-dollar trade surplus of today.

Not to forget, also, another factor, the capacity for sophisticated social organization based on a sensitivity to the needs and feelings of others which goes a bit beyond "live and let live" to the realm of "help and be helped." Even the gangsters had an elaborate etiquette to enforce their own aberrant ethical code, and a pride in spectacular displays of impulsive generosity to underpin it. The tofu makers never sought the custom of anyone who lived less than seven doors away from a rival tofu maker (*how*, one wonders, could they ever have agreed on seven?). The rice dealer who was compassionate about the bills of the unfortunate found the rice he had cast on the waters returned in full measure when his house was ruined by floods. The people of Ibaragi do not have a reputation for gentleness. Nearly a millennium ago the region produced more than its fair share of the rude warriors who destroyed the power—and with it the civilized culture—of the Kyoto aristocracy. It produced the most bellicosely intransigent Confucian scholars in the mid-nineteenth century, and the most murderously fanatical right-wing agrarian radicals in the 1930s. But hotness of blood is supposed to be related to warmness of heart. And the capacity for social solidarity—for organized social solidarity—is not something they lack.

So this is a book to savor, and a book to learn from. We should all be grateful to Dr. Saga for the days he went wandering with his tape recorder. And we should all be grateful to Garry Evans, too, for his wonderfully vivid and readable translation.

Ronald Dore
London, 1986

INTRODUCTION

When he was in his sixties, my father decided to take up painting. His hope was to be able to accurately recreate in his pictures how Tsuchiura, his birthplace, had looked thirty, forty, and fifty years ago. Around the same time I began the complementary task of trying to recreate what had lain beneath the surface of the street scenes my father had painted. I talked to hundreds of old people in the town, and in their reminiscences and stories a vivid mosaic of everyday life in Tsuchiura before the war began to emerge. The customs, superstitions, and experiences they recalled for me had existed in Japan for many hundreds of years, but in the mad rush of change during the last four decades, they have almost disappeared without trace.

Every day, after finishing work in my clinic, I would go out on foot around the town visiting one elderly person after another, a portable tape recorder in my medical bag. The people I talked to came from all walks of life: day laborers, tradesmen, farmers, fishermen, *yakuza* (gangsters), and geisha. Both in their attitudes and in the experiences they had undergone, they provided the sole surviving links with the feudal period which ended with the overthrow of the last shogun in 1868.

Only forty or fifty years ago, poverty was a real and widespread fact of life here. In the memories of the old people in this book lies the story of the hardships Japan had to go through to reach its present position as an economic superpower. But amid all the poverty and unhappiness of those days, there also existed a strange kind of serenity which today seems to have been lost entirely.

Throughout the town there were countless communal wells where the women of the neighborhood would gather for a good gossip and where the children could play, their voices ringing through the narrow side streets. During the annual festivals, the whole town, young and old alike, would pour out onto the streets in a happy throng; dozens of stalls selling food and drink would be set up in every alley; and the sound of wooden clogs clopping along the paving stones would echo through the town until late into the night. There was a spirit of togetherness in Tsuchiura then, a true sense of community.

But in the space of less than half a century everything has altered utterly, beyond recognition. The long streets of low timber buildings and the old-fashioned open-fronted shops, little changed since the seventeenth century, have been transformed into stark concrete office buildings and apartment blocks. Most of the rivers have been filled in and turned into highways. The small local festivals have mostly died out and the little wayside shrines have been abandoned. People have become much wealthier, of course, but the very foundation stones that produced the wealth in the first place have been knocked away. The whole face of the town has been remodeled. And not only the face: the residents' life-style and even their ways of thinking have been revolutionized, for good or for bad.

The only place this other wealth—of experience—could still be found was deep in the memories of people who, born in the early years of this century, had both seen the old Japan and lived through all these changes. My hope was that by recording their memories for posterity, the gap in perception and experience between the traditional Japan of past centuries and the Japan of today might be closed just a fraction.

Sadly, in only the few years that have passed since they told me their stories, a number of the people have died. Perhaps the most remarkable storyteller was Fukusaburo Takagi. I visited him regularly for almost eight years to record his reminiscences. By the end he had become so weak that he was unable to eat, but he stubbornly refused to go into hospital. He was a patient of mine and I went to see him almost every day; I began to realize that telling me stories of the old days had become the only joy left for him in life. "Outcasts," translated here, was the last of almost a hundred episodes he remembered for me. He died two days later.

Tsuchiura is a small, very unremarkable town. Towns like it can be found throughout Japan. In countless other areas there must have been thousands of people who lived and thought in a way very similar to that described in this book. They, too, will have seen change arrive with the same frightening force. It would not, then, be an exaggeration to say that the Tsuchiura depicted here in the stories of about sixty old men and women and in my father's drawings is symbolic of all that Japan has experienced during the past century. However, the life of a community is also undeniably affected by its own particular geography and history, so while the everyday happenings described here are similar to what took place in the rest of the country, they are to some extent colored by the character of the locality in which they occurred. Thus, a brief description of Tsuchiura and its surroundings is called for.

Tsuchiura is forty miles, or an hour's train ride, northeast of Tokyo. Its present population is approximately 110,000. Records show that the population grew from 5,000 at the beginning of the nineteenth century to 14,000 by the 1870s, but sixty years later, in 1935, it was still no more than 19,000.

Five miles to the west of Tsuchiura is Tsukuba Science City. Into what had formerly been an area of low hills, dense pine forest, and tiny villages was transplanted a mammoth technopolis, housing two universities and no less than forty-five high-technology research institutes. Some fifteen miles to the northwest of Tsuchiura stands Mt. Tsukuba. The town is bordered on the east by Lake Kasumigaura, the second largest freshwater lake in Japan. Twenty thousand years ago the lake was part of the sea, which formed an inlet reaching as far as the foot of Mt. Tsukuba. For the last two or three hundred years, all the villages around the lake have been prey to frequent and severe floods, for which the shogunal government in the seventeenth century is directly to blame. The River Tone, the third longest river in Japan, originally emptied into Edo Bay, but since this meant that Edo (present-day Tokyo) itself was often hit by floods, the government decided to change the course of the river so that it flowed out to sea some forty-five miles to the east. The work of rechanneling the river took more than sixty years to complete and succeeded in saving Edo from any further flooding. The redirected river, however, began to cause catastrophic floods in the area around Tsuchiura. In addition, the large quantities of sand and mud brought down by the River Tone from its upper reaches finally blocked off the main waterway joining Lake Kasumigaura to the sea, and rapidly turned it into a freshwater lake. A narrow channel still linked one part of the lake to the open sea, and, because of this, saltwater fish such as smelt could still be caught there in fair numbers until quite recently. However, in 1973, the sluice gates between the River Hitachitone and the sea were closed so that salt water could no longer flow into the lake.

Lake Kasumigaura is now divided from the sea by a long, narrow stretch of land, near the southern tip of which stand two ancient "grand shrines," Kashima and Katori. When the hierarchy of Shinto shrines was first regulated more than a thousand years ago, only one other shrine in the whole of Japan (at Ise) was designated a grand shrine, the highest rank. Kashima is dedicated to the god Takemiikazuchino, who in the *Kojiki*, Japan's oldest mythological and historical chronicle, is described as being the bravest of the gods.

All the evidence points to the fact that powerful rulers, with close connections to the imperial court, lived in this area from earliest times. The region also had a reputation in the Nara (646–794) and Heian (794–1185) periods for producing particularly fierce and loyal warriors. The province of Hitachi, in which Tsuchiura was situated, played an important political role during the first thousand years of recorded Japanese history. Why, then, did this once proud province disappear from the center stage of Japanese history and turn into an agricultural backwater? The answer lies in the events of the Tokugawa period (1600–1868). To ensure the survival of their regime, the Tokugawa shoguns drove the most powerful warlords as far away from Edo as possible. One of the strongest anti-Tokugawa clans in the vicinity of Edo was the Satake family, based in

Tsuchiura, and they were forcibly removed to Akita, on the very northern tip of the main island of Japan; their domain was then given to pro-shogunate clans that had no connection whatsoever with the area.

For much of the Tokugawa period the domain was ruled over by the Tsuchiyas, an illustrious clan. Tsuchiya lords played a significant part in the politics of the shogunate throughout the Tokugawa period: the clan had a hereditary seat on the shogunal government council, and several members of the family served as chief minister to the shogun. As a result, the clan was concerned exclusively with central politics, and it regarded its domain purely as a source of revenue. The fact that, throughout the almost three hundred years of the Tokugawa period, Tsuchiura saw no notable cultural development or artistic achievements testifies to the lack of interest shown by the Tsuchiyas in their lands.

In 1868 the Tokugawa shogunate was overthrown and the new Meiji government set about the task of building Japan into a modern, Western-ized nation. The Tsuchiura area had no part in influencing the social revolution that took place, however, merely accepting the changes passively. Many of the samurai left and the castle fell into ruins. Newly rich merchants built themselves splendid mansions and storehouses. With the capital they accumulated, they bought up vast tracts of land and then rented the same land back to the peasants in return for a large percentage of the crop.

The greed of these people is perhaps best demonstrated by a story concerning the tenements built by many of the landowners. Before the war, the main streets of Tsuchiura contained many impressive-looking houses and fine shops, but the back alleys, running behind the major thoroughfares, were full of rows of mean, cramped tenements. Most of these terraces were set up by wealthy landowners for one specific purpose: to obtain a ready supply of fertilizer for their fields. Night soil was the cheapest and simplest fertilizer, and a landowner who built a tenement could put the excrement produced by its inhabitants to good use.

Rural farmers could afford to eat only things like potatoes and millet which were low in nutrients, so their excrement was not particularly useful as a fertilizer. The residents of the terraces were themselves extremely poor but even they ate more nutritious food than the peasants, and their night soil was that much more effective. The landlord had his employees regularly collect the stuff from the terraces; it was then taken out into the countryside and stored in giant vats in every hamlet. The tenant farmers were then charged for using it on their fields. These vats of night soil could be a hazard, though: several people have told me that occasionally a villager would get blind drunk and end up falling headfirst into one. There are better ways of dying, surely!

In addition to the merchants and poor laborers, a number of professional men—doctors, lawyers, priests, and teachers—lived in the town, but since they had little interest in local affairs they hardly influenced the community at all. Accordingly, culture and the arts in Tsuchiura remained at a comparatively low level, and few public amenities of any note were built.

In contrast to the lack of intellectual activity in the town, however, more "vulgar" amusements, particularly the red-light districts, flourished. In the Tokugawa period Tsuchiura, being a post town on one of the main highways to the north, had been crowded with taverns and lodging inns, where the maids doubled as low-class prostitutes. These inns were still in existence, albeit on a rather subdued scale, well into this century, but the arrival of the naval air squadron changed the situation completely. In the 1920s the Japanese navy established a pilot-training school on the shore of Lake Kasumigaura, about seven miles south of Tsuchiura. The Kasumigaura Naval Air Squadron, as it was known, went on to become the largest air base in Japan and achieved fame (or notoriety) as the place where the kamikaze pilots were trained. The base had a profound effect on Tsuchiura's economy and society and in particular brought great prosperity to the red-light districts. As a result, the authorities decided that, in order to stop the men running wild in the town, they should move all the brothels and geisha houses to a single large amusement quarter on the southern outskirts of Tsuchiura.

Girls from all over Japan poured into the town, and in its heyday the district was populated by more than eighty geisha and a hundred prostitutes for the lower ranks. This book contains stories by several women in their seventies and eighties who before the war served some of the highest-ranking officers in the land. But at the end of the war, the base was closed down, the employees of the amusement quarter moved away, and Tsuchiura once more became a dull country town.

The rural areas around Tsuchiura have become prosperous in the last twenty or thirty years, but not all their problems have disappeared. The country folk remain very wary of strangers and still stick stubbornly to many of their old ways and customs. In a sense, though, they have perhaps been able to preserve something of their own identity only by behaving so defensively. There does remain the faint shadow of a lost age in their way of life.

This book was first published in 1981 under the title *Tsuchiura no sato* (My Hometown, Tsuchiura). The reason I decided to have it translated into English was that it seemed to me the stories revealed something about modern Japan very little understood by the rest of the world, and perhaps not even by the Japanese themselves. Namely, that the Japan which now prides itself on being an advanced, high-technology nation had, until only recently, a very different type of society; and that indeed it was this very society, backward though it may have been, which created the basis for what Japan has become today.

The English translation is due to the remarkable efforts of Garry Evans, a graduate in Japanese studies from Cambridge University. The book presented a number of special problems for a translator. All the stories were in the local dialect, for example, making the translation of the Japanese—no easy task, in any case—doubly difficult. I was genuinely impressed by Garry's knowledge and his enthusiasm for the task. I would like to express my sincerest gratitude to him.

I would also like to thank Mr. Yasuhiko Doi, editorial writer for the *Sankei Shinbun*, who gave me invaluable help with questions arising from the translation and publication of the book. Without him, *Memories of Silk and Straw* could never been published. My thanks go, too, to Mr. Alan Pinnel, first secretary at the British Embassy in Tokyo, Mr. Stephen Shaw, senior editor of Kodansha International, Professor Kazuhiko Hirose of Takushoku University, and Mr. Takashi Iwasaki.

Finally, a special word of gratitude is due Dr. Nobuo Otsuka of the Ome Keiyu Hospital for his encouragement and, in particular, his financial support of this project.

Junichi Saga
Tsuchiura, 1986

Note on currency:
In 1917 one yen (100 sen) = 0.5 U.S. dollars

AROUND
THE TOWN

Now Tsuchiura's main street

The Fudo Terrace

Mr. Ryutaro Terauchi (1905–)

In Tajuku, next to the Fudo Terrace, there was a rice shop called "Hirose's" that my grandfather owned. I was adopted by him at the age of fifteen and went to work in his shop as an apprentice. I stayed there until I was twenty, so got to know the area fairly well.

The people living in the terrace were all terribly poor. Working in the rice shop, you see, I knew just how hard things were for them. A wife would wait till her husband brought home the day's wages of maybe forty or fifty sen and only then—though it might already be late in the evening—could she go out and buy some rice. If she could afford it she'd buy five pounds, but more likely she'd only have enough money for three or four. I doubt if there was a single household in the terrace that could afford as much as ten pounds of rice at a time. We couldn't keep the shop open all night, though, and often in the early hours of the morning, when we were closed, someone would come knocking on the shutters calling out, "My family's hungry—sell me some rice."

When it rained hard, the men couldn't find any work and no money came in, which usually meant an empty rice bowl. No doubt some people will say we should've let them have a bit on credit when they needed it. But if we'd started doing that, there'd have been no end to it: there were dozens of poor families in the Fudo Terrace and also in the Nakasei Terrace, the one next to it along the same tiny back street, and if all these people had been given rice on credit, it would've been the shopkeeper who went bankrupt. So no one was given anything on tick. The terrace folk understood this, and nobody ever came along in floods of tears begging for help. When all their money had run out, they managed somehow to find a way of filling their bellies, either by pawning some of their stuff or borrowing small amounts of food from their neighbors.

The item you could hock most easily was a *hanten*, a short coat printed with the trademark of one of the town's large shops. However old and tatty the *hanten* was, the pawnbroker would happily advance you money against it. The reason for this was that, no matter how badly worn the

A typical back alley

coat might be, the shop that had had it made could always be relied on to buy it back. There was a well-known story behind this. A man, who'd been given a *hanten* by a large grocery store when he worked on the building of their warehouse, had later pawned the coat but hadn't been able to pay back the loan. His pawnbroker put the dirty old thing up on a pole and hung it out over the street. Every time the wind blew, the *hanten*, with the name of the shop printed on it, flapped in the breeze and after a few months it began to tear. This didn't do the store's reputation any good, so the owner got one of his clerks to hurry out and reclaim it. All the large shops took considerable pride in their own *hanten*, you see, so pawnbrokers were only too pleased to take them as security for loans.

But if the rain continued for more than a few days, there'd be nothing left to hock and people would be reduced to eating rice gruel. Families that didn't even have any gruel would eat steamed barley, with maybe just a little soy sauce poured over it. In the town, though, no one made do with millet, however hungry they were. It takes a bit of an effort to imagine now, but it was quite common to go without food at all for a couple of days, and you'd have considered yourself lucky to have proper rice cakes more than once or twice a year.

Once a year, in fact, the terrace people were given what they called "dung cakes." A local farmer used regularly to bring along a cart and buy up all the night soil from the communal toilet; then, at the end of the year, he'd take them some of the special rice used for making rice cakes to thank them for the year's supply of "dung." Everyone flocked out into the alley, and the rice was pounded with a pestle and mortar borrowed for the occasion. It was pretty lively. "You can see 'business' has been good this year—there are plenty of dung cakes," we'd joke to each other. There was a great din of excited voices as the rice was worked over. The children couldn't wait for the cakes to be finished and would sneak up to the bowl and snatch handfuls of the half-ready stuff. I remember them running up and down the alley in great high spirits—you could really sense

Pestle and mortar

that New Year was coming. It was good to see everyone having such fun.

There were no cooking ranges inside the terrace houses, so everybody had to do their cooking out in the street under the eaves. Those that didn't have a portable clay stove would build themselves a makeshift one out of tin, waving a fan at it to keep it alight.

Since every family did its cooking on the front doorstep, the people in the terrace all knew what everyone else was having for supper that night. No one had enough money to buy anything particularly fancy, but occasionally someone was given something as a present and this would always be shared out among the neighbors.

None of the houses had rain shutters either, so with only paper-covered sliding doors to protect them from the elements it was obviously bitterly cold in winter. The windows and doors were all badly fitting and the wind blew in through the gaps. The roof was thatched with twigs, and as the tenants didn't pay much rent, the landlord never bothered to mend it when it leaked. I really don't know how anyone managed to live in a place like that. I suppose they just had nowhere else to go and, after all, as they say, "Home is home." Everyone was poor together, we all helped each other out and got on well together. Perhaps in many ways this sort of life-style's better than having to live in a cold, impersonal block of flats.

The Village Blacksmith

Mr. Horokichi Numajiri (1888–1983)

My grandfather was an agricultural blacksmith. He rented a shop on the main street in Omura where he made and mended hoes, rakes, and other farm tools. All farmers in those days plowed by hand and, after many years of use, these implements got worn down. A farm tool could be mended only by grafting a new piece of metal onto the worn part of its blade. Grandfather must have been pretty good at his trade because people from as far away as Oda used to bring him their old sickles and hoes, wrapped up in carrying cloths.

The furnace for firing the iron was fueled by charcoal; Grandfather always insisted that only pinewood charcoal was good enough. The bellows was operated with your right foot and right hand: a length of string was tied to your big toe and this you pulled in alternation with another piece of string held in your hand. The other hand was then free to hold down and turn the piece of iron you were working on. At the same time, another blacksmith would hammer away at the red-hot iron, flattening and beating it out.

Eventually, when my grandfather was so old he could mend no more than a couple of hoes a day, he decided it was time to retire. He was an excellent blacksmith, though, and his work was sorely missed.

I was about seven when the war in China started in 1896. Four or five men from the village went off to serve in the army, and I remember everyone went down to the banks of the River Sakura to see them off. Back then, however, there was no bridge across and the men had to use the ferry. Getting horses across was more of a problem: the ferry was too small, so they were made to splash down into the river and wade to the other bank.

There were almost no carts on the roads in those days: it was only after the war with Russia in 1904 that handcarts and horse-drawn vehicles first appeared on the main roads leading into Tsuchiura. It was about that time, too, that Suijin Bridge was built across the Sakura.

There were about thirty families living in our village then; of these maybe ten owned their own horse. At the back of the house belonging to the village headman was a piece of ground we called the "repair yard," and at a certain time each year the villagers brought their horses here and a vet, paid for by all the villagers, would come along and clip the horses' hooves. Alongside the "repair yard" was a building where the old people of the village used to meet; they'd pray there and then chat together over a cup of green tea.

In Oshita, one of the staging posts along the highway, there used to be a tea house. The place today is just waste ground where buses are parked, but back then we had a small one-story building with three whores working in it. It was a long trip into Tsuchiura then, made even more difficult because there weren't any bridges across the river, so all the young men from the surrounding countryside used to come to this house for a bit of fun. But it's become much easier to travel into town now, and the tea house, along with much of everything else, has disappeared.

My father died suddenly, mainly from overwork, when I was seven, and from then on, young as I was, I had to go out into the fields and help my mother. Since we were tenants and didn't have any land of our own, there was no alternative. The annual rent for land that yielded about twenty-four sacks of rice per acre was twelve sacks, so it was damned hard work for tenant farmers to make a living. Still, there were so many people who wanted to rent a field or two that the landlord could tell you, "If you think the rent's too high, you can always leave"; you had no choice—you put up with the conditions and got on with working the land as hard as you could.

If the weather throughout the summer had been bad, some of the tenants would be forced to go along and beg him, with tears in their eyes, to reduce the rice rent a bit. And like as not the reply would be: "If you can't afford to pay, you'll just have to get off the land." In bad years you had no choice but to give the landlord most of your harvest, though this was really meant to feed your own family.

Threshing rice

Some of the landlords were so plain cruel and heartless that their tenants were driven to murdering them. The villagers in those days used to make a type of firework called a "lightning," which was let off as part of the celebrations during festivals. The firework was made by putting gunpowder into a wooden tube, and fixing a bamboo hoop firmly around the end to stop it splitting. One landlord, apparently, was killed by a "lightning" that someone threw into the room where he was sleeping. Another was beaten to death up in the mountains. These things all happened a long time ago, of course.

Once you'd paid in the rice rent, even in a good year you were lucky if you had enough left over to keep your family going for as much as six months. Rice for the rest of the year had to be bought with extra income from doing casual work, in the gravel pits or with a road-mending gang.

Many houses in our village didn't have their own bath. People without baths would wash at home in a tub of cold water most days, and then once every week or so they'd go along and use a neighbor's. Yes, I suppose that out of the thirty or so houses in the village, only five or six had their own baths. I don't know about other villages, but in our area the problem was that, even if you could put up the money for a proper wooden tub, there just wasn't enough fuel available to heat the water. If we'd had some woodland of our own, we could have cut down some trees and used the timber for fuel; around here, though, trespassing in the landlord's woods in the mountains was forbidden, and even collecting fallen leaves wasn't permitted. We certainly couldn't afford to buy firewood, not even for cooking, and instead we had to burn straw, usually bundles of rice straw. But we could never get hold of enough of it, so we used to go and cut dead reeds on the riverbank and use those too. And since there would never have been enough fuel to heat a bath as well, most families were left without one.

When it rained, the farmers in those days used to wear straw raincoats and bamboo hats. During the hottest months of the year we wore *himino*, short coats made of thin straw, used for keeping the sun off. The *himino* let the air circulate around your body and kept you surprisingly cool. They were worn by peasants in this area until as late as the 1950s.

Because everyone was so hard up around here, "thinning out" the newborn was quite widely practiced. The number of children killed just depended, I'm told, on how strict the local policeman was. An officious and bloody-minded cop might well notice that a woman, whom he'd previously seen several months pregnant, no longer was, but there weren't any new babies around. If he'd started poking around for reasons, it would have caused all sorts of trouble for the villagers. So with this sort of man in the neighborhood there was nothing for it but to let an unwanted baby live. On the other hand, if a slack new policeman was appointed to the area, the "thinning out" rate would rapidly increase. The situation was so bad that the number of kids in each grade of the primary school varied a good deal, depending on who'd been the local constable at the time they were born.

You know, I remember when I was at primary school we used to use a wick dipped in kerosene for light. Some families used proper oil lamps, but more common were simple wicks because they needed a lot less oil. My family sometimes couldn't even afford the kerosene for a wick; so to provide the light to do my homework by, I often had to go out into the fields and collect fireflies, which I put in a paper bag. In those days, near the paddy fields, there were an awful lot of fireflies, so many in fact you could feel them brushing against your face as you walked along. If you put them into a bag they gave off a palish glow. I'd hold the bag near my exercise book, and it would give off just about enough light for me to practice writing my Chinese characters.

The Carter

Mr. Tamotsu Kimura (1902–1980)

I was born in Tsukiji-machi near the River Tsukiji. The people in our terrace were all dirt poor. A number of the houses along the river were of reasonable quality with thatched roofs, but the people who lived in them were almost all day laborers, plus a handful of carpenters and plasterers. Most of the men got paid only about forty or fifty sen a day, and had to support a whole family on that. People nowadays just couldn't imagine how hard life was back then. When you think that a bowl of noodles cost three sen and a haircut fifteen, you can understand how low the wages were.

My father ran a poultry business. He used to buy chickens and eggs from farmers and then sell them to shops like "Tochigiya." To get the birds to weigh as much as possible before selling them, he used to stuff them with sweet potatoes to make their stomachs swell up; but the potatoes got stuck in the chicken's throat, so he had to pour water into its mouth and then blow into its beak to make the potato go down. The bird would then swallow the thing with a look of surprise on its face. My father did a bit of farming as well, to help make ends meet.

When I was nineteen, my father died very suddenly from some infection. The work I was then doing as a bicycle repairer didn't pay enough for me to support my mother and all my brothers and sisters, so I got a job with Marugo Transportation, which had a depot next to the railway station. As I remember, the biggest transport firm in Tsuchiura at that time was Marutsu and there were three other firms—Kakutama, Marusa, and Marugo—in the same business. All transportation was by horse and cart, of course. There weren't any trucks around at all.

To become a carter, you had to provide all the necessary equipment yourself. You had to buy your own horse, and have a cart built. If you couldn't afford a horse, the only thing was to become an ordinary porter and carry stuff around on your back. Some people, known as *hikiko*, hired a horse and wagon from the company but they only took forty percent of the payment for a job—the rest went to the employer.

When I was twenty I was called up into the Utsunomiya Regiment for two years, but as soon as I got back from military service I bought a horse and cart. Having your own horse involved an awful lot of hard work. I was living in a terrace house at the time, and of course I had to rent a stable with a shed for my cart as well. And a horse, unlike a motorcar, is a living creature—if you don't make a fuss of it all the time, it'll go sick on you. Every evening, come rain or come shine, after getting home from the day's work, I had to fill a tub of hot water and wash it. After it had worked hard for me all day, pulling a cart fully loaded with maybe thirty-two sacks of rice, if I didn't at least do this much to look after the animal, it would've refused to do what I told it. I could carry thirty-two sacks when I was delivering in the town, but if I had to go up the steep hills at Manabe or Takatsu, about twenty was all the horse could manage.

In the morning it was fed as soon as I got up, before I even had my own breakfast. I generally gave it straw, cut up and mixed with either rice or wheat bran. Horses are funny creatures—if they don't fancy what you're feeding them, they won't so much as look at the food; they can get mean and start lashing out, kicking at the stable walls. And if ever a tiny spot of its piss was left in the straw, the thing wouldn't touch it, however hungry it was. But I reckon if you take good care of a horse and show it affection, it can understand you better than any human. My eldest son, when he'd been scolded by me and told to get out of the house, would often run out to the stable and lie under its stomach, crying, and the animal would nuzzle up against him, almost as if it was trying to comfort him.

Carters in those days wore *hanten* and either a straw hat or a headband; in the summer, some wore just a loincloth, but most had breeches. None of us ever wore shoes. And when it rained we used to put on straw coats. I covered an area in a radius of about twenty-five miles around Tsuchiura and it wasn't unusual to have to go as far as Mito. There was a carters' inn in Mito near the lake where they'd put up the horse for the night as well.

Porters, with horse and cart

In those days none of the roads were surfaced and, whenever it rained, they weren't much better than paddy fields; if you were pulling a heavy load it wasn't at all easy to keep moving. And there are plenty of hills in this area: on the way to Kandatsu, for example, you had to go up and down three or four steep ones. From Manabe to Ishioka there must have been at least twelve hills. Along that road, though, there were several watering places where you could rest the horse. At midday, I'd stop at one of these and have my lunch. I carried the horse's feed in the cart, so it got its bran mix in a bucket.

Horses are pretty sharp, you know: after they've done deliveries around the streets for a few months, they get to know what's sold in each shop. My horse would always stop suddenly each time it got to Isamu Ono's place in Sakura-machi and, however much I hit it, it wouldn't budge: it knew he sold carrots. As soon as I fed it one, it'd be in a good mood again and would walk on quite happily. Then, on hot days, it liked a drop of beer as well: whenever it was plodding along wearily I'd stop somewhere and buy a bottle. When I poured the beer into its mouth, the thing would stretch its neck up high and gulp it down as if it was loving every drop. And if I then rested it for a few minutes it would soon be its old self again.

What did make me angry was when I'd fussed over a horse but it didn't take a liking to me and wouldn't do as it was told. I'd try thrashing and whipping it, and would end up swearing helplessly . . . "You miserable bastard," I'd shout at it. This sort of language would get to be a habit, and I'd find myself swearing at my children in the same way. After a while I'd begin to hear that the woman next door had been saying, "What a horrible man that Mr. Kimura is." But with most horses, as long as you were kind to them, they'd obey you OK, and I could get on with my work quite easily.

Racehorses are said to be at their best around three or four years old, but horses that young are useless for putting in harness; they're still too frisky. Any horse more than five or six years old can be trained, provided it's healthy, but by the time it reaches seven or eight it becomes much easier to handle.

I had the horse's shoes changed once a month. There was a blacksmith called Kubota in Takatsu and another, Mr. Otsu, near the railway crossing in Manabe; both of them did a good trade. It took the blacksmith half a day to shoe all four feet. The hooves were cut with a thin, sharp blade and reshaped, then the shoes were put on and made to fit the foot. I used to squat on the floor and watch. The packsaddle also had to be mended once a year when it began to lose its shape and hurt the horse's back. If the horse got saddle sores it couldn't work, so as soon as the saddle started looking tatty, I took it to be mended; there was a saddler's in Omachi. The cart wouldn't last more than five years either. After all, it was used every single day and always weighed down with heavy loads. If you didn't look after it properly, it would start to creak and rattle in no time at all. Persimmon juice was painted on all over to stop the wood rotting, but the protection from this only lasted several years.

So this is how a carter lived. You could never hope to make much money in our line of work. They used to say that "a carter's eaten out of house and home by his horse." You had to spend all your money on the horse and cart and, once you'd fed your family as well, there was never anything left over.

But I suppose the reason I never packed it in was that I was too fond of my horses. I remember one evening I got very drunk on *shochu* and fell asleep splayed out in the back of the cart. The horse managed to find its own way home and, outside the house, it neighed to let everyone know it was back. I could swear they understand some things just as well as we do.

How the Wealthy Amused Themselves

Mrs. Iku Miyazaki (1896–1982)

There are still plenty of rich people around nowadays, but fifty years ago they behaved far more extravagantly than the wealthy of today. Let me give you just one example. A good patron of mine when I was a geisha, a man called Gihei Okamoto, used to visit a friend of his once or twice a year, a Mr. Asano, who lived in the Fukagawa area of Tokyo. He never made the trip alone, though: he always took a couple of clerks, three or four shop boys, and five or six of us geisha with him. Okamoto's firm sold fertilizers, coal, and gravel, and also had interests in shipping. Asano owned the Joban Colliery, and the two had become close friends through their business association.

Once he'd fixed the date for his trip to Tokyo, Okamoto would buy each of the geisha a new set of kimono. All the geisha going with him were given a complete outfit—new kimono, sash, and everything else right down to their footwear. For example, if the visit was in summer, we might be given a kimono of figured cloth with a quail design on a gray background, a half-coat of dappled cloth, a light gray sash with gold stitching, and a crepe *obi-age* pad with a pattern of cherry blossoms on it. And different outfits had to be made to suit the personal tastes of those coming on the trip. When the clothes were ready, we'd go along to Okamoto's house and each of us would be given our outfits by his wife. She was a very well educated, attractive lady; he also had a mistress, a great beauty called Tamafune, whom he'd set up in a splendid house behind the Tokoji temple in Tajuku. Tamafune was a former geisha. She didn't usually join him on these excursions, though.

The day before we were due to leave, the geisha would go off to the hairdresser's and have their hair done in one of the more elaborate, top-heavy styles. And that night we slept with our heads on box pillows, being even more careful than usual not to disturb our hair. At the foot of the bed we laid out all the kimono and sashes we'd been given, ready for the morning.

On the morning of my first trip, we were up and had finished put-

Front gate of a landowner's residence

ting on our makeup before it was even light. All the geisha went down to Okamoto's house together by rickshaw. By the time we arrived, the houseboys had finished cleaning the garden and entranceway; everywhere was so spotless there wasn't so much as a single leaf left lying on the ground. We waited in the garden, and after a short while Okamoto came out with a number of clerks and servants. Behind them came his wife. Okamoto looked us up and down and said cheerfully, "Yes, with you dressed like that, we could go to the most fashionable parts of Tokyo and not be disgraced."

From his house we all made our way down to the station in a convoy of ten or more rickshaws. The stationmaster came out to meet our party and was very polite and respectful. We got on the train at seven, and it took us about three hours to get to Tokyo. After arriving at Tokyo Station—it had only just been built—we had a meal in the station hotel. I had a steak for the first time in my life. But I had no idea how you were supposed to eat Western food. I tried copying the way the clerks were eating, but unfortunately, perhaps because I put my knife and fork down in the wrong way, a waiter came along and whisked the plate away before I'd finished eating. Even now it makes me sad to think I never managed to finish that meal!

It was quite some distance from Tokyo Station to Mr. Asano's house but we traveled all the way by rickshaw. His mansion was absolutely enormous; it was surrounded by a high wall and had huge iron gates at the front, with ten or more stone steps leading up to them. Around the wall and on either side of the steps shabby-looking men, who could have been either casual laborers or tramps, were hanging around—it was really rather frightening. One of the clerks told me they were all men who'd come to find work with Asano. Just at that moment, the iron gates swung open and one of Asano's clerks, a man called Ryozo, and a number of maids and houseboys came out to meet us. Okamoto politely returned their greetings, and we all went in. Just as the gates were about to be shut, the men waiting outside began running toward them, shouting. Ryozo, without a hint of sympathy, quickly ordered the servants to shut the gates, and he bawled at the men outside, "Wait a bit longer." Ryozo explained to us later that Asano's agents distributed "tickets," which were in effect licenses to work for him, in various poor areas of the city, but they only gave out the same number of tickets as the number of men they needed. The men who hadn't been given any work would come along to the house in desperation and sit outside all day long. Every day tickets were distributed to ten or twenty of them, and they were given odd jobs to do.

Asano's estate was so big that, if I'd walked around on my own, I'm sure I'd have got lost. There were dozens of tall trees growing in the grounds and, hidden among the trees, a number of little cottages. You know, even now I can still picture the huge entrance hall of the house and the bright red carpet that covered the wide corridor off it from wall to wall. In Tsuchiura before the war, not even mansions like Okamoto's were carpeted, so it seemed awfully fashionable to us. I remember we exchanged glances with each other, and I even wondered whether it was all right to walk on such a fine carpet.

All I can remember about the rest of the estate was that there was a beautiful garden on the east side with a whole border full of Chinese bellflowers, all in bloom. Since we'd come with Okamoto, we weren't expected to do any shamisen playing or singing, and instead were served splendid meals by the maids of the house. Everything was just so different from even the grandest of the wealthy houses in Tsuchiura—we felt as though we were being entertained in a palace. In fact we were so excited and overawed by the place that we hardly touched any of the food they laid on for us. After lunch, Asano and Okamoto went into a separate room to talk, and we were shown around the house and garden by Ryozo.

In the early evening, dozens of men with brooms came into the garden and began sweeping everywhere. These were the men who'd been waiting outside that morning, and who'd finally been given work. They'd come to the house after finishing the work allotted to them, and had to sweep and clean the garden till it was absolutely spotless. When that job was finished, I saw them go to the back door of the house, get down on their knees with their foreheads scraping the ground, and each say in turn to the foreman, "Thank you very much, sir. Please remember me when you need men in the future." I was watching from the shadow of the trees, and it made me sick to see men having to behave in this degrading way.

I remember another occasion when we all went with Mr. Asano down the Joban coal mine. Okamoto went too, of course; there were six geisha in the party altogether. The mines in those days were terrible places, and the men who worked in them lived wretched lives. Asano said to us, "It mightn't be a bad idea if you saw for yourselves just how difficult it is to mine coal," and so, still wearing our kimono, we followed the light of a miner's lantern down into the pit. The men stood staring at us; their faces were pitch-black except for their eyes which seemed to glare at us out of the gloom. They were obviously shocked by the sight of geisha, wearing kimono, down the mine there with them. After a while, though, we all began to complain of feeling sick and not being able to breathe properly, so we turned around and came back out again. Hardly any geisha—at least not the ones I knew—came from coal-mining families.

Mr. Asano used to come to Tsuchiura occasionally too. He always dressed very simply—so simply, in fact, that he didn't appear at all rich. He always wore a cotton kimono with his family crest on it, but his half-coat was usually of plain black cloth, with no crest or anything at all. So, from a distance, it looked as though he was wearing just an ordinary kimono. But whenever he thought it necessary, he'd take off the half-coat to reveal his family crest. And in the summer, for example, he never even asked the geisha to fan him; he always said, "It's only natural it's hot—it is summer, after all. Fanning up a breeze might make me cool for a second or two, but it can't do more than that."

Okamoto was much fonder of show and luxury than Asano and, as far as we geisha were concerned, that was all to the good. He was always

Mrs. Miyazaki

great fun to be with, and looked after us well—we all liked him a lot.

Sometimes he'd go out for a picnic on Lake Kasumigaura with some of his business associates, perhaps the owners of big Tokyo stores or officials from the Bank of Japan, and we'd always accompany the party. Okamoto was the only person in Tsuchiura who had a houseboat with glass sliding doors. I remember one time, on a very hot day at the end of July, when we all went down on the boat, with some people from the Bank of Japan, to Itako. As the boat crossed the lake, Harukichi, Kochiyo, Mitsuyo and myself—about six or seven geisha in all—and Sakamae from the "Nisshin" inn played music on the shamisen, drums, flute, and gongs. We thoroughly enjoyed ourselves. Okamoto said, "Why don't we catch these Tokyo chaps some nice fresh whitebait?" so we anchored near a sandbank and the houseboys started fishing the whitebait out of the water with small dip nets. We were all so excited we couldn't bear just to watch, and we rolled up the hems of our kimono and poked around in the sand with our toes until we'd caught a load of shellfish. We boiled them up and made them into soup—it was delicious. When we arrived in Itako, we all went to the best restaurant there and ate in their private dining room. Since we were with Okamoto's party we could just sit and watch the geisha from the restaurant dancing and singing.

Back then the rich entertained themselves far more gaily and lavishly than most people now could even imagine.

The Mansho Estate

Mrs. Hisa Goto (1905–)

The present members of the Goto family are the eighth generation. The fifth head of the family, Shosuke Goto, apparently made the family's fortune from his rice business in the Fukagawa district of what's now Tokyo. My great-grandmother told me that when Shosuke was sixteen he went down to Fukagawa with nothing more than the knife in his belt and a few sacks of rice, and started a trading business. But when I say trading, in fact the rice was sold and resold very rapidly, in a way more like gambling than business. During Shosuke's lifetime the firm grew considerably, and he began dealing in drapery, cooking oil, candles, bleached cotton, and haberdashery as well. But in the second half of the nineteenth century the retailing side of the family business didn't go very well, and by the time I was born we had already pulled out of everything except rice.

The Mansho estate owned land in thirteen different towns and villages around Tsuchiura, but it was completely dissolved in the land reforms after the Second World War. After the rice had been harvested, the tenants on the parts of the estate nearest Tsuchiura would bring us the share they had to pay as rent on little handcarts. Tenants who lived some distance from Tsuchiura obviously couldn't deliver the rice themselves, so in the various sections of the estate there were men appointed as agents, who collected the rice rent, paid the taxes owing on it to the local government tax office, and then delivered it by *takase* boat to the shore of Lake Kasumigaura and from there in ten or twenty large wagons into Tsuchiura itself.

The Mansho estate was so big the owner had to employ a number of estate managers. These men were known as "the Mansho five," and at the end of the year they'd meet and, with a large map of the estate spread out on the floor, they'd make decisions: buy a new plot of good fertile land here and sell another piece there, one field gets too little sunlight, so get rid of it and buy a new field somewhere else, and so on and so forth. Discussions like this would go on day after day for more than a month.

Luckily there were no tenancy disputes on our estate, but the land around Tsuchiura was so low-lying and marshy (people used to say that "even when the frogs pee, it comes out as water") that ten days' continuous rain in the summer could cause all sorts of trouble. The situation sometimes got so bad that many of the tenants would camp themselves in our entrance hall begging us to reduce their rents. And it wasn't just the tenants from the Tsuchiura area who came, some turned up from as far afield as Inashiki and Namegata. It was quite a problem.

During the weeks when the rice rent was being paid in, each day we'd have to cook an enormous cauldron full of rice. We'd also buy a box of salmon from the shop next door and the maids, wearing aprons tied with pretty red sashes, would slice it up and cook it on a clay stove. From early in the morning right through the day, tenant farmers would appear to pay in their rent, and the custom was that each farmer would be given a meal of all the rice and salted salmon he could eat, even if he'd only paid in a single sack. The farmers would happily scoff their way through a big slice of fish and four or five bowls of rice before going back home. You see, in those days country people only ate fish on very special occasions, at New Year and during festivals. A large cask of saké, the sort with straw wrapped around it, was opened as well—these farmers could drink a terrifying amount of it.

When more than fifty sacks of rice had been paid in, an inspector from the local government office would come and assess the quality of the rice. We'd lay a straw mat on the ground in front of the shop, taking up half the roadway, and the inspector would decide which rice was grade one, grade two, and so on. Of course, before the official assessment the clerks in the shop would've been able to tell at a glance roughly which was which, and the farmers who'd brought us grade-one rice would have been given gifts of saké, *hanten*, or rolls of cotton as a reward.

Once our agents had collected all the rice rent and brought it to Tsuchiura, they'd come to my father's office with the account book that recorded all income and expenditure for the year. When an agent arrived at our house, he'd go straight into the office and sit and discuss business for a while. When the meeting finished, my father would thank him for his hard work and give him a number of presents. These were on top of his wages, of course. The presents varied from year to year: they might include tea services, side tables, small charcoal braziers, porcelain, fancy-colored plates or fine glasswork. The back room in our house was filled right to the ceiling with these gifts, and my mother and the clerks would decide what to give each agent. There used to be as much stuff in that room then as in a small shop.

The agent would be as pleased as punch with the things he'd received. He'd load them up onto his cart, and drive as slowly as possible down the main street without any cover on the cart so that everyone could see what he'd got. When he went past a shop he knew the owner of, he'd call out, "Look what I've got this year." The shopkeeper and all the assistants would come out to examine the presents, and tell him how lucky he was; they'd probably have had a cup of tea together too. So we obviously couldn't give our agents any cheap, shoddy stuff. The man would call on so many friends in Tsuchiura it'd be almost nightfall by the time he got out of town. Agents who came from particularly far away would stay the night at an inn on the way home or might go and enjoy themselves in a geisha house. . . . You know, when I think back on it all now, it really seems like an entirely different world.

A Spending Spree

Mr. Masujiro Tsukuda (1906–)

In Nakajoura, the narrow street that ran behind "Daitoku," there used to be a number of brothels, geisha houses, and restaurants—about six in all. When I was young I once worked flat out for forty days drying silkworm cocoons for "Toyoshima's" and, when I'd finished the work, I went and spent every penny I'd earned in a brothel in Nakajoura.

But, first, can I explain how the drying was done? Most of the year "Toyoshima's" was a department store, but in the silkworm season it ran a cocoon market. The sales counters in the shop were taken out, the building was emptied, and a large wooden auction table, about fifteen feet square, was set up. The cocoons that farmers had brought in for sale were spread out on it and the dealers—about twenty altogether—stood grouped around the table and decided which specimens to buy. People came to the sale from all over northern Japan, as far away even as Nagano.

The auction went like this: once the dealers had decided which cocoons they wanted, they wrote down their bids on the inside of a special plate, rather like a rice bowl, and threw it to a man called the "reader," who called out the bids in a loud voice: "Mr. Yamato—fifteen sen; Mr. Narato—twenty sen." The deal was clinched by the farmer who owned the cocoons shouting "Sold!" to the dealer who'd made the highest bid. The cocoons the man had bought were then pulled across the table with a pole and put into large baskets. These were carried to the back of the room and dumped on a conveyor belt that whisked them up to the drying room on the next floor. A piece of paper, with the name of the dealer who'd bought the batch written on it, was put in the last of his baskets.

In the drying room the cocoons were tipped into a net that moved slowly from one end of the room to the other along a rail. At various places in the net there were holes you could put your hand through to test how well the cocoons were drying. This was a job for an expert: you squeezed a cocoon lightly with your fingers and then slit it open to look at the grub inside. When they didn't seem to be drying fast enough, you'd get through to the boiler room and ask them to stoke the fire up a bit.

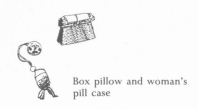

Box pillow and woman's
pill case

After about four hours, the work would be done. But if the cocoons weren't properly dry by this stage, they'd either rot later or make only poor-quality silk, so we had to take great care over the drying. The cocoons were then put into sacks and stored in a warehouse before being sent off to the mill for processing.

Some of the dealers, you know, were even able to borrow money merely on the security of cocoons stored in a warehouse. For example, if the Okatani Silk Mill had bought two tons but then found they were a bit short of ready cash, they'd go along to the bank and ask for a loan equal to the value of the cocoons. If the silk merchant was trusted they'd normally lend him the money; but if his business had been in trouble in the past the bank wouldn't even give him the time of day. In fact, once a dealer lost his credit, he'd almost certainly go bust.

I worked in the drying room for forty days solid without a single day off, and came away in the middle of June with fifty yen in my pocket. I even owned my first ten-yen note. Ten yen in those days was worth something like a hundred thousand in today's money, so fifty seemed an absolute fortune. I'd never had so much money in my life.

As soon as I got the money I went straight to "Toyonoya," the little brothel just behind "Toyoshima's." I stayed there right through July and August until the autumn cocoon season started at the beginning of September. It only cost fifty sen a night back then. The woman I spent all my time with was called Okiku. She wasn't exactly a youngster—she must have been a good twenty years older than me. As far as I remember, she wasn't particularly pretty either. No, and there were quite a few young girls in the brothel too. But not many customers arrived with fifty yen in their pocket, intending to stay several months, so I was treated like a king.

The girls had a hard life. They had to find a customer every night or they got into trouble. If no one had come along asking for her by nine o'clock, the girl would have to hang around in the street trying to persuade passersby to come inside. She was expected to stand out there till

The red-light district

midnight or even later. You can imagine how nasty it was in the winter: the girls had to wait outside dressed only in thin kimono—they got frozen to the marrow. They were so desperate they'd even grab some drunk who just happened to be passing, and wouldn't let him go until he promised to come in. There was even one time, apparently, when a woman taking her sick husband to the doctor was stopped by them; she had a terrible struggle to keep him from being dragged inside. It was no joke. When they did manage to get a customer, the owner of the brothel kept seven-tenths of the money and the girl only got what little was left. So even if she worked all night she couldn't earn more than fifteen sen—it was a hell of a rough way to make a living.

Anyway, since I was there every night, Okiku didn't need to look for other business. We behaved almost like a married couple while I was living in the brothel: if I went out during the day I'd quite often bring her back a nice *o-dango* cake as a present. And the girls really looked after me well. My meals were served to me individually on beautiful lacquer trays— I felt just like a millionaire.

The brothel was built and furnished like an ordinary house. But, compared to the other places in Nakajoura, "Toyonoya" was rather classy, with its own entrance gate and a little garden at the front. On your left as you came in there was a curtain hiding the office where the brothel keeper always sat. A corridor ran right through the middle of the house, and on either side of it were the girls' own individual rooms. In those days, none of the brothels made the girls sit with their faces close to the lattice doors so that new customers could see them—that practice only started after the red-light district moved to Sakae-cho.

The sort of men who slept with whores back then were mostly casual workers and day laborers or, at best, clerks—the kind that liked to live life to the full. And the women barely scraped a living from prostitution. But the women and their customers were all poor, so they found they had a lot in common. A strong sort of solidarity often grew up between them.

43

The Gangster

Mr. Shozo Ijichi (1897–1978)

I've done some pretty bad things in my life: I've been in dozens of fights, I was picked up by the police for gambling a few times, and I even committed murder. I've seen the inside of a good many jails, too, I can tell you. As I've got older, I've begun to realize how lousy and pointless my life's been, and every day now I pray to the statue of Buddha I've got set up at home. But when I die, there's no doubt I'll go straight to hell.

Let me tell you how the gangs operated in the old days. Today's *yakuza* are mixed up in the construction business, in loan-sharking, and all kinds of things, but before the war we made all our money by running gambling rackets. I first got involved in crime as a kid. After finishing a spell behind bars for some minor offense, I went and joined a gang in the old Asakusa area of Tokyo. It was one of the most powerful mobs in the capital. All the same, the boss lived in a very ordinary house and the boys were told to keep a low profile in the neighborhood. Everyone knew we were *yakuza* of course, but we took great pains to make people think we were decent guys who'd always help them out if they ever got into a scrape. We particularly did our best to keep in with the local tradesmen. We'd even go so far, for example, as to buy fish from the shopkeeper for more than it was really worth. In this way our reputation for fairness spread around the area and people began to say, "They may be tough, but they're regular guys." And so men who were normally too scared of *yakuza* to join in our gambling sessions would feel OK about coming along.

The gang world was a hard one. The rules we had to follow were drummed into us by our seniors in the gang (our "elder brothers" or *aniki*, we used to call them). They were incredibly detailed: for example, we weren't supposed to piss against people's walls. Also we were banned from mucking about with respectable girls—we had to stick to whores, bar girls, and the like. If you broke any of the rules, they could throw you out on the spot. The relationship between the boss and his men was one of absolute obedience.

As you can see, I've got two fingers missing. In the *yakuza* code—even nowadays—if you break the rules, you're expected to cut off one of your fingers as a sign of regret for what you've done. One of the fingers I lost was the result of a big misunderstanding. But I reckon it was only my own fault for letting myself be misunderstood. I lost the other one on account of a woman. I'll tell you what happened.

I was twenty-six. In a town near Tokyo—Funabashi—the local boss was having trouble with a new gang that was trying to muscle in on his patch. He asked my boss to lend him some men, and six of us went up there. It was a lively place with a large red-light district full of cafes, restaurants, and brothels. One Western-style restaurant was specially popular, partly because it served good food, but mainly because the owner's daughter, who worked there as a waitress, was a real stunner. Her name was Omitsu. Of course, a pretty girl like that was sure to have a patron, and in fact she was connected with a very big name indeed, a man called Makuda who, though he wasn't a *yakuza* himself, was associated with one of the largest construction companies in Japan.

I didn't know this, though. After we turned up in Funabashi, the rival gang got cold feet and steered clear of us. We had loads of time to kill and I gradually became friendly with this Omitsu. Since she worked in a restaurant in the red-light district, you could hardly call her "respectable"; so I thought it'd be safe to see her. She must have been about twenty, I suppose. But the other boys in my gang got to know about us, and one of them came up to me and said, "I'd pack it in if I were you. Didn't you know she's tied up with some big shot?" I had no intention of stealing someone else's woman so I asked Omitsu about it. "That's only what *he* thinks," she replied. "I don't even like him." Then she told me she loved me, and begged me to take her away.

Now, when a girl says that to you, it's not exactly easy to refuse, is it? In the end, we set off for Tokyo together. I felt too scared to face my boss, so I went to see a senior member of the gang instead. I asked him what I should do. "Hell, you're in trouble," he said. "Makuda's not actually a

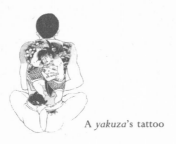

A *yakuza*'s tattoo

yakuza but he's pretty closely connected. He carries a lot of weight, you know. If a girl he claims is his has run off with someone else, he's not going to let the thing rest there. If you were in the right, we could back you up, but as far as I can see you've not got a leg to stand on."

I stayed there one night and then moved on, so as not to cause my *aniki* any trouble. The girl and I wandered from place to place. She never once complained, though. In fact, I think the more she realized how difficult it was to escape from things, the more she fell in love with me.

There's a custom among *yakuza* that, when you arrive in a new area, you have to announce your presence to the boss of the local gang. Most *yakuza* have such good spy networks they know immediately if anyone has entered their patch and why. So each new town we arrived in, I had to go straight to the local gang's headquarters. I'd leave the girl waiting in a restaurant nearby.

In *yakuza* circles the way of paying your respects—*jingi*, it was called—was quite a ritual. It may have come from the samurai idea that it was polite to announce your own name before asking the other person his. I'd start by saying, "I have come to pay my respects to your boss Mr. So-and-so. Please allow me to introduce myself." The gang member who'd answered the door would reply, "No, please allow me," I'd stand my ground and say "No, please allow me," and the other guy would come back with the same thing. This exchange had originally been meant as a test of willpower but it had eventually become just part of the ceremony.

After a bit more of this, the man would stop and let me introduce myself. First I'd say where I came from: "Born in Utsunomiya City, in Tochigi Prefecture, an area famous as the last resting place of the great shogun Tokugawa Ieyasu . . ."—it was usual to add a few words like this, pointing out how proud you were of your birthplace; then I'd announce which gang I belonged to: "I left my home province to serve Dewaya in Asakusa, Tokyo. Shozo Ijichi by name, I am glad to make your acquaintance, and hope for the benefit of your approval." The guy would thank me and disappear inside to discuss with his boss whether to let me stay or just give me some money and ask me to move on.

That was the end of the ritual. When the man came back, he'd speak normally: "Sorry to keep you waiting. There's not much around here worth seeing but, well, enjoy your stay," which I'd acknowledge with, "I was just passing through, but thanks all the same." The phrase "I was just passing through" had a special meaning: it signaled that I was on the run and couldn't hang around very long. The other guy would immediately get the idea and reply, "Well, I won't keep you any longer, but here's something to help you on your way"; and he'd give me some money. He'd add, "My boss and his wife are both out right now, so this gift's from me personally." He'd say this so, if there was any trouble over the matter later, the boss could claim he knew nothing about it.

The girl and I wandered around the countryside from August to the end of October. It wasn't much fun, I can tell you. We couldn't move when it rained: the country roads got so muddy you could hardly tell them apart from the paddy fields. We'd just lie around all day in an inn. We were in love with each other, I suppose, but we couldn't exactly stay in bed screwing forever.

Sometimes, when we'd run out of money, we'd have to sleep on the floor of a drafty old temple, with just a single straw mat to keep us warm. Most of the time we were hungry as hell and we got bitten half to death by mosquitoes. We couldn't even light a fire in the temple to keep the insects off in case someone spotted the flames and reported us. But Omitsu never showed she was upset, and never once complained. I've known a few women in my time, but never one as tough as her. Those few months we spent tramping around the countryside together taught me a lot about life.

In the *yakuza* world, ties between friends are often very strong, and men will really put themselves out to help others in trouble. I remember even now a good turn someone did me at that time—a man called Saburo,

who I went to see while I was on the run. He was beginning to make a name for himself in *yakuza* circles, so I was surprised how poor he seemed. His house was tiny. He made me some tea and a meal, and, after I'd eaten, I said I was traveling with a friend and should be moving on. "Who's the friend?" he asked and I had to explain the whole story. When I'd finished, Saburo whispered something to his wife. She went and unhooked the mosquito net hanging up in the next room, and took it outside. I reckon she must have hocked it, because when she came back she was carrying a bag of money. Saburo handed me the cash and said, "This won't get you very far, I'm afraid, but we want to chip in something for the journey." I was so touched I almost cried. "It's a bit of a dump we live in," he said, "but at least we've got a roof over our heads. So take the money. And if you ever come back this way again, come and see us." Saburo went on to become a big *yakuza* boss and I never forgot my debt of gratitude to him.

As time went on, our journey got tougher and tougher. I felt guilty because I knew that, if Omitsu hadn't fallen in love with me, she'd have been living in style, eating good food, wearing fine kimono, and going out to the theater or the movies as often as she wanted. I couldn't even provide her with enough to eat—we'd got to the stage of having to beg at farmhouse doors for water. We were just drifting, living from day to day. Mind you, it never for a moment crossed my mind to commit suicide together: it would have been a terrible disgrace for a *yakuza* to kill himself over a girl. Besides, I had ambitions to become a gang boss myself someday.

After a few months of this I said to the girl, "Look, you'd better go back to your parents. I'll sort things out myself somehow." She started crying and said, "I don't want to go back—I'd rather die." Omitsu cried and cried, and I stood there not knowing what to do. To tell the truth, I'd been thinking she must be fed up with the whole thing and secretly longing to go home, but it seemed now I was wrong and that she meant what she said about dying together. When it came down to it, I began to feel the same way too, and all night long we lay in each other's arms in a dark pine forest.

When I woke up next morning she'd gone. I suddenly felt terribly afraid and alone. I ran through the forest barefoot looking for her, but I couldn't find her anywhere. She must have run away, I thought, and I began to shake all over; I've never in my life felt as lonely as I did just then. I looked for her a bit more, but it seemed pointless, so I sat down for a rest on the steps of a shrine. Then I saw her walking toward me.

"Where the hell have you been?" I called. The relief I felt at seeing her again made me feel quite weak and trembly. She laughed: "I just went to get some rice balls from a farm over there." I can't go on like this, I thought; it's not fair to make such a good woman go through what she has over the last few months. This isn't the way a real man should behave. I decided that, if I really loved her, I should split up with her.

I took her back to her parents' place. "When you've got things sorted out, you will come for me, won't you?" she said. "Please!" I just nodded.

I went into a restaurant near Makuda's house. I asked them to lend me a carving knife. They brought me the knife, and there and then I cut off the little finger on my left hand. The waiter was pretty surprised, I can tell you. I didn't have time to think about the pain; I just wound a bit of rag around the stump, wrapped the finger in a piece of paper I borrowed from the restaurant, and went along to Makuda's house.

One of Makuda's men came out to meet me and obviously knew who I was. "I've come to apologize," I said. He gave me a murderous look and said, "How the hell d'you think you can apologize for what you've done?" I passed him the piece of paper, with the finger wrapped in it. The man immediately realized what this was. "I see," he said. "Wait here a minute," and he went in. I stood outside. I think Makuda must have been at home, but he didn't come out. His house wasn't all that big but it was still pretty grand, and from around the back I could hear women's voices, perhaps

Mrs. Makuda and the maids. After a few minutes my finger began to throb and hurt like hell. I felt sweat all over me—my shirt was soaked.

After a while the man returned. "The boss told me to say he 'understands,'" he reported. "Will you now please leave." I thanked him, bowed, and got the hell out of there. I'd been expecting worse—even that Makuda might bump me off—and I was almost disappointed I'd got off so lightly. When a *yakuza* says he "understands," you can take it to mean that the affair's considered closed. Makuda must have been a very generous man. I genuinely felt sorry for what I'd done.

After that, I went straight back to my boss's place. "You're going to have to grow up and learn to control yourself," he said, but he left it at that—no punishment or anything. I never saw the girl again. I thought it better not to: a man can weaken when he sees a girl crying. Besides, the fact that Makuda had forgiven me and been so decent meant I had a duty not to cross him a second time. Still, I did hear a rumor that Omitsu ran away from home again later. But at the time I was in jail, so I don't know whether she came looking for me or not. None of the other members of the gang ever mentioned anything, but maybe they were just keeping their mouths shut. What ever happened to the girl after that, though, I've no idea.

Outcasts

Mr. Fukusaburo Takagi (1898–1981)

About a mile north of Manabe there was a gloomy, heavily wooded, hilly area called Mt. Daitoku. The area has been developed since then and the pine forests have disappeared, but less than thirty or forty years ago it was such a spooky place that people were afraid to go anywhere near it.

A lot of strange tales are told about Mt. Daitoku. Large numbers of outcasts, known as *sanka*, lived up there in the depths of the forest, for example. They roamed from place to place in the hills and along the dry beds of rivers that flowed down onto the plain, living like savages. When I was young, they even used to wander into our village occasionally. They made rough bowls, baskets, ladles and other household goods and would come down into the villages around the mountain to sell them. They weren't exactly tramps—it's just that, for some reason or other, they weren't listed in the official census. And, strangely enough, many of the women were very good-looking. I'm not entirely sure but I've heard that these *sanka* once lived in the capital and that, hundreds of years ago, they were outlawed and forced to roam the countryside.

The outcasts up on Daitoku used to kill and eat wild dogs. In those days even low-class meat such as horse or rabbit was almost impossible to get hold of, so when, for instance, someone was ill and needed extra protein, even townspeople would be forced to go along and buy some dog meat from the *sanka*. Today that sort of thing would seem unthinkable, but back then poverty drove people to desperate measures.

The outcasts also used to hold gambling sessions in the hills and these were attended by laborers from the town. I knew an old man—he died not so many years ago—who told me he used to supply these sessions with saké: he'd buy a five-gallon cask in the town, carry it up the mountain, and sell it to them. With a good slug of alcohol inside them, they'd play right through the night. There were in fact a couple of betting joints in Tsuchiura, too. Gambling was actually prohibited by law, but the police used to turn a blind eye to it. These joints, though, were a bit risky: for one thing, they were run by gangsters and since, strictly speaking, they were illegal, there was no guarantee you wouldn't end up in jail. But the police never went out into the mountains, so if you'd set your mind on a bit of serious gambling you could go up there without anything much to worry about.

You know, there were plenty of beggars around here in the old days as well. Up in the mountains they dressed fairly normally, but when they came down into town and went from house to house begging for money, they deliberately wore the filthiest, most tattered rags they had. Most Japanese were devout Buddhists in those days and believed that by giving to the poor they'd acquire virtue for use in their next life. The beggars got to know which households were generous with their alms and would return there regularly time after time. You could actually make quite a decent living by begging.

There were sometimes lepers, too, on Daitoku, and others with bad infectious diseases. There were no hospitals for those people back then, so when someone got leprosy, for example, he'd be forced out of his village and end up drifting around the countryside. After a while groups of them would get together, and they'd build makeshift huts and start a small camp. They never stayed long in one place, though: you could go up the mountain one week and see a thriving little colony, but when you went back a few days later it would have disappeared without trace. God knows where they all went. The sick were treated lousily in those days—it was pitiful to see them. I was often asked to go along and burn the old clothes and rubbish that the lepers left behind.

The body of anyone who died of an infectious disease was burned at the foot of the mountain, though people used to hate the idea of cremation, and they'd beg the doctor to fiddle the death certificate. Even now burial is far more common than cremation in many of the country areas around Tsuchiura; in the town, too, not so long ago cremation was very unusual.

The body was burned on a simple pyre, and extremely hard work this was too. When I worked as a casual laborer I was usually asked to help out. Before lighting the pyre we'd pile up a number of wet straw mats beside it, so that if the flames got out of hand we could dampen them down with the mats. When the fire was too hot only the flesh of the corpse would burn, leaving the bones intact.

There were four or five of us, lighting the pyre as the sun began to set and working right through till dawn the next morning. It was a very grim, depressing sort of job—up there on a pitch-dark mountain, lit only by the dim glow of a single lantern, burning a disease-ridden corpse—so we'd have a few drinks to cheer ourselves up. Mind you, after you'd done the work a few times, you got completely hardened to it; it's frightening how callous you can get about things.

Around 1920 an isolation hospital was built where the crematory had been, and the burnings were done a bit higher up. The hospital was tiny, with room for only four or five patients suffering from things like typhoid fever or diphtheria. Miles away from any village and with very little medical care, the patients were absolutely miserable. In those days most people were terribly prejudiced about disease—folk nowadays are much more open-minded.

There used to be five small ponds up on Daitoku, which collected the water from mountain streams. Dozens of other little streams spilled down the mountainside toward the villages at its foot. But the area has now been completely dried out, and all the ponds have disappeared. That's progress for you, I suppose.

The Last Executioner

Mr. Fukusaburo Takagi (1898–1981)

My grandfather, on my mother's side, lived in Tozaki on the outskirts of Tsuchiura. Just outside Tozaki, on the little winding road that led into the center of town, there used to be an execution ground. The executions ended with the fall of the last shogun, and by the time I was around all that was left was the cemetery and a memorial. I remember seeing prisoners from Tsuchiura jail coming out to the site and being made to clean the cemetery and pull up weeds. They were kept roped together by a number of guards.

We kids were scared to go near the cemetery even during the daytime, and at night we'd always sprint past it. They later built a cinema on the spot and, when the foundations were being dug, the workmen came across piles and piles of bones. The folk from Tozaki all came along to have a look. In the end, they decided they'd better get a priest out to pray for the souls of the victims. And one of the reasons why they built a cinema, rather than some more practical building, you know, was to entertain the ghosts of the men executed there. Bored ghosts can become spiteful, it's said. But all those bones—God knows how many people must have been killed on that site.

My grandfather was the public executioner. He was an enormous, terrifying-looking man—people tended to keep well out of his way. When I was a boy, he was in his eighties and had long since retired. He often used to take me out and show me how to kill small birds with a blowpipe. The pipe was about ten feet long; he used three-inch darts with little paper flights. A blowpipe might sound rather primitive but it was in fact deadly accurate: Grandfather could hit a sparrow on a roof twenty-five feet away with a single dart.

He was also an excellent shot with a matchlock. As well as having been the executioner, he worked as a gamekeeper for old Lord Tsuchiya; he often had to go out onto the marsh and shoot a duck for his lordship's table. Sometimes he'd take me with him. If a flight of duck had been spotted there, a local farmer would come along and tell my grandfather. He'd then take his old matchlock down to the gamekeeper's hut on the edge of the marsh and make one bullet. He never used ready-made shot, my grandfather, and he only ever made his bullet after the birds had been sighted.

How was the bullet made? Well, he'd just melt some lead down and roll it into the right shape and size. He couldn't be bothered to make more than one. He'd then fill the gun with powder, load the bullet, and row out onto the marsh in a small boat. He had a clever way of trapping duck. He always kept a long rope in the boat: he'd gradually lower this into the water so that it made an enormous circle around the birds. He'd then shoulder the gun and tell me to slowly pull in the rope. The circle would get smaller and smaller and, when the rope was just about touching them, I'd give it a hard yank and they'd take off from the water in surprise. As the ducks rose into the air, Grandfather would shoot one down. He never missed.

I remember one day we'd been out shooting and had got back to dry land when three or four tough-looking tramps came up to Grandfather and shouted at him to hand over the duck he'd shot. Grandfather glared at them and said, "If you're hungry, I don't mind giving you something. But I'm not going to be threatened. Ask politely." They really flared up at this—started yelling and waving their fists; they didn't actually hit him, though. Just then one of the locals turned up: "You're crazy," he told them. "If you lay a finger on that old man, he'll kill you." And they took to their heels.

Grandfather was also master of another weapon, the sickle and chain. The idea was to knock the opponent's sword out of his hand with the chain and then cut his head off with the sickle. Grandfather would whip the chain, which was a good fifteen or twenty feet long, around and around his head so his opponent couldn't get near him. You'd never have believed he was an old man of eighty, he looked so ferocious. He'd sometimes arrange a match with the local fencing master and people

Tozaki

would gather round to watch. They didn't fight to the death, of course: the fencing master only used a wooden sword, not a steel one. The crowd usually went home disappointed that they hadn't seen any blood. There were a lot of former samurai around when I was a child—they liked nothing better than watching a good duel.

My grandfather didn't talk about his work as an executioner, but just once or twice he did tell me something about it. Mind you, everyone in the village knew precisely what he did. Criminals were usually beheaded in the old days. The executioner stood directly behind the prisoner, took a good look at the man's neck, and then brought his sword down with a single blow. Grandfather told me you had to be careful to cut between the bones in the neck, otherwise the sword wouldn't go right through and the man would be left there with his head hanging half-off, screaming in agony. Criminals apparently even used to ask specially for someone capable of killing with one stroke. My grandfather's reputation was pretty good, I hear. He could even cut off a prisoner's head on the run. This wasn't really allowed, he told me, but he used to do it occasionally to test his own skill.

The day before the beheading, a couple of outcasts who used to lend a hand at executions would walk around Tsuchiura announcing the sentence. They'd go into all the large shops, and in each they were given a certain amount of money. There was a reason behind this. Once the sentence had been carried out, the criminal's body was wrapped in straw matting and lugged around the town by the same men. This was meant as a warning to others not to commit crime. And when they got to a shop that had refused to give them anything the day before, they laid the corpse down and sat on the doorstep pretending to rest. And they wouldn't budge. Blood would trickle onto the ground and a crowd would collect. You can imagine what damage was done to the shop's trade with a corpse propped up on its doorstep. After a while someone would come running out and give the men money to drive them away.

56

What did they do with the head? I never got around to asking my grandfather that. Grandfather was nearly ninety when he died. He certainly lived a long time—"too bloody long," he used to say.

In and Around the Rickshaw Station

Mr. Ryutaro Terauchi (1905–)

When I was a child my parents ran a rickshaw business from our house—at times we had as many as eighteen men working out of our station on a hire basis. During the twenties, a number of taxi and bus companies started up and rickshaw operators were gradually put out of business, but until then it'd been a really thriving trade.

Just inside the entrance to our house was a spacious earth-floored area where rows of rickshaws were kept. The men sat around there waiting for customers, smoking or playing chess, and as soon as a servant turned up with an order, one of them would grab a rickshaw and be on his way. When he returned, he'd tell the boss what fare he'd taken; the boss kept twenty percent of this for the hire of the vehicle, and the remainder went into the fellow's own pocket. In our business it was unthinkable that any of the men should try to cheat by claiming, for example, that they'd only received a one-yen fare when in fact they'd taken two. It was fairly unlikely you'd be found out at once, but if you tried this sort of fiddle for any length of time, you'd be sure to slip up eventually and you'd never find work as a rickshaw man in the same town again. A circular would be passed around all the rickshaw stations to the effect that "So-and-so's dishonest—please take note," and once the news had spread, nobody would take you on.

Our best customers were doctors and geisha. I never actually pulled a rickshaw myself, but on many occasions I went with Dr. Araki on his rounds. Araki had previously been a ship's doctor and really wasn't too clued in to what went on ashore. My job was to carry his bag around for him. He was very popular as a doctor, being devoted to his patients, but like all doctors in those days he had his problems: patients only paid their medical bills twice a year, at *o-bon* in the summer and on New Year's Eve. I was sometimes asked to help out with his office work and it'd be my job to try and collect his fees.

When I think back on it now it seems an incredible state of affairs. I'd go along to one of the terrace rows on New Year's Eve to pick up the money, but everyone would've disappeared—there'd not be a soul around. I'd rush about looking for them, and eventually midnight would come and the temple bells would start ringing in the New Year. Once midnight struck, you couldn't collect the debts. If someone called out "Happy New Year" to you, you really had no choice but to say "Happy New Year" back, whoever they were. And once you'd started exchanging greetings, you could hardly begin pestering the person to pay his debts. That was the custom, you see. The poorer people had to sneak about from place to place till midnight, but as soon as the bells rang out they could stroll back home as cheerfully as they liked. I knew what sort of financial situation Dr. Araki was in, so I did my best to collect as many debts as possible, but a lot of people were hard up then and getting your hands on the money wasn't easy. . . .

The Omachi Canal flowed past the back of our house and came to a dead end just by the bank of the River Sakura. It's now been filled in and made into a road, but it used to be a good eight feet wide and children were always fishing in it. The canal was surrounded by rice paddies, so water ran into it all along its length. At the western end, near the statue of the god of travelers, a number of small streams flowed into it and, after a spell of rain, water would pour into the canal. It wasn't exactly clean but it wasn't a stagnant ditch either. When I was a child I often swam there in the summer. I'd dive into the canal, and when I surfaced again I'd find pieces of straw or weed stuck to me; we never felt the canal was dirty, though.

It must have been in about 1911 or 1912 we had the terrible floods; the whole town was a shambles. The level of the Sakura rose, the river water started rushing along, and Zenikame Bridge was in danger of being washed away. Back then all bridges were made of wood, of course, and the only way to stop the whole thing lifting out of the riverbed was to weigh it down. Everyone in Omachi was asked to fetch out all their two-gallon barrels—maybe a hundred or a hundred and fifty of them in all; the

Main street at dusk

fire brigade then filled the barrels with water as quickly as they could, and piled them on top of the bridge. There was terrible panic and chaos. All the roads in Omachi were underwater. The River Bizen, to the south of the Sakura, was even worse affected: all along it, from Zenikame Bridge to the hill at Shimotakatsu, there was a high wharf, and during the floods you had to walk along the top of this to avoid falling waist-deep in swirling water. The rivers have since been widened and bridges reinforced with steel struts, so there's no longer any real danger of flooding, but in the past, whenever it rained, people were terrified it might result in floods. . . .

One tradition I remember from my childhood that unfortunately no longer survives was what we called "untying the string." When one of the children in the neighborhood was about to celebrate a seventh birthday, all the other kids would join hands and, with the birthday child in the middle holding a lantern, they'd walk through the streets singing—for example, "Come to Terauchi's house tomorrow for *oshiruko* [sweet red beans]." The next day the children would come around to my house and be given a party. Kids didn't get much in the way of sweets at that time, so it was exciting—as much *oshiruko* as you could eat. Plates of rice cakes and bean jam were also taken around and given to neighbors and relatives. They'd give a little token something in return and later on, after the child had made the ceremonial visit to the local shrine, he'd visit all the houses in the neighborhood, and at each he'd have some money tied onto a piece of string that he carried with him.

At New Year the children used to walk around the streets carrying paper lanterns, calling out "Happy New Year" at each house. People loved this, of course, and they'd give them small sums of money. The adults also went out making New Year calls, and the people who'd been called on first would later make a return visit. With everyone visiting back and forth like this, one felt a greath warmth and friendliness filling the town. Just giving money for *shichigosan** as they do nowadays has some sort of meaning, I suppose, but you certainly don't get the feeling any longer that everyone in the town is celebrating for you.

* Literally, "seven, five, three." A celebration for boys aged three and five, and girls aged three and seven, held on February 15 each year. Both this and the custom of "untying the string" were a mark of thanks for a child's survival in an age when many of them died young.

The Omnibus and the
Horsemeat Butcher

Mrs. Yasu Someya (1921–)

My shop is now a butcher's, but in my grandfather's time the Tote Omnibus Service, running between Tsuchiura and Toride, operated from it. Until the Joban Line was built at the turn of the century, the only way of traveling, even when you were going as far as Tokyo, was on foot, by rickshaw, or in a four-wheeled carriage. So there must have been an awful lot of people who used my granddad's horse-drawn buses. From Toride you could get a boat to Tokyo that arrived by six the next morning. I imagine the boat must have gone up the River Tone and then via the River Edo to the Fukagawa area of Tokyo.

My grandfather pulled out of the bus business before I was born and started a wholesale butcher's, specializing in horsemeat. In the area around Tsuchiura there were only two shops selling horsemeat wholesale: ourselves and "Komatsuzaki's" in Fujisawa. We owned stables by the end of the canal and kept more than ten horses there at times. I wonder if I can remember where the stables were exactly. On one side of Tamachi Bridge, just on the corner of the street to your right, I remember there was a baked potato shop, which also sold vegetables. Everyone called it the "three day shop," because they only brought in new supplies of vegetables every three days. And if you then turned right down the little side street past "Tosaya's," the rice cracker shop, you came to "Kuwabara's," the large paper makers, and, a little further on, a public bathhouse and then a cemetery, next to a small temple devoted to Amida. Yes, our stables were on the left, on the far side of the bridge next to the temple. They were surrounded by paddy fields.

We used to buy old broken-down horses from farmers; sometimes we went out looking for these nags ourselves, but often farmers brought us ones they wanted to get rid of anyway. In the old days, buyers used to bring young horses all the way down from Iwate and Fukushima and walk around the villages near here till they came across some old nag in a field. Then they'd find the farmer who owned the horse and offer to buy it off him, and sell him a young one in return at a reduced price. It was sort of like buying a new car in part exchange for your old one.

We also had a buyer working for us, who'd go off to Namegata by steamer, and walk from there to Kasama and as far as the borders of the next prefecture to get horses for the shop. When he'd bought a horse he tied a straw mat over its back and led it home to Tsuchiura. And when he had to lead two or more of them at the same time, he'd wind a bit of rope around the bottom twelve inches of one of their tails, and fold the bound part up and tie it with more rope to the top of the tail, making a loop. The lead rope of the second horse could then be tied onto the tail of the first without any danger of its coming loose.

When a horse was going to be slaughtered, a man would come and take it off to the abattoir in Tanaka. He put two large boxes he would later use for the meat onto the back of his cart, tied the horse behind it, and led it there over the bumpy roads. At the abattoir the horse's throat was cut, its carcass was chopped into four lengthwise, put into the boxes, and brought back to our shop. The slaughterman would skin the carcass for us and salt the skin to preserve it. The skins were piled up in our storehouse, and every February a drum maker from Tokyo used to come along and buy up the lot.

Back then lots of people ate horsemeat, so we used to keep the shop open till at least ten o'clock at night. But after about seven, customers only came in a trickle, and I'd have time to get things ready for the next day's business; I'd make up packs of meat, wrapped in plaited bamboo-grass containers, about eighteen inches wide—this would take me until ten or eleven.

There were two retail horsemeat butchers': a little one called "Te-kane," which sold meat supplied to it by "Komatsuzaki's," and our retail branch near the railway station. Behind the "Matsubakan" inn was a noodle shop called "Tamotsu." If you went down the flight of stone steps just next to it, you'd find our shop at the bottom.

I suppose you could get about 400 or 450 lbs. of meat from a single horse. The horse's tongue was sold cheap as offal. The spine contained a type of marrow that looked rather like blancmange; there was a very attractive woman—I've no idea where she was from—who often came to our shop just to buy the bone marrow. Goodness knows what she made from it.

There was a statue of the horse-headed Kannon in Tanaka; we depended so much on horses for our livelihood that we also had a stone statue of this goddess set up in our garden. We used to make offerings and pray to it for the souls of the horses we'd slaughtered.

BOATMEN
AND
FISHERMEN

Takase boats, with the lake beyond

The Water Nomad

Mr. Susumu Fujii (1911–)

Let me tell you about life as a fisherman.

All modern fishing boats are fitted with engines, so the strength of the fisherman has no effect on the speed you can get out of the boat. But when I first went out fishing with my father at the age of sixteen, the boats were still rowed with a single oar at the stern. And that—believe me—was backbreaking work. I'd messed about with my friends in small rowing boats from almost before I could walk and rowing was second nature to me, but unfortunately there was a lot more to becoming a fisherman than just being able to row. It was a very tough life.

What can I say to give you some idea of how hard it was? Well, for a start, to get out to the fishing grounds you had to row straight into the wind for five or six miles. The boats we used were about twenty-five feet long and they were weighed down by the mast, sail, nets, and other tackle, so you can imagine what a strain it was keeping the boat moving at all. In the summer I'd be wearing nothing more than a loincloth but I soon found myself dripping with sweat and, to make matters worse, the sweat would stick to me as it dried, and I'd end up caked in salt like a pickled herring.

We usually set off from the shore just as the sun was going down, and by the time we arrived at the fishing grounds the sky would be crimson. We lowered the nets, hoisted the sail, and got ready to start fishing. The area of the lake where you could find the most fish varied from day to day, depending on things like the wind and the temperature. So before setting out, each of us would size up the weather conditions, decide which spot was likely to give us the best catch, and then row out as fast as we could in that direction. The trouble was, though, that experienced men tended to think alike, with the result that most of the boats headed off on the same course, competing to get to the best fishing grounds first. Fishermen are all bloody-minded: they can't bear being beaten to the best spot. So there'd be a mad scramble as we all rowed flat out.

The speed of each boat depended mainly on the strength and skill of the fisherman, but it could also be affected quite a bit by the quality of the oar and other equipment. Good oars had plenty of give in them. If you had top quality, the boat would glide over the water and cut through even the largest waves. But if they were anything less than the best, most of the rower's power was used up by each wave that hit the boat. The best wood for making them was evergreen oak, but you couldn't get this in the Dejima area, so the timber had to be brought up from Choshi. I used to get my oars made for me by a shipbuilder called Sugasawa. His were superb: after rowing a few strokes with a new one, you could tell just how well made it was.

When I first started in the fishing business, you used to be able to make about ten yen from a night's catch. On a good night the deck would be piled so high with smelt and other fish that the boat looked in danger of capsizing. Mind you, with oars costing ten yen apiece, once the equipment and other overheads had been taken into account, you could hardly make a fortune from the business.

To anyone not a fisherman the sight of boats bobbing on the lake with their white sails filling in the wind must have seemed all very peaceful and romantic. But for us the life was anything but peaceful. The more boats there were, the fiercer the rivalry became; there used to be some serious fights. "Everyone else can get lost: I'm out to get what I can," was the attitude of most of the men. A fisherman's only thought was how to catch more fish—he didn't give a damn about anybody else.

Let me give you an example. Suppose there were two boats on the lake competing with each other. The one rowed by the stronger man overtakes the second. They drop their nets and start fishing, but the first boat begins to drift backward with the wind. You might expect them to drift at the same speed and not get in each other's way, but in fact the first boat moves more quickly and the one behind has to head away to avoid being rammed. The reason the first boat drifted more quickly was that, since the fisherman was a better rower, he always got the best position and caught

Fishing boats

more fish; so with the extra money he could afford to keep his boat in good shape and buy a larger sail and a better oar. The mast on the boats was, on average, about twenty feet high and the sail about fifty feet across, but this could vary according to a man's skill.

Fishing was done from sailing boats from July till December, but toward the end of November the catches got much smaller. Eventually we packed it in and went out alone in small boats instead, wandering around the lake from place to place, fishing for bitterling and the like with fixed shore nets. This was known, in the local dialect, as *wadari* ["itinerant fishing"]. I often didn't come home for two or three months at a time.

I'd put up a few poles on my boat and build a makeshift roof to keep out the rain, and I lived, cooked, ate, and slept entirely on the boat, alone, for months on end. During the day I'd row around the rivers that flowed into the lake and fix my nets at various spots and, when I'd finished the day's work, I'd tie the boat up among the rushes for the night. Next morning, I would get up early to go and check the nets, and if I'd caught a fair number of fish, I used to take them to the nearest village and sell them there. With the money I got I'd buy rice, *miso*, soy sauce, firewood, and other essentials, then move on and set my nets somewhere else. I was totally self-sufficient: I don't think I once stayed in an inn or ate in a restaurant. I didn't even have a lamp because I couldn't afford to buy oil for it; after dark, I just had to rely on the light of the moon. Besides, being on my own, there was nothing to do in the evenings anyway, so I used to go to bed as soon as it got dark. It was really quite warm on board if you spread some loose straw on the deck, laid a rough straw mat over that, and put your mattress on top. In any case, after you've been out fishing for a few years you get used to the cold.

I fished in some very out-of-the-way places. This side of Sawara there used to be a large area of marshland called Yodaura. It's now been drained and not a trace remains, but it used to be an eerie place: miles and miles of nothing but reeds and rushes—no sign of any human life, not even any animals. Even in the daytime you almost expected a ghost to jump out at you suddenly. The marsh was so far off the beaten track I couldn't take the fish I'd caught straight to a shopkeeper—there wasn't one near enough. I had to drag the fish behind the boat in a keep net and, as I moved from place to place, the catch got larger and larger. After a week or so I'd get fed up with working the marsh; I'd throw away any fish that had died, and take the rest off to the nearest village.

I sometimes called in at the little port of Itako on these wanderings of mine. I probably wouldn't have had a bath in two or three weeks by the time I got to the town—I'd be filthy—stinking. I'd have liked to have baths more often, but the public bath cost one and a half sen and I just couldn't afford it. The part of Itako that stretched along the river was full of brothels. Every street you walked down had a row of brothels on both sides; in front of each there'd be a tout trying to get people to come in-side. But when I walked past they never so much as gave me a second glance: they could tell just by the way I was dressed that I wouldn't be able to afford a woman. Even in Itako I kept well away from inns and board-ing houses. I just used to moor my boat by the riverbank on the outskirts of town and spend the night there. After dusk the brothels would begin to fill with customers. The lights of the inns along the river flickered on the water, and I could hear the twanging of shamisen and women laughing in the distance as I fell asleep.

I steered clear of anything that involved money. But though I couldn't have any fun in the brothels of Itako, I did manage to make friends with quite a lot of farmers around the lake. I often used to go along to some nearby farm with a bag of fish, and in exchange they'd give me a meal or a cup of tea. But I usually had problems the first time I went. I was dressed virtually in rags, my face and body were black with dirt, so I suppose I must've looked like a tramp. Often the farmer's wife would open the door and then step back in horror at the sight of me. But once the people got to know me, I normally got on very well with them and we'd sit for hours chatting together. Some people even invited me in for supper and let me use their bath.

I never had time to be ill. No one unhealthy could have stood these trips: it would've killed them. Fishermen seemed almost to belong to a different race from townspeople. We all had powerful muscles, huge hands and feet, and dark, weather-beaten faces. Fishing folk hardly ever got sick. Even in winter I never wore more than a pair of thin cotton shorts. And we never wore shoes, either: both farmers and fishermen went barefoot all the year round. It was only after the war that country people started wearing shoes, and I reckon it's one of the reasons why they're so feeble these days.

But just once when I was out fishing I did have some trouble: I got this terrible ache in my belly. The pain became unbearable and in the end I had to moor my boat in the rushes. I lay there on board for a whole week, moaning in agony. I'd get up just once a day to have a drink of river water, but apart from that I lay there motionless all day long. Little by little the pain went away, and after a week or so I was able to get up. I rowed the boat down to Ushibori and went to an old friend of mine who lived there. He said I should go and have moxa treatment. He took me along to a place he knew, and a girl, who was really pretty I remember, made me strip and applied the stuff. After that I was right as rain again. My friend let me use his bath, and after a good wash I felt as though there'd never been anything wrong with me. But it's an experience I shall never forget.

Tragedy on the Lake

Mr. Takamasa Sakurai (1903–)

I had my first rowing lesson when I was only five. My grandfather tied a rope around my waist so I wouldn't fall in, gave me a good shove off from the bank, and just told me to "Row!" The only problem was that the single oar was so much bigger than me, all I could do was dangle it down into the water. My grandmother laughed: "If you row the boat like that, you'll just go around in circles." From then on I practiced rowing every day and, after a while, I got the knack of making the boat go forward in a straight line.

It was important to get a feel for the lake while you were still young. If you wanted to survive, you had to be able to recognize the telltale signs of danger and know what to do in a difficult situation. My parents drummed these sorts of lessons into me day after day until I could feel their advice oozing out of my ears. The old fishermen knew the lake like the backs of their hands and they'd happily go on fishing even in the strongest winds—it was almost unheard of for a fisherman to drown. The only people who ever died in the lake were the ones who didn't realize how deadly it could be.

My father could predict the next day's weather more accurately than the forecast on the radio. In fact success as a fisherman depended a lot on this gift. Unless you knew what the next day's weather was going to be, it was impossible to work out where the shoals of fish would move, so your catches would always be poor. To take just one example: at the beginning of winter, rather peculiar clouds—dark and fast-moving—used to pass over Mt. Tsukuba, and if you looked carefully at the way they moved, you could roughly judge the speed of the wind on the lake and predict how the weather would change. I mean, there'd be days when the sky overhead was clear and blue, and the fishermen would look at the clouds over the mountain and reckon it was wiser to head for home.

But the clouds on Mt. Oda were next to useless as a warning. The wind would start gusting across the lake as soon as the first clouds appeared over the peak, and there wouldn't be time to get back before the storm

blew up. You'd have to row as fast as possible to the nearest bank, drive the boat into the reeds or shelter up a little side stream, and wait there till the storm passed.

The fishermen had so much confidence in their own forecasting they even ignored typhoon warnings on the radio and went out fishing. "With a cloud formation like that, we won't get a typhoon," they'd say. And they were never wrong, either.

We also reckoned you could tell the weather by listening to the sound of the sea in the distance. If you could hear the waves off Kashima to the north, you knew a storm was on its way. In those days smelt fishing was done in the early hours of the morning, and we fishermen would hang around down by the shore late into the night chatting and waiting to see whether we'd be able to go out. As it got chilly we'd wrap ourselves up in the sails, with just our heads poking out, talking and occasionally dozing off. And then all of a sudden we'd hear the distant roaring of the sea from the far shore of the lake. If the sound came from the northeast we knew the weather would turn bad, but if it was from the southeast, even though there might be a few spots of rain, we could be sure it'd clear up after a while.

My grandfather told me I should think of the lake as a pot of boiling water: if I ever fell in I wouldn't have a chance. This, particularly in winter, meant that fishermen always kept a sharp eye on the weather before deciding to take the boats out. And as far as I can remember there were only two fatal accidents on the lake.

Let's see: the first happened when I was about nineteen. As you might expect, it wasn't fishermen who were killed, but men who didn't realize how dangerous the lake could be. It happened one day in January. A terrible westerly wind was blowing, and the men had decided that any fishing was impossible; they were drinking and chatting in the wholesaler's office. Someone looked out over the stormy lake and noticed a large boat had put out from Oyama on the far side, and was heading westward.

"What the hell's he think he's doing?"

"That's the boat from the naval air squadron. It's enormous—can carry as many as fifteen men apparently."

"I don't care how big it is, it's never going to get anywhere in this wind."

The fishermen dropped everything and ran down to the shore to watch the boat battle against the wind and the huge waves. In that part of the lake there's a sandbank about two or three feet below the surface that can be really dangerous, particularly when the wind's blowing from the west. The south side of the sandbank might be relatively calm, but as soon as you rounded it and came out on the north side, the waves slammed into you. In a westerly gale the fishermen always avoided that area like the plague.

We all stood and watched in horror.

"The idiot. Surely he's not going to try and round the sandbank."

Everybody knew exactly what'd happen if the boat kept on the same course. It began to turn the tip of the sandbank and was suddenly pounded by the waves, and stopped moving forward altogether. The skipper presumably thought he wasn't going to get anywhere headed in that direction, so he swung the boat around and tried to go back. We stood rooted to the spot, watching. Suddenly the boat disappeared from sight.

"Oh God, it's gone under." The boat had capsized. But in that storm there'd have been no point in going to their rescue. Everyone on board was drowned, seven men in all. One man—a flight sergeant—managed to swim the eight hundred yards or so to the tip of the sandbank, where there was a target used by the air squadron for bombing practice; but having got there he dropped dead from exhaustion. We helped search for the bodies afterward—it was more than three weeks before we managed to find them all.

I remember another incident in March 1924 when a seaplane—again from the air squadron—crash-landed on the lake near Magake. There was a strong wind that day too, but the local fishermen managed to put out four or five boats and tow the plane to the shore. But the squadron brought out a tug, tied a rope to the plane, and tried to tow it back across the lake. The water was still very rough, though, and the plane shook violently in the wind and was battered by the waves. It was only a small single-seater with two flimsy floats, and it looked in serious danger of breaking up. For some reason—I suppose to try and stabilize it—an airman was made to sit on each of the wings. They towed the thing back past Magake and on toward the sandbank. But as soon as they tried to pass it they stopped dead, beaten back by the waves. They decided to turn around. But almost immediately both the seaplane and the tug capsized. Five men drowned. The two who'd been made to sit on the wings never had a chance. I mean, if you're stupid enough to go out in that kind of wind, what else can you expect?

Those military people thought they knew it all back then. In fact they hadn't a clue about conditions on the lake, and wouldn't listen to the locals. They only had themselves to blame.

A Fisherman's Wife

Mrs. Yasu Nemoto (1899–1982)

I married a fisherman when I was twenty-five and came to live near Lake Kasumigaura. I've been here ever since, and I'm eighty-one now.

We did a little farming as well, but it was fishing that gave me all these wrinkles. You know, I remember taking one of the kids out with me once. He was playing around splashing the water, when suddenly he leaned too far out and fell in. I didn't even notice, but a man on another boat shouted out, "Hey, your kid's fallen in the water." I must have turned as white as a sheet. Luckily I'd thought to tie a long piece of cloth around the boy's waist just in case anything happened, so I managed to drag him out before he drowned.

We used to set off well before dawn, around two or three in the morning. We always took a large tub of rice along to keep us going through the day, which meant I had to get up at about one to draw water from the well, carry it back to the house, and cook the rice. We couldn't have started any later: every family got up as early as they could to grab a good position on the lake.

So, you see, life for the wives wasn't ever sweet and easy: I was up not long after midnight, I was out on the boats till mid-afternoon, then, after getting back from the lake, I had to cook and clean the house—and there were the paddy fields to be tended too. The only chance I ever had to do any laundry was at ten or eleven at night, and I'd end up hanging it out to dry by the light of the moon. Mind you, clothes weren't washed anything like as often as they are now—there just wasn't time.

Before I came here as a new bride, I had no idea what I was letting myself in for. I was miserable—hopeless—for the first few months. I felt dead-tired all day long and hated going out on the boat, and I often thought about running away. "But if all the other wives manage to put up with it," I thought, "maybe I ought to try and stick it out a little bit longer"; and after a while I got used to the life, and stayed put.

We really did catch lots of fish. We never hauled up the nets without them brimming over. We sometimes even caught too many: I remember

one time we netted so many carp that the wholesaler refused to buy them all. The only thing we could do was take them down to Ishioka and see if we could get rid of them there. We loaded all the fish onto a handcart, my mother-in-law pulled and I pushed from behind, and we started out.

After a few miles we got to the steep hill at Owada and, with a lot of puffing and panting, we managed to drag the cart up the hill, but we were so done in we could hardly move another inch. That day we'd left home without any breakfast, so we were low on energy. We struggled on a bit further through the fields, but after a while both of us got completely out of breath, and our arms felt all shaky. We couldn't go on, and we hadn't brought any food along that might have perked us up a bit. But we were in luck—just then we met a man we knew. We explained the situation to him and he kindly said, "OK, I'll pull your cart for you. Mine's empty, so you two pull that." We were delighted, but even pulling his empty cart we still found the going pretty difficult.

We eventually made it to Ishioka but, after all that effort, the fish sellers there just laughed at our load. "Where did you pick up these mangy things?" they said. "They're all damaged—they're not fit to be eaten." They refused to buy any of them. We were hopping mad. My parents, though, lived on the outskirts of Ishioka, so as a last resort I went to them and persuaded them to sell the fish for us. My mother was rather curt: "God knows how you managed to bring a load like that all this way. But I don't want to get a bad reputation in the neighborhood, so I'd rather you didn't ever bring any fish here again." She seemed very put out by the whole thing. I'd learned my lesson too, and that was the last of any sales trips to Ishioka.

Even when I was nine months pregnant, I still had to go out fishing. In fact, with my second daughter, I was out on the lake when my contractions started, and we didn't make it home in time—the baby was born on the boat. We called her Urako ["child of the lake"]. She was a healthy girl and she's grown into a fine woman.

Fishing Nets Three Miles Long

Mrs. Hama Suzuki (1906–)

You know, in the old days the water in the lake was so much cleaner than it is now. The fishermen's houses stood in a long line along the shore and all the families used the lake water for cooking and washing; there was no need to dig any wells. The water was so clear you could see the bottom out to some distance.

The front was always a lively place then: the sand white in the bright sun, men shouting and heaving on ropes, women carrying huge baskets of fish, and kids playing and getting in the way or sometimes lending a hand. There was life in that scene. But nowadays the lakeside's almost empty; it's a sad, dead sort of place.

I suppose I must have been a bit of a tomboy when I was small: I remember in the summer I used to run around the beach naked all day long playing in the sun. Where we lived, the lake was quite shallow and, if you waded in up to your knees and grubbed about in the sand with your toes, you could find lots of shellfish. We'd collect as much as a large bucketful in less than an hour.

Our village, Aso, had at least two fishing bosses who used *daitoku* nets. These were up to two or three miles long, and could be used either from the shore or from boats out on the lake. As a kid I often went and joined in. The money you could earn was quite good, so all sorts of people —farmers with a few hours to spare, women, and even the old folk—used to help out. Farmers in those days, you see, worked in their fields every day but never actually got any money till the harvest was in. But if you worked for one of the bosses you were paid in cash the same day, so for farmers this sort of job had an obvious appeal.

The *daitoku* fishing began at dusk and went on right through the night until dawn. The net was taken out on a large boat into the middle of the lake and, when the men reckoned they were in a good spot, it was lowered over the side with the boat moving slowly, so that finally it enclosed a large area of water. The boat then went back to the shore, and the work of winching in the four ropes on each end of the net began. The

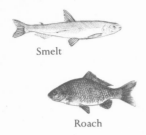

Smelt

Roach

net was incredibly heavy and it took eight wooden winches, each attached to one of the ropes, to pull it in. The men were always in high spirits as they slowly cranked the winches around and wound in the ropes. With each heave, they'd stamp their feet on the ground, chanting as they worked—and sweating like pigs. The women would clap and sing to keep up the rhythm.

As the net got closer to the shore, the men left the winches and everyone waded out into the water to grab the draglines and haul it onto the beach. We kids were always being shouted at by the fishermen for not pulling hard enough: "Don't let the net just dangle like that; heave on the damn thing." Once all the net had been dragged right up onto the beach, the women would put the fish caught in it into baskets. But as soon as it was empty, it was loaded up onto the boat and taken out into the lake again. The net might be lowered and hauled in three or four times in the course of the night and, in the summer at least, all the fishermen and their families worked nonstop right through until first light. If you got completely done in, you could go home and have a lie-down for a couple of hours, but then it was straight back down to the beach again.

There were all kinds of different fish in the lake: smelt, whitebait, roach, eels . . . we even netted the occasional octopus, turbot, or salmon. The fish were sorted by the women and each type put into a separate basket. Whitebait, smelt, carp, and eel were the most profitable, but we caught some varieties, roach for example, in such quantities that we couldn't get rid of them and often had to turn them into fertilizer. Most of the smelt were boiled in brine and dried, then sold to the dealers in Tsuchiura in little plaited straw bags.

The boiling was done in enormous cauldrons that belonged to the boss. These were at least three feet across and eighteen inches deep—the boss had five of them in the kitchen of his house. In each cauldron you heated up a mixture of three parts water to one part salt. You put fifteen pounds of smelt into the brine for two or three minutes, boiling fiercely,

and then fished them out with a net and left them in baskets to cool. After you'd done several batches you'd find a layer of grease floating on the surface of the water, and you had to skim this off carefully to stop it ruining the smelt and turning them a nasty reddish color. The boiled fish were then dried on the beach in the sun. Whenever the weather was good, hundreds of straw mats were laid out end to end right along the beach, all of them covered with smelt slowly drying out under the hot summer sun.

The boss's house was always full of people coming and going; a cheerful place. But the nice thing about going there was that you'd always be given a good meal. If ever one of the farmers in the village had an empty belly, he'd go and lend a hand with the nets just for the meal he'd get afterward. On the day of the festival of the God of Wealth, the boss was even more generous: practically the whole village was fed by him and everyone was given as much saké as he could drink. That was definitely the best day of the year in the fishing villages. The boss himself seemed almost like a god to us.

But everything's changed nowadays, of course. The lakeside will never be the same again.

Bathtubs by the Lake

Mr. Minoru Hida (1924–)

Our house was right next to the lake. You could look out of the window and see the reeds waving in the wind, and listen to the reed warblers. But now they've built a flood wall between our house and the shore, so the view's nothing like as nice as it used to be.

In the old days we used the water from the lake for absolutely everything: the laundry, bath, and cooking. There were two wooden steps down from the bank into the water. The lake rose and fell as much as eighteen inches between low and high tides; usually you could reach the water from the top step, but sometimes you had to crouch down on the lower step. But after the floodgates across the River Hitachitone were closed in 1973 the lake stopped being tidal altogether.

It's hard to imagine how full of fish Lake Kasumigaura was in those days. When you sat there washing the rice for supper, you could see dozens of huge carp swimming around just by your feet. There were loads of gray mullet too. They swam around in shoals of up to two or three thousand, and you could tell where they were because one patch of the lake would turn a different color—fish churning the surface. When the mullet were just offshore the kids would swim out around them and, when they'd got the shoal surrounded, they'd suddenly start making a terrible din and splashing in the water. The fish would try to escape and dozens of them would throw themselves onto the beach in panic. The gray mullet's a very attractive fish—its scales seem to glitter in the sun. Full-grown mullet are about a foot long, and they put up a good fight if you hook one on a rod.

It was a nuisance having to haul buckets of lake water for the bath all the way into the house, so from April to November we used to leave the tub by the lake. A little roof of plaited reeds was put up over it to keep the rain off. And to heat the water, you could use driftwood picked up on the beach; sometimes we burned straw or dry reeds instead. The fishing families on the lake all had their baths like this. Some of them couldn't be bothered to put up a roof so, when it rained, they'd either just sit there

Gray mullet

holding an umbrella or would stick a pole in the ground and tie the umbrella to that. But when the weather was fine it was a lovely feeling sitting there in the bath gazing up at the stars or watching the moon rising over the lake.

The bath wasn't hidden by screens or anything, so you were in full view of anyone who happened to be going past. The girls used to bathe there too, of course, and the lads in the village—me included—used to sneak from one tub to another, trying to get a glimpse of naked bodies. But it was pitch-dark down by the lake, so as often as not we'd end up falling about in the water or being bitten to death by mosquitoes. Playing Peeping Tom wasn't always as much fun as it sounds!

When winter came, the bathtub was taken back inside. Mind you, bathrooms were so basic back then it hardly made any difference whether the bath was inside or out. The "bathroom" was no more than a single stone slab you squatted on to soap yourself before soaking in the tub. The only washcloths we had were filthy; people today wouldn't even use them as cleaning rags. There wasn't any soap or shampoo either; women used to wash their hair in clay.

After dark the bathroom was only lit by a candle left on a ledge or stuck in a lantern. Not a single house had electric light to wash by, though after the war some used light bulbs with long cords that could be moved around and taken into the bathroom when they were needed.

To Tokyo and Back in a Month

Mr. Hachigoro Yamaguchi (1901–1970)

Both my father and my grandfather were boatmen on *takase* riverboats. The work involved transporting goods such as rice, firewood, and straw sacks to Tokyo, and cereals and other cargo back to Tsuchiura.

I was born in a house very near the Kawaguchi lock. The river around there was full of boats then—flat-bottomed riverboats, small rowing boats, and steamers—and dozens of them were always moored along the bank end to end.

I started work on my father's boat as soon as I left primary school. Even children had their uses on board: I had to cook the crew's meals. You see, children in those days were treated rather differently from kids today: from the age of twelve or thirteen we were expected to be able to manage any job an adult could do. On a lot of the riverboats, the wives and families lived on board too, but in our case it was just my father, my three elder brothers, two crew members, and myself; Mother stayed in our house in Kawaguchi, and spent most of her life waiting for us to return from a trip.

Takase boats relied very much on the wind. If you had a strong, favorable wind you could make it to Tokyo in only three days; but that was rare, and sometimes the trip lasted as long as a week or even ten days. The reason was that when it rained heavily the River Tone became really treacherous and also, when the wind was too strong, it was dangerous to hoist the sail. It was impossible to make even a rough estimate of how long it would take you to get to Tokyo. Of course, the *takase* boats did have some good points or we wouldn't have used them. In fact they were very well built and, particularly if there was a good following wind, they were able to cut through the water fast even if you didn't have the sail up.

But when there was no wind at all the boats were useless. And, even worse, in heavy rain with a head wind blowing, all you could do was run out a rope and wait for the weather to change. We'd moor the boat at the side of the river—it could be miles from anywhere—cook ourselves a meal, and just lie around on board till the storm died down. When our food ran out, someone would have to walk as much as two or three miles to the nearest village to buy some more—if you walked far enough you could usually find some sort of little village shop. Most of the shopkeepers were dark-skinned and looked like peasants; but once they realized you were a boatman they'd be friendly enough.

If we were stuck somewhere for several days we'd get fed up being on the boat all the time and would do a bit of sight-seeing. In Takasaki, for instance, there was a famous old tree—you ought to go and have a look at it sometime, I think it's still there. It's supposed to have been planted by Mito Komon, the famous local lord, two centuries ago.

Also, there used to be an old boat we called the "bathboat" in Ohori. It was a barge with a roof added on, and inside it a public bath and several rest rooms had been built. The water for the bath was pumped out of the river.

The bathboat was moored there permanently, and the riverboats used to tie up around it. From early afternoon till late at night there'd be men just soaking in hot water and others gambling in the waist of the boat. Hardly anyone lived in Ohori apart from a few boatmen and the like, so the police very rarely set foot in the place, and you could play dice or whatever without any of the usual risks.

For us it was a fantastic place, somewhere of our own to feel snug in, playing and drinking. No, there weren't any girls on board—you had to go to the brothel in Toride for that. The men used to cross the river in one of the small skiffs when they wanted a woman; large boats always pulled a skiff behind them wherever they went. The prostitutes had a strange way of attracting customers: they used to sit behind lattice screens and blow smoke from long clay pipes in your direction.

So we used to go down the river at a leisurely pace, and we'd feel pleased with ourselves if we managed the round trip from Tsuchiura to Tokyo inside a month. Still, we made enough money from just one trip a

month to feed and house ourselves all right. In fact there can't have been many jobs in those days quite as easy and pleasant as working on one of the riverboats.

Mind you, in the bitter cold of midwinter it wasn't quite such fun. A freezing west wind would blow up off the river and, standing on deck trying to steer wearing only a quilted jacket, I used to find my hands and feet turning to ice before long. I'd be so cold I couldn't even move my lips to speak. And you couldn't let go of the tiller just because you felt cold, of course. I do wonder sometimes how we managed to work in such conditions without getting any serious illness.

In 1918 I went down to Tokyo and started working on barges transporting coal, rice, and cereals. My wife and kids came with me and we lived on board the boat.

One night we'd just set off from Omori, where I'd loaded up with a cargo. Sleet had begun to fall and the deck of the boat became terribly icy. My wife came up on deck with me. I was concentrating on steering when I suddenly heard a splash. I looked around and saw my wife had disappeared. I rushed to the side and peered into the water: she was floating on the surface, bobbing up and down with the waves. We were just passing the Omori Gas Company and the lights from their factory, which were left on all night, lit up the surface of the river. My wife couldn't swim at all, and I realized if I didn't get to her quickly she'd drown. I cut the engine and jumped straight in. After only a few seconds I found her and managed to drag her head back above the surface. I started pulling her toward the boat when I heard a person on the bank shout, "Someone's fallen in the river," and dive into the water toward us. I shouted back, "It's all right—I've found her." "Thank God for that," the other man answered, and after a few minutes he rowed out in a small boat to pick us up. I'd managed to save my wife's life.

The children also fell overboard on several occasions, with me diving in to save them too. Luckily nobody ever drowned. But it does make me wonder, every now and then, how I ever managed to bring up kids in those conditions.

Nowadays there are hardly any boatmen left, not even in Fukagawa in Tokyo. And in Kawaguchi, where as many as twenty or thirty families once lived on their boats, there's not a single one left. When I was young, it seemed just a part of life that rivers should be full of boats. But now all the rivers are almost completely empty. It makes me sad to see an empty river, so these days I try not to go anywhere near them.

By Sail into Town

Mr. Yukio Komatsuzaki (1902–)

We hadn't much choice: we used the rivers for transport, and used them a lot. Every village in the Dejima area had a riverboat making regular trips into Tsuchiura, mostly for moving goods to and fro but they carried some passengers as well.

When my family started in the business in 1919 or 1920, there was already a boat running from our village, Kawajiri, into Tsuchiura: this was the *Asano Maru*, owned by a Mr. Asano, who'd started the service twenty or more years earlier. The *Asano Maru* could carry sixty bags of rice at a time; our boat was a newer, larger type and could carry seventy. You see, there were a number of fairly important stores in Kawajiri, and there was plenty of work hauling goods just for the two biggest: "Yoemon," a grain and fertilizer wholesaler, and "Kanegawa," the leading fish seller in the whole Lake Kasumigaura area.

Our boat left Kawajiri at eight o'clock each morning and usually got back just after three. Most of the villagers were too busy in the fields to be able to get into Tsuchiura to do their shopping themselves, so if there was something they needed they'd call in at our house the evening before and ask me to buy it in town the next day. I used to have to get all sorts of things for people: salt, sugar, soy sauce, clogs, straw sandals, cloth. . . .

Sometimes I was even asked to go to the bank and draw out or transfer money. Of course, the person would have to give me his bankbook and seal. And if someone had something like a fixed-term deposit that had come to maturity, I'd be told perhaps to withdraw the interest earned, or to reinvest the money for another year, or even to take out a certain amount and buy something the customer wanted with it. But when I was working for either "Yoemon" or "Kanegawa," for some reason they wouldn't let me withdraw money from the bank to pay for the stuff they wanted; they insisted on giving me the money in cash. Sometimes I had to look after very large sums indeed.

Until the end of the 1920s all the boats on the river were rowed, so, depending on the wind, it took a bit over an hour to get to Tsuchiura.

If there was a following wind, we used to put up a small sail to help the boat along. In the winter it was so cold we kept a little charcoal brazier on board and made tea on it, using the water from the river, to serve to the passengers.

The round trip cost ten sen. I seem to remember the fare was the same throughout the twenties and thirties right up till the war. Ten sen might seem quite cheap, but when you think most farmers in those days only got paid in cash once a year, after the harvest, it was in fact more than most of them could afford.

In the old days Tsuchiura was far more prosperous and go-ahead than it is now. There were always dozens of riverboats like mine moored along the quay in Kawaguchi, and hundreds of people, down from the surrounding villages, poured off them into town. We also had *takase* boats, steamers, and sight-seeing boats, all full of passengers and cargo, coming in and out of Tsuchiura all day long.

Once I'd moored my boat, the passengers would go their separate ways into town, and until two o'clock they'd spend the time shopping or visiting friends. So I'd set about buying the various things the villagers had asked me to get. Let's see: I bought salt from "Nomura's" in Uchinishicho, sugar from "Nomura's" sugar shop in Nakajo, and soy sauce from "Nagai's," or later on from "Shibanuma's" in Mushikake. For most things I just had to telephone from Kawaguchi and a shop boy would deliver the order to the boat by bicycle.

After I'd had my lunch, I went back to the boat. By then, everything I'd ordered would've been delivered and stacked up on board. And one by one the passengers would straggle back too. When everyone who'd been on the boat that morning had arrived and all the goods had been delivered, I'd say, "Right, let's shove off then, shall we?" and we'd head for home.

I only ran one regular return trip to Tsuchiura each day but, depending on how much cargo I had to take into town, it wasn't all that unusual for me to do two journeys a day. Naturally, when it was really windy we canceled the run. But sometimes it happened that, though there'd been little wind on the outward trip, by the time I wanted to set out from Tsuchiura the wind would've got up and sailing was out of the question. In that case I had to ask the passengers to go back by road, and I myself would spend the night on the boat, still moored in Kawaguchi.

I didn't usually go up the River Sakura, but on sunny days in the cherry blossom season I used to take parties of villagers on the boat, and we'd go under the railway bridge, past Nioi Bridge, and all the way up the Sakura to Mushikake. That stretch of the river was a tunnel of flowers; I don't think there's anything to match it elsewhere in Japan. The lines of cherry trees continued along both banks up as far as Mushikake Bridge. Fancy barges would float by with rich parties from Tsuchiura in them, dancing and singing and having fun with geisha. On both sides of the river there'd be rows of little stalls selling food and drink to dozens of sightseers. In full bloom, it was spectacular.

But the riverboats all went out of service a few years after the war. With so many cars and trucks around, people began to use the roads for transporting things. Most of the River Kawaguchi was filled in and made into a road, and the cherry trees along the Sakura have all disappeared. Only cars run along the Kawaguchi now. Everything's changed so much, in such a short time. . . .

The Business Side of Fishing

Mr. Shunichi Hotate (1914–)

The Tsuchiura Sea Fishing Company was owned by a man from a former samurai family who also had a fish market. The company was managed by twelve directors, and there were two vice-chairmen: Tohachi Okubo, who ran a greengrocer's as well as being tied in with the company, and Hachiemon Numajiri, who also owned a grocer's shop in Omachi. You probably think it's strange that grocers were involved in a fishing business, but in those days, remember, fish shops sold all sorts of stuff, not just fish.

You see, trawlers were much smaller then, so if the sea was at all rough they couldn't put out. When that happened, of course, we in Tsuchiura wouldn't get any deliveries of deep-sea fish. With nothing to sell, the fish shops supplied by the company couldn't do any trade, so instead they'd buy up whatever had been delivered to Tsuchiura on the steamer in place of the fish. The steamer would arrive piled high with groceries, radishes or something, the company would buy the whole batch, and the fish shops would have to go hawking the goods around the town. Sometimes, even, Lake Kasumigaura was too rough for the steamer to cross to Tsuchiura, and then they were forced to buy up leeks and other vegetables from the villages nearby and sell those.

There's one funny story I remember about those days: once, when the fishermen on the coast had failed to catch anything, a whole consignment of cherry saplings was sent up on the steamer. The fishing company had no choice but to buy them and get its men to walk around the town trying to flog them. But no one wanted the trees, so in the end, just to get rid of the damn things, they planted the whole lot along the banks of the River Kawaguchi. They grew, and that's why, before the war, the banks of the Kawaguchi in spring were smothered in cherry blossom.

The fishing company started up in 1881 and was in business for over forty years. All the fish was brought upriver by steamer from Choshi on the coast. Bonito and sardines were transported in bamboo baskets, the slightly higher-class turbot and bream were put into large barrels, and shark or tuna were just laid out loose on the deck of the ship. But this

The Choshi steamer

doesn't mean that before 1881 no sea fish got to Tsuchiura at all. It got here all right—it was brought up from Choshi by *takase* boat. Even the steamer took eight hours to get from Choshi to Tsuchiura, so the *takase* boats must have taken more than a day to make the trip. Some of it even reached here by road, piled up on handcarts.

Our shop made fish sausages—we used to sell them in Utsunomiya. There was no such thing as preservatives in our time, so the stock had to be sold within three days of being produced. And since it took a whole day to cart it to Utsunomiya, once you got there you had to get rid of it all in a day or two or you'd find yourself with a load of rotting sausages on your hands. Luckily the Utsunomiya area used to get absolutely no deliveries of fresh fish, so they didn't produce any sausages either and it was easy enough to unload them there. Too easy, probably: the young lads from the shop who took the stuff down to Utsunomiya often stopped off in Tsukuba on the way back and spent the night with a woman—they were always coming home with a lot less money than they should have had.

Our biggest headache, though, was how to keep fish from going off. We tried all sorts of ways: we built a stone storeroom under our house and in the winter we'd take a cart up to Lake Suwa to fetch ice. It was about a three-week trip, there and back. We'd pack the ice with sawdust to keep it from melting, and in summer it was put in the cellar with the fish. Eventually a company started up in Kamitakatsu producing ice, but it was very expensive. We also had a number of big, wide tubs made for us; if you put masses of salt and water in them you could keep any sort of fish fresh for a while. But that still wasn't long—maybe a few days at most, if you kept changing the water.

So a spot of food poisoning was no great surprise to anyone in those days; it was actually very common. The trouble was that people would quite happily eat even fish that tasted off. When the stuff made you ill, you'd probably just make a joke about it, like "I should have had a servant try it first!" You wouldn't have made the sort of fuss that someone with food poisoning would today. Think about it: in those days the shops bought fish that had already traveled a whole day up from the coast. By the time the boys took the stuff out around the town to sell, it obviously wasn't going to be a hundred percent. It really is something that nowadays you can eat raw fish safely anytime, even in the middle of the summer.

When the Kawaguchi District Thrived

Mr. Yoshimatsu Sekozawa (1908–)

Many of my early memories—I grew up in Kawaguchi—are of swimming in the river there, which until the 1920s was clean and clear. As soon as school was over in the afternoon I'd get my mother to give me ten sen and, leaving my clothes on one of the willows in front of our house, I'd dive into the river, then swim down under Asahi Bridge along to "Ogata's," the large fertilizer merchant. If the water was fairly high I'd usually climb out onto the bank thereabouts, but it was steep and I might have to drift on a bit further to "Tsuruta's" wharf and haul myself out there. There was a cake shop near the bridge, so I'd go and buy something to eat.

My next destination was the Watanabe Shipping berth, where I would hitch a ride down to Lake Kasumigaura on one of their boats. The owner was a close friend of my father's, and the crew always allowed me on board; but I was the exception, since other kids—unless they were with me—were kicked straight off, so I often had a little gang of five or six trailing along. We used to ride several hundred yards downriver, then dive off and swim back home.

Oddly enough, my parents weren't the least bit worried about me swimming in the Kawaguchi; but I remember asking once if I could walk to Tsukuba and for some reason they seemed to think it was dangerous and wouldn't let me go. In actual fact the river in front of our house, being near the lock, flowed past at quite a rate and wasn't safe at all; the police had even banned children from swimming there. So if we saw a policeman coming while we were splashing about, we had to scramble up the bank, grab our clothes, and run like hell. That part of the river was so deep, you know, we could do backward somersaults off the lock gates without touching bottom.

Until the 1960s, when sluices were built at the mouth of the River Hitachitone, Lake Kasumigaura was full of fish, and water flowed in and out the whole time from all the rivers and the sea.

In 1922, 156 red dace were brought up from Lake Biwa, near Kyoto,

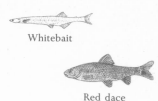

Whitebait

Red dace

by the Fish Research Center and released in the River Sakura; within only five or six years they'd done so well that local fishermen were catching them in vast quantities, there and in the lake. One trick was to tie up a bundle of bamboo grass and drop it in the water; shrimp and shellfish would burrow into the grass, and you could catch the dace that came to feed off them.

Red dace laid their eggs inside mussel shells. Kasumigaura was fairly shallow, so sunlight reached right to the bottom of the lake, the mussels grew quickly, and the eggs inside the shells also developed well—in fact the fish are supposed to have bred far better in Lake Kasumigaura than they did in Lake Biwa.

My father bought dace from the fishermen and sent them out for sale all over Japan. In the late 1930s he sold more than forty tons of them a year just in Tokyo, shipped in large drums with a special contraption that allowed oxygen to get in. But it was in the Osaka area that he sold most, the custom there being to eat dace on special occasions, while in Tokyo sea bream was more common. We were even catching more red dace here than where we got them from originally, and we began to reexport back to that area. We also sent consignments to Nagoya, where they were usually eaten broiled in soy sauce.

When eels were sent off for sale, they were put in large bamboo baskets and piled onto a freight train, four on top of each other. If the weather was hot, ice was packed in with them and they could then travel as far as Hokkaido without any problem. To be on the safe side, though, in summer we'd often arrange for someone to meet the train at Aomori Station on the way and pour buckets of cold water over the eels to make sure they were still alive when they got to the other end. Every year we sent between thirty and thirty-five tons of them to Tokyo alone. You see, in those days you could easily catch a ton of eels at a time in a single large net.

In places, the Hitachitone was literally crammed with eels, so much so

Kawaguchi: the wharf

that the fishermen often caught too many and had trouble getting rid of them, and they'd end up being used for fish stew or even spread on the fields as compost. We used to buy all our eels from a broker. And to keep them alive until they were transported, we put them in baskets and left them in the river. Around where the main car park in the center of Tsuchiura is today there used to be row upon row of our eel baskets, strung right across the water.

We also sold whitebait. Whitebait were caught in large quantities from about September onward. They were packed into casks with ice, each holding forty pounds, and sent out to all parts of the country—five casks usually going to each area. We could probably have sold as much as ten or twenty, but we reckoned that if we sent too much at a time people would soon get fed up with the fish. So instead we sent small consignments frequently to several different regions. But the trouble with this was that we could never get hold of as many casks as we needed, and we often had to make do with empty soy-sauce barrels.

We didn't sell much smelt in the Osaka region, because there they only ate the very large kind—strange people! Most of it went to the Tokyo area, though a certain amount was sold in Gunma; but, there again, they seemed to prefer the larger sort, and our nice standard ones weren't all that popular. Compared to red dace the market for freshwater smelt was small—they didn't even fetch a particularly good price—this partly because dried smelt didn't sell at all well in Tokyo.

Roach were so common I wouldn't even like to guess how many were caught in a year. The fishermen were always pestering us to buy some from them. Even when we said we didn't want any, they'd go off and store the fish in baskets in the river to keep them fresh, and a few days later they'd be back trying to sell us the same fish again. Sometimes they just stuffed them into eel baskets and tried flogging them from house to house.

We sold both natural and farm-bred carp. These were caught in vast numbers too. There are even records of three tons of carp being caught in a single net, and we were always hearing stories of fishermen who'd netted so many they couldn't drag them out of the water. But there was a steady demand for carp: in Namegata it was eaten at all celebrations, and in Inashiki it was served at wedding parties.

But when they shut the sluice gates at the mouth of the Hitachitone, blocking the lake off from the sea, it became impossible to catch dace, roach, or anything like that around Tsuchiura. All the mussels died off, so the fish that laid their eggs inside the shells were wiped out too. And fish like smelt and eels that swim up from the sea are now so few and far between they're pretty well extinct around these parts as well.

SHOPKEEPERS
AND
TRADESMEN

A tofu seller

Shopping by Rickshaw

Mrs. Fumiko Hirose (1903-)

I used to live in Fujisawa, and whenever there was a sale on in Tsuchiura I'd go into town shopping with my grandmother. On the way in we'd walk all along the River Sakura, but usually we got a rickshaw to take us home. Sometimes we caught the horse bus in, but unfortunately it ran only very infrequently. I think the bus stop was near the Fujisawa Shrine. There was a little sweet shop there that sold lemonade and a kind of jelly called *tokoroten*; we used the place as a sort of waiting room. An hour or more waiting there, looking out at the dusty road with the sun beating down on it, always made me awfully thirsty and I sometimes persuaded my grandmother to buy me a bottle of lemonade. Soft drinks were never chilled back then, and they didn't even sell ices in the shop. But though the lemonade was lukewarm it tasted delicious and I can still remember the feeling as it slipped down my throat.

The horse-drawn buses held about eight people. The road to Tsuchiura was terribly rutted and uneven and, especially if it had been raining, the bus would shake and rattle—it was so bad that one moment you'd be sitting there quite happily and the next you'd almost bang your head on the roof. The stretch from Fujisawa to Manabe went right through the mountains. The road was narrow and the pine trees seemed to go on forever; even on sunny days it was as dark as nighttime there. Apparently people in the old days were quite often attacked by bandits along that lonely mountain trail.

When the new Tsukuba Railway opened in 1914, the bus service was stopped; still, the railway was run in a fairly casual, friendly way. I remember once, when I was going to Tsuchiura to have a sewing lesson, I was walking along still quite some way from Fujisawa Station when I saw the train coming in. I started running and the stationmaster called out to me, "Where do you want to go?" "Manabe," I shouted back. "Right, I'll get your ticket and hold the train up. You get straight on," he said. I rushed down to the track as fast as I could, one of the passengers hauled me on board, and the train immediately set off. The conductor brought

my ticket along, and he told me I could pay the stationmaster for it when I got back.

Almost all our clothes-shopping was done at "Daitoku." Drapers' shops back then all had *tatami*-mat floors, so you took off your shoes before you went up inside. Customers were greeted by an assistant who'd get one of the shop boys to bring down various items and lay them out in front of you. "No, I don't really like this. No, this isn't quite what I want," the customer would say—you could spend several hours looking at everything the shop had to offer. It might have been different for people living in the town, but country women like my grandmother came into Tsuchiura with the intention of spending the whole day there and so they didn't mind in the least how long it took to buy what they wanted. The shop assistants were in no particular hurry either, so, far from being annoyed that we took such a long time, they were always nice and showed us everything they had in stock. When Granny finally decided what to buy, the assistant would work out the bill on an abacus, and my grandmother would ask him to wait a minute while she went across the road to the Goju Bank to draw out the money.

By the time she'd paid, it would be gone midday, so we'd be asked to stay and have something to eat. This was served in a room at the back of the shop. When they had a sale on, both the room at the back and the shop itself would be packed with customers having lunch, and the maids would be so busy that, even if the weather was cold, they'd be sweating. Serving meals to so many people, they must have got through a good three sacks of rice a day, I should think.

After lunch, rather than just go straight home, we'd spend some more time browsing around the shop. And at the end of the afternoon, "Daitoku" would call a rickshaw to take us back to Fujisawa. Actually, we needed two or three of them to take both us and everything Granny had bought—the fare was terribly expensive. Granny always came home with piles of shopping, so I think she must have been really quite well-off.

99

When my mother came along as well, she used to joke, "We'll be all right today—we've got old moneybags with us."

The rickshaws always took the road along the Sakura. As the sun went down and it began to get dark, the men would light lanterns on long poles and hang them on the rickshaws, where they'd swing from side to side as we trundled along. And on summer evenings, thousands of fireflies swarmed around, blown like sparks. Sometimes you could hear frogs croaking: they'd suddenly stop as the rickshaws got near, but once they were past they'd start up again. It was wonderful, with the sound of running feet on the dark path and the moon over the distant mountains.

"Daitoku," the Draper's

Mr. Masao Ogata, brother (1912–1986)
Mrs. Utako Murase, sister (1906–)

Masao Ogata: Apparently the first owner of "Daitoku"—Kazuma Ogata—was the son of a priest from Katori Shrine. Why a priest's son should have come to Tsuchiura I've no idea, but he started as an apprentice in a soy sauce shop, a famous one that made the soy used by the shogun; worked his way up to become head clerk; and finally set up in business on his own in about 1763.

Utako Murase: But it was the third owner of the shop, wasn't it, who really got things going?

Masao: Yes, that's right. He came from Ishioka and was adopted as an Ogata when he married the eldest daughter of the family. With us, it's always been a tradition that the shop is inherited by the eldest child, whether it's a girl or a boy. If it's a girl, her husband runs the business. The second, third, fourth, and fifth owners were all outsiders adopted into the family when they married the eldest daughter. Our mother was the first bride to come into the family for more than two hundred years.

Anyway, the third owner, Tokuhei Ogata, used to buy all his supplies in Edo and have the goods brought up to Tsuchiura by river. But at the end of 1865 there was a terrible fire in Nakajo—almost all the buildings were razed. As it happened, Tokuhei had been making plans to build a house for his own parents back in Ishioka, and all the wood was cut and ready. So, after the fire, the wood was moved to Nakajo, within three days they'd built a new shop, and "Daitoku" was able to open again using stock from the old storehouse, built in 1842, which had survived the fire.

Utako: You know, when I was a child the shop looked exactly as it had in the eighteenth century. At the front were shutters—these were only closed at night—and, behind them, very thin latticework doors. Just inside the shop there was an earth-floored area about twelve feet wide. At night a solid wooden shutter, which was kept out of sight during the daytime, was pulled down from the ceiling to close the entrance area off from the main part of the shop and stop anyone breaking in.

The left-hand side of the place, as you looked toward it from outside, was called the "upper shop" and the right-hand part the "lower shop"; in between the two was an earth-floored passage, about six feet wide, that ran right through to the back. The upper shop sold silks and better fabrics, and the lower shop muslins and so on. Some customers bought what they wanted from the edge of the *tatami* floor without coming into the shop itself, but many of them did come inside and took their time looking at various articles before deciding what to buy.

Masao: In the old days we didn't use display cases at all. When customers came in, one of the assistants would go and greet them, and then he'd shout to a shop boy to bring out particular items. The boy would go into the storeroom next to the lower shop and bring back whatever he'd been told to fetch. The assistant spread the articles out on the *tatami* to show the customers; they'd have a good browse over the stuff and, if they decided they'd like to look at something else, the shop boy would run off to the storeroom again. Older lads worked in the storeroom, passing down goods from the shelves in a container known as a *hariko*: this was just a bamboo basket covered in cloth, with handholes to make it easier to carry. They often played nasty tricks on boys they didn't like, such as deliberately dropping heavy *hariko* or passing down the wrong things.

The shop boys were all given nicknames ending in "-kichi," and when they became full apprentices the ending changed to "-suke": for example, Sakichi would become Sasuke. But once you became an assistant you were called by your proper name with "-san" after it.

So, you see, things were only brought out when they were needed, and most of the time the main area of the shop was completely bare. Admittedly, it was a damn nuisance having to drag the stuff out every time someone came in, and then take it all back afterward. I suppose it was done partly as a precaution against fire and theft.

Utako: Yes, it certainly made a lot of work for the shop boys. They were kept running backward and forward and were always in such a hurry they

"Daitoku"

didn't have time to use the gangway over the corridor between the upper and lower shops—they just leaped over the gap. The assistants were all good at their job too: they had to be able to tell as soon as a customer came in who he or she was, where they were from, and what they were likely to buy. You see, they'd then know what to get out to show the customer. The assistants all carried a little writing box, with a drawer in it, and an account book. The shop boys would line up at the back behind the assistants so they could nip off on their errands. And at the very back of the upper shop was an office where the deputy manager, who was in overall charge, sat keeping an eye on things.

In between the lower shop and the storeroom was a long *tatami*-mat room where the shop boys could take a break. Also customers who'd come to buy wedding presents, or something like that, used the room to have a careful look at what we had in stock. In the corner were five or six desks, and in the evening the older employees would teach the young lads reading, writing, and how to use an abacus. There was also a large cupboard for bedding in a corner of the room; at night, when all the work was finished, the mattresses were taken out and laid on the floor of the shop—the assistants sleeping in the upper shop, apprentices and shop boys in the lower one.

Masao: In those days people didn't have a lot of furniture or decorations in their rooms. When you needed something, you got it out of a cupboard or storage and put it back when you'd finished with it. So rooms never got cluttered up with junk and no space was wasted.

Utako: There was also a night watchman who patrolled the house and grounds every night on the lookout for fires and burglars. He had a little hut by the old storehouse where he slept during the day. In the late afternoon he'd get up to light the fire for the bath and then go back to sleep a bit longer until it was dark. All night long he wandered around with a lantern attached to his belt, banging a pair of wooden clappers every now and then. Sometimes if a plasterer or carpenter was working in the house,

Another draper's

the watchman would stay awake during the day too, to keep an eye on him and make sure he did his job properly. It was very important to have a good night watchman.

During the spring and autumn sales, at *o-bon* in August, and at the end of the year, we'd open up an additional four rooms at the back of the shop. Everywhere would be packed with customers. There were rooms above the shop as well, where we could put up people who'd come from a long way off. During a sale all the fabrics were laid out along the walls, and a gramophone with an enormous fluted horn blared music out of the windows. On my way back from school I could hear the music from as far away as the little shrine to Konpira—it made me skip, I was so happy.

Masao: The maids' bedroom was upstairs at the top of a narrow back staircase. Parents felt that when their daughter became a maid in our house she was our responsibility until she went off to be married; so if anything ever happened to the girl we'd have been in trouble. At night the watchman would often sit in the kitchen to check that no men went up the back staircase.

Next to the maids' room were three more large bedrooms. The senior maids slept in the middle one, and the other two belonged to my grand-parents and my mother and father. This was a convenient arrangement because the maids in the middle could wait on the rooms on either side and also keep an eye on the girls at the back of the house.

Utako: In those days, whenever a member of the imperial family came to Tsuchiura, he always slept in our house. Princes apparently had to have a suite of three rooms wherever they stayed. The prince slept in the eight-mat room at the back, his attendants in the ten-mat room near the front staircase, and the middle one was left empty. The maids' bedroom was used as an antechamber for people waiting for an audience. We also had to build a new bath in the courtyard with a curtain around it, for the prince to use.

Masao: I remember we used a hand pump to draw water from our well—

104

it ran along a tin pipe into the kitchen sink and the bath. Good, clean water it was, too, wasn't it?

Utako: Our bath was enormous—do you remember? It was so big you could have got at least three or four people in it together. The boy in charge of the bath seemed to be stoking the fire up all the time—there was always masses of hot water.

Masao: Back then it was the custom that men bathed before women: Father would go in first, then the shop assistants, followed by the apprentices and the shop boys. When all the men had finished, my elderly grandmother, my mother, and my sisters could have their turn. Even the male servants went in before the women.

Utako: They kept it filled to the brim—it always slopped over when I got in. It seemed such a waste of hot water.

Masao: Clothes were dried on the roof of the bathhouse. Next door to it were storerooms for rice and pickles, and past them was Mr. Yamaguchi's house. This had once been a government inn where feudal lords and officials stayed. Around 1910 our family bought a piece of land at the back of it for a woodshed.

Utako: The narrow lane that ran alongside "Daitoku" was always crowded. You see, there were a number of geisha parlors there: "Suzunoya," "Sakasei," and others; a bit further along was a large restaurant called "Koyokan." It was like a miniature red-light district, but in the 1920s they all moved to the town's official entertainment quarter. Various other people moved in and new shops opened up, but many of them left again later—the area around our house has changed so much over the years.

Masao: The drapery business has changed completely too, of course. There aren't any shops nowadays still run in the traditional way. But I suppose it's only natural that business should have to move with the times.

The General Store

Mrs. Iku Sato (1897–)

Nowadays every little town and village has a small supermarket, but in my time there'd have been a general store instead. It's more than sixty-five years now since I married a man from Tsuchiura and came to live in the city, but I was born and brought up in Shishido—a small castle town, though by then the castle was a pile of stones; it was just an agricultural center, and any military importance it might have had was long since gone. My parents ran the general store there, so let me tell you something about what it was like.

Our shop—a wooden two-story building—sold absolutely everything: bedding, fabrics, clothes, salt, sugar, dried fish, *katsuo bushi* [fish flavoring used in soups], medicines, shoes, pickles—everything. And we were one of the few places in town with gas lighting. You see, farming families only did their shopping after dark, since they were out in the fields during the day. So, until electricity arrived, we used acetylene lamps to light the shop; before that, we'd used oil lamps.

On January 2 each year we held a grand sale—I can remember it as clearly as if it was only yesterday. My brothers and sisters and I all went to bed early on the evening of the first, and at midnight we'd be woken up by one of the shop boys running around the house shouting at the top of his voice, "The sale's starting, the sale's starting. Wake up, wake up." I'd rub the sleep out my eyes and force myself to get up. When I went downstairs the place would already be buzzing with excitement and the boys putting the final touch to things. Outside in the dark there'd be a bonfire burning; I could see the flames dance and spit in the freezing wind, and dozens of people around the fire, pushing and shoving, impatient with waiting for us to open.

Inside the shop were five or six hundred "lucky bags" stacked in piles reaching almost to the ceiling. Customers came from miles away to buy them. They only cost fifty sen each and were full of all sorts of odds and ends like scraps of belt material, slightly damaged underwear, hems for slips, waistcloths, smocks, aprons, and loose bits of cloth. The contents of

A general store

the bags were worth anything between three and five yen at normal prices, so people would begin queuing outside from early in the evening on New Year's Day to make sure they didn't miss out on such a bargain. Many of them walked, or came by horse and cart, from villages up to ten or fifteen miles away.

Right through the morning the number of customers milling around gradually built up. The shop boys shouted and greeted them from every corner; it was like a fairground. It made our department stores today look very drab and boring.

Upstairs we'd put on sideshows to entertain the customers. In one of these a maid, dressed up in a sumptuous costume as the goddess Amaterasu, would suddenly emerge from behind a large rock. The audience loved it. . . .

But, let's see, what else went on? At the end of the nineteenth century the shop had begun to sell stuff on an installment basis. In all the villages around Shishido, associations were formed and the head of each one took responsibility for collecting the payments on goods his members had bought. One day each year all seventy or eighty farmers in a village association would come down to our shop, either on horseback or on foot, and decide what they wanted to buy. We had to serve them all lunch—we were rushed off our feet.

In the summer we used to give them enormous bowls of noodles, chilled in the cool water from our well. But however much we gave them, they'd always wolf it down in a few seconds. I often used to wonder what on earth their stomachs were like, to be able to eat such a lot so fast.

Sugar wasn't used in everyday cooking back then, but for holidays and festivals people made cakes and rice dumplings stuffed with sweet bean jam. The day before the holiday the shop was always full of customers buying sugar. We stored it in sixteen-gallon barrels in the lower shop. Three of the assistants manned the sugar counter and spent the whole day weighing out scoopfuls of it on the scales. They got so practiced at this that the amount they scooped up would always be exactly the weight the customer had asked for. (And if the sugar was for someone the assistant knew, he might throw in an extra spoonful free.)

We also sold medicines—I'm not really sure what sorts we kept, though. But I do remember farmers often came and banged on the shutters in the middle of the night, shouting that their kid had come down with a fever, and begging us to open up.

Sometimes a customer would ask my father to get a top-quality kimono for a formal banquet. If the kimono was needed really urgently Father himself would make the long trip to Nihonbashi in Tokyo to buy it. I remember once he got back late at night and the last train from Tomobe to Shishido had already gone; he had to walk all the way home with the huge package, containing the kimono and all the other fabrics he'd bought in Tokyo, on his back.

My grandmother was born and raised in Tsuchiura and came to Shishido as a bride when she was only sixteen. Her sewing was superb, and farmers' wives who didn't have time to make clothes themselves would ask her to sew up a kimono for them from cloth they'd bought in our shop. A number of young girls, mostly from farming families, came to the needlework classes my grandmother gave. They'd start by learning how to sew up simple things like everyday work clothes and, by the end of their training, they'd be able to make their own bridal kimono. I often made tea for the girls and served them steamed potatoes.

But what a crowd we were: our house was usually bursting at the seams. I had six brothers and sisters and, as well as my parents and my father's parents, a dozen or so clerks and shop boys, four or five maids, and a couple of nannies also lived with us. There was an old laundrywoman, too, who worked for the family for years and years right up until she died. Having to do everybody's washing, in the heart of winter, must have been very tough work—I remember she had the most horrible chilblains, and her skin was as hard as tree bark.

A sewing class

We also employed a woodcutter and a plasterer; they both lived over the shop too. The woodcutter had his hands full felling trees in the hills we owned behind the house and producing firewood and timber for us. The plasterer also had plenty of work to do on all the buildings in the grounds. As well as the shop and our house, there were a couple of storehouses where we kept stock for the shop, a store for salt and another for rice, a cottage where my grandparents lived, and a stable.

We were always being visited by horse traders. We didn't actually sell horses at the shop but Grandfather used to deal in them as a hobby. The traders would turn up in the early hours of the morning with twenty or thirty horses loaded onto heavy wagons—they always made a terrible din. They'd tie the things up in our yard, then start an informal horse sale. Luckily the yard was nearly an acre in size so there was plenty of room. After a few hours, news about the sale would get around and farmers from other villages would begin to arrive.

We owned three horses ourselves; they were looked after by a stable lad, whose name was Kinji, I seem to remember. My grandfather was very keen on horses but he couldn't actually ride, so he used to get Father to try out new ones for him. Father could ride even the fieriest horse bareback; he'd gallop the thing up the steep hill behind our house to see what sort of condition it was in. And even if he fell off and hurt himself, he'd climb straight on again without turning a hair. He loved rough, dangerous sports, was good at them, and made a successful businessman as well.

The reason our shop did such a good trade was partly because there were few other stores nearby, and also because it was almost impossible to get to Tokyo or even Tsuchiura to do your shopping in those days. Now, looking back, it's hard to believe that Shishido could have been so isolated. In some ways it's a good thing the countryside's been opened up so much, but . . . I mean, progress does have its drawbacks too.

Eggs by Special Delivery

Mr. Hideo Komatsu (1918–)

I wonder if I can remember. I think there were four big egg wholesalers in Tsuchiura before the war: my own shop; "Tochigiya"; "Torisei's" near the station; and "Iijima's" at the foot of Asahi Bridge.

We had a number of lads working for us whose only job was to carry eggs from our shop to Kitasenju in Tokyo; they went backward and forward on the train, and did three or four return trips a day. Each boy had his railway pass hanging around his neck. With an enormous pack on his back and bundles in both hands, one boy could carry as much as 180 lbs. of eggs at a time: 100 lbs. on his back and forty in each hand. Of course the amount each of them could manage depended a bit on how strong he was.

Their packs were boxes about eighteen inches square and three feet deep—they were just like climbers' backpacks, really. Hemp rope and old cloth were wound around them so they didn't rub the shoulders. A layer of rice bran was put in the bottom of the box and on top of that a neat, single layer of eggs; you then put in another layer of rice bran and another layer of eggs and so on, to a depth of about a foot or eighteen inches; after that you could pile on the eggs without any bran. When the box was full, you put an extra frame around the top to extend the depth by another ten or twelve inches and added more eggs until this was full too. When the eggs reached the top of the frame, you began to pile them on in a pyramid shape and like this you could stack them up another twelve inches or so. You then tied a piece of cotton cloth tightly around the whole lot and heaved it onto your back. Provided the eggs were stacked like this and you didn't handle the pack too roughly, they never got broken.

To save time, we had someone else carry the loads, either on a bicycle or a handcart, to the station for them, so the lads on the train spent the whole day doing nothing but going backward and forward from Tsuchiura to Tokyo. Not that it was ever a cushy job: they had to catch the first train in the morning, at four o'clock, and with four return trips, between them three boys might have to deliver almost a ton of eggs in a single day. Incidentally, it was against railway regulations to travel with such enormous packs, but they weren't too fussy in those days and the conductor would turn a blind eye to it.

The shop sold chickens as well as eggs. We sent other boys out around the dozens of villages in the Tsuchiura area buying up birds, which they delivered to the shop in the evening. The chickens were then stuffed into baskets and sent off by train to Tokyo—in fact there used to be a special chicken train that ran from Tsuchiura to Tokyo. Our local birds were pretty much the mainstay of the Kitasenju market. The baskets were oval, about four feet across. They didn't have lids, but were covered with plaited ropes that made it easy to get the birds in and out (and kids, too—ours were always playing in them). You could get fifteen or twenty of them in one basket. To start with, we only used baskets from southern Japan, but later we had a local man produce some specially for us. We needed them: by then we were using at least ten a day, and sometimes as many as twenty or thirty—sales being really pretty good.

Mind you, it wasn't easy. I mean, today you have breeders producing chickens on a massive scale, but back then most farmers only kept a few chickens and it was a matter of going around and buying one or two birds at a time from each. On their own our people could never have managed to buy up enough of them, so we also bought some birds from chicken dealers.

The dealers sometimes came from miles away, mostly by bicycle. They all had large bicycles with luggage racks so big you could load three baskets on them at a time. And they raised the back of the rack slightly so that the baskets rested against them as they rode along, just as if they were actually carrying the load on their back; like this the baskets wouldn't fall off.

The strongest men could carry 250 lbs. of chickens on their bikes. That's about sixty birds, I suppose. It must have been murder hefting a load like that all the way from Iwase and Shimodate—people wouldn't dream of doing that kind of thing today. And the roads were really bumpy as well, not even graveled. So when the dealers arrived at our shop, they'd be worn out by the ride and so hungry they'd even snatch food left outside in a bucket and gobble it down. We always gave them a midday meal but sometimes they couldn't wait. But however hard the work was, they needed all the money they could get, so the toughest of them would make two or three trips into Tsuchiura every day. Even men from Shimodate often made two round trips in a day, and when you think it's something like twenty-five miles from Tsuchiura to Shimodate, they were doing about a hundred miles altogether. And they were carrying enormous loads and riding over dirt tracks. We also got a lot of duck brought in from Oyama. In those days they used to catch any amount of duck and other waterfowl on the lake, using ropes and birdlime.

Once the dealers got their money, they never went straight home—they'd usually stay the night in Tsuchiura for a bit of fun. I knew two of them particularly well: Goro Haga from Dejima and Masataro Tarumi. Both of them were getting on, but as soon as all the birds were sold they made straight for a geisha house to have a few drinks.

These last few years poultry farmers have moved into mass production, rearing tens of thousands of chickens at a time. Hens spend their whole lives laying eggs and never go outside, and birds bred for meat are specially fed to cut down to a minimum the length of time before they can be killed. In my day chickens were reared at a far more leisurely pace, but it was also much harder work. I don't think I ever imagined then that everything would change so much in only thirty or forty years.

The Secondhand Shop

Mrs. Shige Ono (1899–1983)

When I was a child, Tajuku and Omachi were divided by a river with a plank bridge across it. The river's no longer there—it's now a road. It's frightening how fast things change, isn't it? Our house was the third one along on the far side of the bridge, after "Isayama's," the cartwright, and "Iimura's" tofu shop. We ran a secondhand shop. In the old days, this could be very profitable, the reason being that, after the feudal domains were abolished in 1868, the lords and samurai found it difficult to make ends meet and started selling off their family heirlooms: swords, armor, lances, and hanging scrolls.

We bought up this sort of stuff and sold it in our shop. Today you can spend weeks searching for antique bargains, but back then there were lots of good things around that you could pick up for next to nothing. As I remember, we were the only secondhand shop in Omachi, but in Tajuku there was one called "Takano's" and another in Nakajo. And there were several other shops that sold just old furniture and clothes. The poorer families couldn't afford new clothes, you see, so they had to buy other people's castoffs.

Unfortunately we very rarely came across anything of real value or beauty. I don't know whether this was because there hadn't been any famous generals or wealthy samurai in Tsuchiura; maybe there were people like this, but the families simply hung on to their treasures. But when I was about nineteen we did hear that a family living near Lake Kasumigaura owned some really fine pieces of armor, so we went to look at them. They had about twenty suits of armor in all but, as we'd rather suspected, they hadn't belonged to some famous warlord, just a low-ranking samurai. Mind you, we still bought them all. A suit of armor cost us between five and ten yen and we could usually sell it for twenty or thirty.

I don't know what sort of swords we sold because, when my father was handling them, he wouldn't allow any of us girls near. But I often used to stand in the background and watch him selling one: he always wiped the blade with a square of thick handmade paper before he showed it to the

Charcoal brazier

customer—one sees them doing it in period pieces on TV. Lots of the wealthy landowners from the Tsuchiura area came to buy swords at our shop. I can still remember the names of five or six men who were always dropping in just to see if any good bargains had recently come our way.

Lots of other things were sold in secondhand shops—anything from sliding doors to *tatami* mats. This kind of stuff was mainly bought by poor farmers and people from the terraces who couldn't afford to buy new goods of any sort. For example, when wealthy people built a new house, they'd get rid of their old sliding doors and buy new ones, and they'd ask us to come and take the old doors off them.

But the most common way of getting hold of old furniture for our stock was from people planning to skip town. If you think that sounds incredible, ask anyone who was alive in those days. If a family got itself deep into debt and ended up without a penny to its name, the people would have no choice but to sell everything in their house—both their own stuff and things that didn't really belong to them—and get out of town. They'd have run up debts in any number of shops—for rice, *miso*, vegetables, sugar, and so on—and as the season for paying debts got nearer they wouldn't even be able to go out without worrying about bumping into someone they owed money to. It was a desperate position to be in. And after they'd decided to get out, they'd sneak into our shop by the back entrance, tell us they intended to leave town that night, and beg us to come and buy up the whole contents of their house. My father would wait till nightfall and then go along to look over what they'd got. Once he'd decided what everything was worth, he'd hand over the money and have it all brought back on a handcart. The *tatami* mats were sent away to be repaired, the sliding doors were re-covered, and everything was put on sale in our shop.

The carters that were employed for moving house, transporting rice, or whatever all lived in one tiny back alley in Omachi. You just sent word to them and they came straight around. I suppose there must have been about three or four of them living there. These men also had a hard time supporting themselves, so they sympathized with the family skipping out and wouldn't breathe a word of the matter to anyone. There was never any problem asking one of the carters to help out with that sort of thing.

Still, you can imagine how shocked and angry their creditors were when they found the house stripped clean; they'd sometimes even come barging into our shop asking us what the hell we thought we were up to. But we hadn't stolen the goods, after all, so there was very little they could do about it. I suppose we might have been in the wrong, helping people when we knew full well they were about to run off without paying their debts, but the family needed every penny they could get; for them it was a matter of life and death. So, far from being guilty, we felt we were almost saving their lives. We did our best to give them a good price for their stuff. But we never just gave the people money outright—that would've made them beggars.

Try and tell people today how much poverty there was back then and they just won't believe it. If you said someone had "nothing," you really meant they owned not a thing in the world. So when a poor family had to clear out, they often took only a single small bundle with them—they'd even sell all their pots and pans. Of course we felt sorry for people like that, but there were so many people living in poverty then you couldn't do anything about it; and besides, just saying "How unfortunate, oh we do feel sorry for them," wouldn't have done them a scrap of good. We did at least try to give them a good price for their possessions. Some of the people who made a run for it were pretty sharp, though: the night they were going to leave, they'd buy noodles for the whole family to celebrate their departure. But they'd then leave town without paying the shop for what they'd eaten.

You know, I often think poor people today are as well dressed as the richest classes were when I was young. The poor, fifty years ago, had to wear the same clothes 365 days a year, both in bed and at work.

Sewing box

Workmen wore *hanten* and short, close-fitting trousers both summer and winter, and the only extra bit of clothing they had to keep out the cold was a thin stomach band. In period dramas on television you usually see terrace people wearing bright red kimono, with their hair done up neatly—it's absolute nonsense. The women of the terraces in fact just wound their hair around in a rough bun, they used string instead of sashes, and their kimono were made of coarse, blue cotton. Some country women, even, could only afford a piece of old straw rope for a sash. Just by looking at how people dressed you could tell everything about them, from the way they lived to what their houses looked like.

There's one particular incident I remember well, which happened when I was seventeen: we came across a really promising work of art. My father had bought a hanging scroll from an old family in Tsuchiura. It was a picture of a monkey with very long arms and legs, at the top of a persimmon tree, stretching out its hands from the branches toward some fruit that had fallen on the ground. We'd picked it up at a bargain price. Father gave it to me to look after and I took it along to an antique shop called "Yoshizawa's," in the Ginza in Tokyo, and showed it to the owner. He looked at it for a while and then suddenly said, "I'll give you a hundred yen for it." In those days a hundred yen was an absolute fortune. A carpenter's wages were only about sixty or seventy sen a day, and you could even buy a chest of drawers made of solid paulownia for five or six yen. I was speechless for a few moments and my legs almost folded under me. But I was too much the daughter of an antique dealer just to sell the scroll for whatever price the man wanted to give me, so I went home without selling it. After that my father took over. I don't know what he finally got for it, but I'm sure the man in "Yoshizawa's" only offered me a hundred yen because he reckoned it was worth at least three or four times that.

Of course it's just as true nowadays as it was then that, as well as poverty, there's a lot of astonishing wealth around. Secondhand shops in the old days handled a great range of goods, from fine art to compete rubbish, so we saw both sides of society, met all sorts of people. This was the most interesting thing about the business—you didn't find it in any other trade. And look—it all comes flooding back when I sit here thinking about the past like this.

The Rice Cracker Maker

Mr. Torazo Matsuzawa (1905–)

My granddad ran a rice cracker shop in Koshigaya, Saitama Prefecture, and I've been making them in Tsuchiura ever since I moved here in 1935. For a short while after the war, a Rice Cracker Makers' Association existed in Tsuchiura and there were thirty-five or -six shops that belonged, plus several others that weren't members. But almost all the shops making and selling their own crackers have now disappeared, and the rest of them are ones that buy their stock in from outside.

The way mine are made, I first grind up some rice with a millstone. You know, there are people these days who've never even seen a millstone. Anyway, you see the hole in the center? Well, you push the grains of rice through the hole with your left hand, just a few at a time, and with your right you swing the stone around till the rice has all turned into powder. When I was young I used to be able to grind up thirty-five pounds an hour, but now that I'm getting on a bit I can't do it anything like as fast.

Once you've made the flour, you pour hot water over it and knead it thoroughly. It's not easy to explain exactly what consistency to aim for, but I suppose the stickiness of a rice cake is about right. This dough is then put into a steaming basket and steamed for an hour; it's my wife's job to feed the furnace with wood and keep it hot. After the steaming, the dough's put into a mortar and pounded hard with a wooden pestle until it's about the consistency of a dumpling. After a further kneading, the dough's rolled out flat on a board with a rolling pin—not unlike the way handmade noodles are produced. Round shapes are then cut out with a mold and left in the sun to dry.

The molds are made of tin and come in various different sizes. The one I'm using at the moment was made for me by old Mr. Matsunaga, who's been running his own cracker business for years, not far from here. Large-scale manufacturers use machines that can make up to two thousand crackers at a time, but for people like me who have to cut the shapes out by hand, it's a very slow process.

The crackers are dried on a patch of land at the back of the shop—it

Grinding rice

used to be part of a rice paddy. If the weather's bad, it can sometimes take as long as four or five days to do them properly. Some people feel it's OK to use a drying machine but, as far as I'm concerned, rice crackers dried outside in the sun taste completely different. You also have to be careful that the crackers are done to just the right extent: if they're too dry they often crack when you bake them, so the wife and I have to go out back to check them several times a day. And if it starts raining suddenly, we've got to rush out and bring them all inside again. Once this stage is completed, what's left is the "base" of the rice crackers. These finished crackers you can see here are bases that have been baked, had soy sauce brushed on them, and then been baked a second time.

There's also a bit of a knack to baking them. It's best not to do it right away—I put them first in what's called a *hoero* to heat them slowly for about three hours; mine is just a wire mesh box left on top of the baking oven, but it works perfectly well. If they're baked straight away, they tend not to puff up the way rice crackers should. I mean, look at these bases here that have already been done in the *hoero*: when you rub two of them together they make a nice scratchy sound, don't they? Unless the bases are as crisp as that before being baked, the finished crackers don't taste very good. I then bake them over a charcoal fire, keeping an eye on the heat and at the same time flattening out any curling of the crackers with an iron. If you just leave them over the fire they warp at the edges, and to prevent this you have to turn them continuously and press them with the iron.

The wire mesh I use for the baking was made for me when I first started up in this shop, so I've had it for close on fifty years. It seems like only yesterday, but that's half a century, isn't it?—time enough for nearly all the little stores that used to buy their stock from me to disappear. They just seem to have vanished, while I wasn't looking.

Until about two or three years ago I grew all my own rice for the crackers. I rented paddy fields in various places, and for a time I even tried growing rice on the dry part of the riverbed. But because the soil there was sandy, the drainage was a problem—the water all seeped away. It sounds a bit daft to talk about a water shortage in the middle of a river, but in the years when there wasn't a lot of rain, much of the riverbed would dry up and there were times when I had to work till late at night filling buckets with river water and spreading it around. In the end the current would dry up almost entirely, and I'd be left with a trickle in the middle to water my rice plants from.

These days they make all sorts of different crackers that both look and taste nice enough. But I'm glad I've still got customers who tell me that really the old-fashioned ones are still the best.

The Tofu Maker

Mr. Toshiyuki Kuramochi (1929–)

We kept early hours in my father's day. Now almost everything's done by machine, so even if you don't get up till after five you've still plenty of time to make some tofu, but back then we used to get up before two in the morning—more the middle of the night than the morning really!

Let me see if I can remember how ours was made. . . . First we used a treadmill to grind the two sackfuls of soybeans that had been left to cool the night before. This job was always done by my uncle and, if he started just before two o'clock, it usually took him until gone five to grind them up completely. The thick mash that resulted was known as *go*.

This was tipped into a large cauldron of water, thoroughly boiled, and then poured into the special double bag, four feet long by two feet wide, used for squeezing the soy milk from the bean solids. The double bag full of boiling *go* was extremely hot and heavy, so heavy in fact that the women could barely even lift it off the ground. You heaved this bag up on top of a tub and started wringing it—we didn't have any mechanical presses or anything, it was all done by hand. Several pine boards, tied together with straw rope, were fixed over the tub that was going to catch the liquid. The wringing bag was folded in two and you pressed down hard on it with a heavy wooden pole, about five inches thick and six feet long: one end of the pole was stuck into a hole in a wooden pillar, the middle of it rested on the bag, and you sat on the other end and squeezed the bag down using your whole body weight. But if you just sat on it without moving, the stuff wouldn't be pressed hard enough, so you had to jiggle up and down as vigorously as possible. The liquid would drip down into the tub and the bag would gradually empty. You then had to fold it in four and start squeezing again; eventually all that was left in the sack was the lees.

When the bag had been completely squeezed out, you added bittern to the milk in the tub to make it set. Nowadays they use calcium sulphate, but back then we went along regularly to the pickle shop and got the water left at the bottom of barrels of brine-pickled vegetables.

When the soy milk had set, it was scooped out of the tub with a special ladle known as a *bozu* ["a Buddhist priest"] and put into wooden molds; the molds were made of cypress wood, I remember. From one you could get ten slices of tofu. But you could only make two molds, twenty pieces, at a time. Mind you, the slices used to be much bigger than they are now—they were so big in fact you couldn't have held one on the flat of your hand—about seven and a half inches long and at least three inches deep. And to turn the two sacks of soybeans into tofu, we had to complete the same process again seventeen or eighteen times. But once we'd got started and had the water on the boil, everything went smoothly, with everyone doing their particular jobs, and we'd get all of it done by just after five.

Once we'd finished making the stuff, we had some breakfast and then went out selling it from two wooden buckets attached to a pole balanced on your shoulder. Each bucket held fifteen pieces so, with a total of thirty, plus a certain amount of water, the pole bent right down on either side with the weight. We also put a box of various types of fried tofu on top of each bucket; it took a fair bit of skill and strength to balance that lot. The buckets weren't round but slightly oval-shaped, three feet wide at the longest point and two foot six at the shortest, and maybe about seven inches deep.

In those days, tofu sellers didn't blow a horn to tell customers they'd arrived as they do now; they walked around ringing a little bell. You had to take the strain of the pole with one hand and ring the bell with the other. What's more, if we'd sold the tofu only in the town we'd never have made much of a profit, so we used to go all the way out to Manabe, and then on to the area around Hojo. Well, people back then had good strong legs—we thought nothing of going as far as Oda or Hojo. I can't see anyone doing that nowadays, eh?

There used to be tofu shops dotted about all over the town and in the surrounding villages. There was a sort of unwritten rule that you couldn't

Tofu seller

sell your stock in front of, or seven houses either side of, another tofu shop, but you could sell anywhere else.

Fried tofu cost one sen for as much as a woman could hold in one hand; plain tofu was two and a half sen in 1915, but by the 1920s it had gone up to five sen a piece.

The men got back at about two or three in the afternoon—dog-tired—after carrying their loads twenty-five miles or more with nothing but straw sandals on their feet. My father and the others had a bath as soon as they got in, with a meal straight afterward. And, God, did they eat: one man could easily get through four or five large bowls of rice. There were ten people working in the shop and in one day—for breakfast, lunch, and dinner—they put away a good sixty pounds of rice between them. Cooking the rice was my mother's job: every day she'd fill a huge twenty-gallon pot right to the brim, so full that the grains fell out when you took the lid off. And then, once the rice had puffed up nicely, we'd stuff it down. They say these days there's a surplus of rice; in the past we all ate vast amounts of it, but now people don't eat anything like as much, so it's not surprising there's a surplus.

We used to buy a fifteen-gallon cask of saké each month, but even that often wasn't quite enough, so we'd have to go out and buy an extra four-gallon barrel as well. But it wasn't only us and our employees who drank the saké: for example, my mother would often say to the man who brought us the soybeans on his horse and cart, or to the man delivering wood, "Come on, then, have a drink." And if the fish seller or anyone so much as put their head around the door, "Just a quick one," she'd say, and they'd be given a cupful to knock back. So we easily got through fifteen or twenty gallons a month. And in the summer we'd get in some *shochu* as well. My father would always jump straight in the bath after he'd finished work each day, and when he got out, with just a loincloth on, he used to fill his mouth with *shochu* and spray it over himself; being alcohol, it evaporated in no time—he said it made him feel nice and cool.

Those were long, hard days we worked, with scarcely a moment's rest, so we slept like the dead when it was time for bed. In fact, if you asked me generally what it was like back then, I'd have to say that most of us spent our whole lives doing nothing but working and sleeping.

Making *Katsuo Bushi*

Mr. Nobusuke Kikuchi (1904–)

My grandparents on my mother's side owned a fish shop in Ajigaura, called "Kurohiko," and they also did quite a good business making *katsuo bushi*—the dried bonito that housewives shave flakes off to use as soup flavoring. In the area around Tsuchiura, dried bonito's been used for centuries both as a thanksgiving offering and as a gift. But there can't be many people who know how it's made, so I'll try to explain.

The fresh bonito was bought by "Kurohiko" from my own family by what's called an *uchiage* arrangement. This meant that you agreed to buy a fixed percentage of each day's catch; in "Kurohiko's" case it was a third. Doing business this way could be tricky because, for example, you couldn't decide one day you already had enough fish—you had to keep your side of the bargain. It was normally only used between relatives to help each other out. The rest of the catch was taken to market and sold by auction and so, once the market price had been fixed, "Kurohiko" would pay for its third at this rate.

I often went over to my grandparents' to play when I was small, and I remember once overhearing a strange conversation my granddad was having with a fisherman. Granddad asked him what water temperature the bonito had been caught in and the fisherman replied, "Sixty-eight degrees." My grandfather didn't look very pleased. I thought this was rather peculiar so—being a nosy little kid—I asked him about it. "Bonito live in water of between sixty-eight and seventy-two degrees," he told me, "but the ones in cooler water develop a lot of fat and you can't make good *katsuo bushi* out of them." Apparently, when the bonito that were found in low temperatures were dried, they sounded sort of hollow and they cracked when you planed them. A difference of only four degrees was enough to change the quality completely.

So *katsuo* from Satsuma, in the very south of Japan, were reckoned to be the best. Next came Tosa, followed by Chiba and us, and finally Sanriku—in other words, the quality gradually fell as you went from a hot climate to a cold one. But with sashimi the opposite was true: raw bonito from the south of Japan had too little fat and didn't taste particularly good. Bonito were at their best in August and September. The shoals came northward each year, eventually arriving off Sendai in late July or August. Almost immediately they turned back south on the cold currents: bonito caught around this time had a good layer of fat on them and were delicious. But these days, fish are frozen as soon as they're caught, and to my mind this ruins them and makes the meat lose all its taste.

There was a whole team of them making *katsuo bushi* at "Kurohiko." If I list them in the order the work was done: there was one man who chopped off the heads and gutted the fish—he did nothing else. Then a man who removed the fins and the hard scales under the fins, and another who cut the fish in three lengthwise. These three pieces—"tortoises," they were called, because of their shape—were the chunks of bonito that the final *katsuo bushi* were made from. The skill of the man cutting the fish made a big difference to how much money you could make: if the bonito was neatly sliced, the amount wasted was a lot less than if the bones were chucked away with some meat still on them. Bonito weighing four or five pounds were best. Fish of eight pounds or more were too large to make "tortoises" from: you'd have to cut them in four rather than three.

Once the fish had been cut up, it was cooled in cold water (not ice, because that was difficult to get hold of) and then put into a large pot and boiled. The way it was boiled was also a bit tricky. If you didn't use soft water, cracks would open in the fish. The water used by "Kurohiko" was spring water and very soft, so they always managed to get good results; but most other shops in the area mucked up the boiling and produced a lower grade of fish. Not surprisingly, they couldn't understand why the quality should vary so much in the same town, so they came along to "Kurohiko" to investigate, but no one there knew the answer either. Sometime later a researcher worked out that the secret lay in the quality of the water, and he recommended using spring water or rainwater rather than

Shaving dried bonito

hard well water; from then on every shop was able to make a high-grade product. All this happened when I was a kid.

The boiled "tortoises" were allowed to cool, and the next stage was for the women to pick all the bones out with tweezers. There were always lots of tiny bones around the stomach; these had to be carefully removed, one by one. Half the skin was then peeled off. The reason why only half and not all the skin was taken off was apparently because, a hundred years or so before, some shady salesmen had gone around selling blocks of pinewood to farmers, claiming they were dried bonito. At that time real dried bonito was sold without any skin on, and you couldn't tell it apart from pinewood that had been planed to the right shape. The farmers were obviously furious and for a while afterward, even if you were selling the real thing, they wouldn't touch it. But if you left some of the skin on the fish it was easy to see it was genuine, so the practice caught on. Sounds a bit far-fetched maybe, but that's the story behind it.

Anyway, where was I? Yes, once half the skin had been removed the fish were baked. They were put on a frame over a pinewood fire and slowly dried out; it was important to keep the fire stoked up just right or they'd either burn or cook too long. When the baking was finished the fish were put into a barrel, which was tightly sealed. You left them like this for a few weeks and mold would begin to form on the fatty parts of the fish. When the mold had turned white they were taken out the barrel, dried again in the sun, then scraped with a rough hemp brush to knock off all the mold. This job was often done in the middle of the summer, and working outside with the sun beating down was no fun at all. My grandfather often got me to help out, and one day when it was particularly hot I decided to rig up an umbrella to keep the sun off me. But I was immediately told to take it down because it threw a shadow over the fish. So I just had to suffer—no shade, sweat dripping into my eyes; it was stifling out there.

After the mold had been brushed off, the bonito was "rough planed."

It was then dried out once more, and put back into the barrel to make the mold grow again and draw all the fat out from the fish. It was then taken out of the barrel, dried yet again, and given a "second planing." This was repeated once more and finally the fish was given what was known as the "main planing," to finish it off nicely for sale. In "Kurohiko" there were always at least twenty-four men just to do the planing, so you can understand how much work went into making each single piece.

They make them very differently nowadays, but I reckon I can still tell a good dried bonito from an inferior one.

The Rice Merchant's Daughter

Mrs. Kiyo Nakata (1903–)

I can't remember at all where we lived when I was very young. I've been told my grandfather farmed along the riverbank some way past the Tori-den Terrace in Nakajoura, but I really couldn't say for sure. Grandfather originally came from Chiba.

I heard that we also lived near Shinmichi Road for a time when I was small, but that's pretty hazy, too. Still, I do remember one incident that happened when I was about three. I was climbing up the side of a chest of drawers, pulling out all the drawers as I went, and an alarm clock fell off the top and the base of it poked me in the eye. I remember my mother tak-ing me in her arms and running miles with me through the dark streets. We eventually got to a doctor—I found out later it was Dr. Shimizu in Tamachi.

After that we moved once again, this time to the Daikichi Terrace in Nakajoura. The Oyoshi and Tonoshin terraces were in the same area, and between the houses there were lots of tiny alleyways. Life for the people in the terraces was a desperate struggle. My father was a rice miller so we always had just about enough to eat but, as far as clothes were concerned, we had to wear the same things for years on end. I remember even now how happy I was at the age of seven when I was given a new kimono made of cheap cotton; but I'm pretty sure that was the only time I ever had anything new. Apart from very special occasions, everyone wore old clothes, either patched or restitched. But this seemed only natural, and children never tried to pester their parents into buying them new clothes. All the kids in the terrace went around in rags. And as for shoes, we were bought new *geta* twice a year, at New Year and *o-bon*. As December wore on each year, I always used to look at my tatty old clogs in great excite-ment and think, "In only a few more days it'll be New Year."

I loved school right from the start and whenever I was late I'd run all the way there. And I was often late, because I had to lend a hand with hull-ing the rice in the morning. My father would already be at work when I woke up; the boom of the pounder echoed around the house. We used a pedal-operated rice huller. You put the rice in a wooden mortar and the device was set up so that the pestle—which was raised by treading on one end of a long pole—would drop directly into the mortar. It was a very simple contraption.

As soon as I'd finished washing my face at the well by the little shrine, I'd go and help my father. You see, in hulling rice, if you just drop the pounder onto the same spot every time, you soon find you're simply hitting the bottom of the mortar. It was my job to smooth the rice out with my hands just after the pounder dropped. My father operated the foot pedal, so obviously he couldn't do this as well.

We hulled barley too; this would've been left out the previous night to cool and would be slightly sticky—you had to press it down to get it all in the mortar. To start with, the rice and barley weren't any problem: the heap in the mortar could be crushed quite easily. So during this time I was allowed to sleep in. But once the husks started to come away from the grain it became much more difficult, and a helping hand was needed. My mother would come and wake me. Mother herself couldn't spare any time to help: by the time I was eight, she'd had seven children and was so busy all day looking after them and doing household chores, she just didn't know which way to turn. When the hulling started, my little sisters would all still be asleep so I didn't have to take care of them, but as soon as it got light they'd be awake and I had to carry one of them on my back while I helped with the rice.

I went to the Girls' Primary School—it was where Tsuchiura Hospital is today. Whenever the rice hulling wasn't finished by the time I should've left and it looked as though I was going to be late, I'd burst into floods of tears. I understood that my parents were busy and needed my help and that I couldn't ask to be allowed to stop and go to school. But, even so, I was so upset I'd work with tears streaming down my face and Father would say: "If you keep on making that funny face, it'll get stuck like that for the rest of your life." I just had to put up with it and carry on. After a while my father would decide, "All right, then—that'll do. Thanks for your help. You run along off to school now," and in a great hurry I'd grab my things, wrapped in a carrying cloth, and run all the way to school.

Now, let me think: one of our teachers was the sister of the priest at Jinryuji temple; there was another called Mr. Igarashi who lived near the old samurai school, Ikubunkan. We were also sometimes taught by a Mr. Terakado whose house was near Dr. Hiramoto's surgery in Sotonishicho—he was a very elderly man. When I was ten, the girls' school closed down, and I moved to what's still Tsuchiura Primary School.

As soon as I was home again, Mother would get me to look after one of my younger sisters, carrying her around with me piggyback, so I couldn't go very far away to play. At least we were allowed to play on our own. We used to do origami or play marbles or hopscotch; sometimes I would skip with a rope. In the winter I'd wear a cotton quilted jacket. A lot of my friends, too, had their younger brothers and sisters on their backs when they came out to play.

I also used to deliver rice. When I was only ten I had to heave forty pounds of it over my shoulder and deliver it to the rice cracker maker in Omachi—they made delicious crackers there. And from the age of twelve or thirteen I was carrying eighty pounds at a time—just think, eighty pounds is getting on for a hundredweight. It was so heavy I had to stop and rest at least a dozen times on the way.

There was a woman who lived near us whose husband was a heavy drinker, and sometimes she'd come and ask my father to lend her some rice; but he always refused. My father liked a drink himself, but he was too poor to be able to afford it more than once in a blue moon. So he wasn't all that nice about it—in fact we'd hear him shouting, "Who the hell does your husband think he is? He can afford to drink all right, but he can't find the money to feed his wife and kids." Rice was definitely never sold on tick.

We also used to sell rice from a handcart. The sort of people who bought just a few pounds at a time could only come to get it in the evening after the shop had shut, so my father would drag the cart up and down the little lanes between the terraces until late at night. Quite often, I remember, I took a lantern and went out through the pitch-dark streets to meet him.

You know, back then, if a day laborer fell sick there was no way he could afford to see a doctor, in fact he probably wouldn't even have enough to buy any food. If something like that happened to a man my father knew, he'd feel sorry for the family and he might secretly go and leave a little rice outside their front door. I don't know how many people he did this for, but we were hard up too, so presumably it could only have been very occasionally. But the favor was sometimes returned. In 1924 our house was flooded out, and the *tatami* mats and all the furniture got washed away. A lot of people we didn't even know came to lend us a hand, and one of them brought us a huge chest of drawers and told us he was a furniture maker who we'd helped out once in the past. "This is all I've got to give you, I'm afraid," he said, "but please take it anyway." My parents thanked him with tears in their eyes.

WOMEN OF
THE TOWN

A sewing school

The Magistrate's Wife

Mrs. Mineko Toyama (1903–)

For generations a member of my family served as the feudal magistrate in Kitamachi. The house in Takajo, where I was born, had formerly been the magistrate's official residence.

The roof of our house was reed-thatched, not tiled. The drainpipes running along the edge of the eaves were made of thick bamboo sliced in half and with the nodes removed. Seen from the ground, they were a dirty brown color; they were rotting in several places and mold grew all over them. The vertical rain leaders were made of plaited hemp: when it rained, the water came trickling down the ropes, ran over the fine gravel at the bottom, and flowed down in tiny streams into the River Tsukiji which was just behind our house. The building was extremely old.

My grandfather had been the magistrate toward the end of the Edo period but, after the overthrow of the shogunal government and the beginning of the Meiji Restoration in 1868, he lost his feudal stipend like everyone else, and instead was appointed by the new government as the first mayor of Tsuchiura. I don't know very much else about him, though.

My father had been mayor of a rural district in Chiba Prefecture, and after Grandfather died he succeeded him in Tsuchiura. One of the clearest memories I have of when my father was mayor is of the Electric Light Company starting up in Tozaki and electricity being installed in our house. Because Father was the mayor we were the first people in the town to be linked up to the supply. But our single electric lamp was only ten candle-power; it hung from a hook in the ceiling. It also had a very long lead on it, so if you took the light off the hook you could carry it all around the house with you. Thinking back on it, the bulb must have been really very dim indeed, but at the time everyone in town was quite amazed by it. "Have you seen the Hiyama's house?" they used to say; "it's as bright there at night as it is in the daytime." Children, and villagers from the countryside, would come into Tsuchiura just to look at our light. For a time our house became almost a tourist attraction.

Father was nearly always out on town business, so Mother was kept ex-

tremely busy around the house. I could talk for hours about all she had to put up with. But there's no doubt her biggest headache was having to wait hand and foot on her mother-in-law.

You see, from the day she married, my grandmother had always been "the lady wife of the Kitamachi magistrate," and although Japanese society changed in many ways after the Meiji Restoration, Grandmother hadn't the slightest intention of changing herself. At the same time every morning, Mother would have to go along to her room to pay her respects. But she'd never actually go into the room. From behind the sliding door in the vestibule she'd ask, "Are you awake yet?" and she'd kneel there, bowing low.

If Grandmother answered, my mother would quickly fill a metal washbasin for her, put this on a tray together with salt for brushing her teeth, a small bowl for gargling, toothpicks, and a towel, and leave it on a bamboo mat on the edge of the veranda. In summer the basin was filled with cold water, but in the winter months she had to be careful to fill it with hot water at just the right temperature. "I've prepared everything," my mother would say, and Grandmother would slide the door open and come out. Then, sitting stiffly upright on a floor cushion, she'd lean her body elegantly over the basin and begin to wash her face.

Grandmother took all her meals alone sitting at a beautiful low lacquer table. Mother would sit alongside serving her; part of her job was to judge exactly when she wanted more to eat and to serve her a fresh tray at the opportune moment. You see, none of the servants, not even her old personal maid, was ever allowed in. When she'd finished her meal, Grandmother would sit on a large floor cushion in front of the brazier, fill her pipe with tobacco, and puff away at it for a while.

She wouldn't even let the maids into her room to do the cleaning, so Mother was obliged to do that, too. She had to wipe the *tatami* floor and the ledge around the top of the wall with a duster; Grandmother would shout at her if she used a damp cloth, even in the corridor.

Then there was the bath: my mother had to scrub her back for her, though I took over this chore when I was a bit older; and when she got out I used to do her hair as well. She'd got rather thin on top by this time, but I had to run a boxwood comb through her hair, thin though it was, over and over again. If I ever hurried the combing because I wanted to get it over with, Grandmother would be cross and shout, "If you comb my hair as roughly as that, you'll damage it." It made me so angry sometimes when I saw Mother doing everything she was told, without a word of complaint, that I couldn't help cursing the old woman under my breath.

In television dramas you quite often see samurai chatting to their servants; but this is rubbish—it would never have happened. In the feudal period the difference in status between the various classes was extreme, and although these distinctions broke down quite a lot toward the end of the nineteenth century, something of them survived for a long time afterward. Even those distinctions that lasted up until the war would seem quite strange to most people today.

Let me give you an example. One of our maids, a girl called Otsune, left us to marry a man in Tajuku. One day, when I was walking along with my grandmother, we happened to bump into Otsune. She noticed us, looked slightly shocked for a moment, then fell quickly to her knees and bowed with her forehead touching the ground. But no passerby, whether he'd known who my grandmother was or not, would have been particularly surprised at this spectacle. Grandmother looked down at the girl, who was still kneeling there, said "I hear you are well," and walked on as though she'd already put Otsune completely out of her mind. Only a person born and brought up in the feudal period could have behaved like that.

Then again, when all our servants came along at the end of the year and at the o-bon festival to pay their respects, they'd kneel in the entrance hall and, hunching their shoulders in the humblest way, bow right down till they scraped the ground. To me, brought up in a different age and educated in the modern fashion, it seemed incredible they should behave like this.

At the autumn and spring equinox festivals and again at *o-bon*, I used to accompany my grandmother to the local temple to put flowers on our family grave. And there too, if we met somebody we knew on the way, they'd bow down deeply to her, their bodies bent almost double; but she in return would only incline her head slightly to acknowledge their presence and certainly wouldn't have bowed. When you think she was just the wife of a local magistrate, it's impossible to imagine how a feudal lord in the old days must have been treated.

We employed three elderly maids in our house, but from the age of seven or eight I was made to help out with the cooking and washing. In fact I had to do all sorts of chores: cooking rice, fetching water from the well, and stoking up the fire for the bath. I used to pour the well water into an old wooden pail to take back to the bathhouse; but the pail was terribly big and heavy and I was still quite young, so I always had to stop and rest every few yards. When I was about nine or ten, however, we bought a Western-style bucket. I'd never even heard of a "bucket" before, but it was very light and the handle moved freely; it was easy to carry and made filling the bath much less of an effort. I remember being delighted and thinking what a marvelous invention it was.

We were brought up very strictly. If we ever asked one of the maids to do something, Mother would tick us off sharply: "The maid's been working for this family for years. You children are not to tell her what to do." In the morning we all had to help with the housework. My three elder brothers had got married when I was very young, but during my school years there were still eight of us left at home—I was the seventh of eleven children. So every day we had to make up nine lunch boxes: the vegetables for them were picked from the fields behind our place, then boiled and seasoned. The mornings, until everyone had left the house, were a continuous mad flurry of people running backward and forward.

Blowing at a kitchen fire

All the same, since there were so many of us we had a lot of fun too. The River Tsukiji which flowed past the back of our house was wide and pretty deep in those days, and we used to row up and down it in a small boat. Whenever the boat sprang a leak we'd get some oakum—a sort of plaited rope made from softened pine bark—stuff it down the joints in the planks, and knock it into place with a mallet to plug the leak. We managed simple repairs like that on our own. I was well known for being good at punting. We all loved mucking about on the river.

One tends to forget the brighter moments—they fade more quickly—but like every family, I suppose, mine had its share of happiness, and its share of sorrow.

Upper-class Women

Mr. Fukusaburo Takagi (1898–1981)

These days any married woman, the wife of a small shopkeeper or even a laborer, is referred to as an *okusan* ["mistress of the house"]; but in my day, ordinary married women were called *okamisan* ["the missus"] and only the wives of wealthy shopkeepers or landowners were called *okusan* or, even more politely, *okusama*. And these ladies lived in exactly the way the word suggests.

What I'm saying is that *okusan* literally means "the person at the back of the house," and these women really did spend almost all their time in the gloomy back parts of their houses; it was rare if they went outside at all. Even during the annual festivals, they couldn't go out, join in with the crowds, and enjoy themselves. If you watch period dramas on TV, you quite often see scenes with ladies from nice families walking around the streets on their own but, as far as I know, that sort of thing was unheard of.

You're probably wondering how I know all this. Well, you see, the thing is I used to work as a casual laborer and did jobs for many of the large shops in Tsuchiura. So very occasionally I got to talk to the mistress of the house. And more often than not she'd say something like, "I hear there was a festival at the Washinomiya Shrine yesterday. What was it like?" I'd tell her all about it, but she'd know so little about what went on in the world, it would take me years to explain everything. I used to think it was almost as if we belonged to two different races; even our feelings were different somehow.

Even in the Gion Festival, upper-class women couldn't slip outside to watch the floats going past. There was a thin lattice partition between the women's quarters and the shop so, instead of watching the parade like anybody else, the lady of the house would have to sit inside, with a fan in her hand, watching in secret behind the partition. The geisha would file past and the men would heave on the ropes of the floats, singing and shouting as they went, but unfortunately all the lady could see of them was their legs. She'd have loved to go and have a good look, but back then festivals were thought of as vulgar things, only for common people to enjoy, and it certainly wouldn't have been proper for someone like her to be seen joining in and laughing with the crowd.

It was also the custom that, whether a festival was on or not, an *okusan* shouldn't go outdoors in the daytime. And when she did have to go out, maybe on business or to visit a friend, she always went by rickshaw and took at least one maid with her. And even then, if at all possible she'd set out at dusk, just as people in the streets were beginning to light their lanterns.

On the few occasions when she did step out, she'd always wear one of her finest kimono, with a fancy sash and a half-coat on top. One of the houseboys or maids would walk in front of the rickshaw carrying a lantern, and her personal maid would ride inside with her. In those days shops were all open till fairly late so, as the rickshaw passed through the town, people would watch it going by and call to each other, "Quick, come and look; it's the lady from such and such a house." It was as if they were looking at someone from a different world.

Learning to Sew

Mrs. Mitsu Oshima (1906–)

I started at the Kimiyama Sewing School in Manabe as a boarder when I was twenty. There were quite a lot of needlework shops in those days and all of them did a good trade. At Mrs. Kimiyama's we had nine or ten girls like myself who lived in, and more than a hundred others who came in every day from the surrounding area. So we were quite a crowd, and you sat as near the teacher as possible if you wanted to learn anything; the day girls had to get up at the crack of dawn to have any chance of finding a decent seat.

Most of the girls who lived in did so because their own homes were too far away for them to make the daily journey to and from school. My own family were farmers in Chiyoda. As well as learning needlework, the boarders were expected to do all sorts of jobs for Mrs. Kimiyama: cooking, washing clothes, sweeping, cleaning, and fetching water for the bath. We shared the work out among ourselves, each knowing that if it wasn't done properly we'd be given what for.

She was also very strict about manners. For instance, when we were eating our lunch boxes at midday, she'd often tick off a new girl from the country for shoveling her food in: "Putting so much in your mouth at one time, it's no wonder you have to open your mouth wide in that unpleasant way. And if you insist on putting a whole fish in at once, some of it's bound to stick out, which isn't at all nice, is it? You should use your chopsticks to cut the fish up small first."

The trouble was that country girls, who were made to work in the fields from a very early age, had learned to eat their meals as fast as possible so they could get straight back to work; otherwise they were told off by their parents. They even used to pour water over their rice and barley to make it easier to swallow quickly. A girl needed at least two large bowls per meal to keep her going, so she had to get used to stuffing it in. In fact, when matchmakers came around looking for suitable brides, one of the things they took particular notice of was the girl's appetite: if she really gobbled her food down she'd make a good farmer's wife, they said. So it wasn't easy to make the switch to a slower pace. And the food at Mrs. Kimiyama's was remarkably good: the rice had very little barley in it and there were plenty of side dishes, such as fish, to go with it.

Another thing the girls often got ticked off for was saying "yeah" instead of "yes." "The word is not 'yeah,' " Mrs. Kimiyama would declare. "Please say 'yes' correctly." And the offender would do as she was told in a sort of timid whisper. We always did our best to remember everything she taught us, whether it was etiquette or needlework, but it was difficult sometimes.

Our days began very early—with a "wash by moonlight," as they say. Even in winter we were out by the well before five. At that hour of the morning the trains on the Tsukuba Line weren't yet running, which gave the young men who worked next door at Manabe Station time to come over and play tricks on us. They'd put the capes that were part of their uniform over their heads and sneak up behind the hedge, then jump out on us and make silly noises; sometimes they'd even leap over the hedge, creep up behind one of the girls, and suddenly throw a cape over her. This, of course, made her scream, and the station boy's cheery "Good morning, miss—it's only me" didn't help much; so when the rest of us came running out we'd shout "You rotten pig" at him, and other rather unladylike things. Fortunately, Mrs. Kimiyama never seems to have heard about these goings-on.

We used a type of soap in those days that you don't see any longer: it was known as "floating soap." It was about twice the size of the modern kind, and if you dropped it in the water it really did come floating back to the surface. But it didn't produce much of a lather. Anyone my age will remember using it—you ask them.

We never had time in the morning to put on any makeup. The attitude then was that a girl who spent time in front of the mirror was no use to anyone, and certainly no farmer's daughter who did her hair up nicely and put on makeup would've found herself a husband. The ideal girl got

up in the morning, folded her mattress, dressed quickly, and went outside. Then, without even sitting down, she'd quickly run a comb through her hair, wind it up into a bun, and fasten it with a pin. She'd give her face a quick splash of water—she wouldn't have dreamed of using perfume or anything, of course—and, to clean her teeth, she put a bit of salt on her finger and rubbed it hard against them. Once that was done, she went straight off to work. Provided she didn't actually look downright filthy, her appearance didn't matter in the slightest. Anyway, all you had time to think about during the day was work, so you weren't expected to worry about how you looked.

The girls were used to starting early at home, so they carried on in the same way at the sewing school; in fact we competed with each other to see who could work hardest. As soon as the first signs of daylight appeared in the sky we'd all be up hanging out laundry and cooking rice for breakfast.

All the girls brought their own floor cushions, and there was always a great fight to get your cushion down in the classroom first. This was how you saved your place for the day, you see. Sitting right in front of Mrs. Kimiyama made you feel a bit uncomfortable, so we preferred to put our cushions just a little way back from the teacher but in a place where we could get a good view of her hands. The girls who lived in were lucky because they could bag the best positions and sit next to their friends.

So by seven o'clock there'd already be rows of cushions laid out in the best parts of the classroom, and anyone who arrived much later than that had to sit squashed together at the back. Girls who weren't particularly keen to learn wouldn't worry much about what time they turned up, so you could reckon the ones at the back were the least enthusiastic.

Our spare time was spent wandering around the town together or perhaps going along to watch the trains. I was born out in the country, so when I came to the school at the age of twenty, I'd still never seen a train. We used to walk from Manabe through the rice fields, and in spring all the flowers would be out, with larks singing in the sky. And beyond, as we followed the ridges between the paddies, we'd see a train puffing along the track with black smoke pouring out of its stack. I was fascinated by them; "What wonderful machines," I always thought. I used to go and watch the trains most Sundays.

After we finished work in the evenings, we went straight to bed, but—being young, perhaps—we were often too hungry to sleep. Sometimes we nipped down to the cake shop or the sweet potato seller before we went to bed and, when we were all supposed to be asleep, we'd have a secret feast. If I'd bought rice crackers, I used to put a thick cotton jacket over my head and eat them underneath it so I didn't make too many crunching sounds. As I munched away someone might hiss at me, "Watch out, teacher's coming," and I'd have to stuff the rest of them into my mouth. Obviously, Mrs. Kimiyama wouldn't have approved of these midnight snacks.

There wasn't much, though, we got up to behind her back. For one thing, she had a temper, and you wouldn't believe how often she lost it with us. But in my day teachers were really respected, so if they told you to do something, you got on with it, without messing around.

Another thing I remember very clearly from those days is the frustration I felt when I was given, for example, a kimono of *habutae* silk to sew up and worked on it for a solid week but still couldn't get it right. The biggest problem was making the neck. *Habutae* kimono were made of two pieces of material laid on top of each other and, when you came to the neckline, even if you tried bending the end of the needle, it was impossible to get the pieces of silk properly aligned. The only way to do it was to lay the kimono on the floor with the sleeves spread wide, then stretch the material as much as possible, stitching it along the seam in a dead straight line with your hand moving as fast as it could go. But however many times I tried, the two sections never seemed to match. "Oh, I'm giving up," I used to think, but there was a competitive streak in me, and I couldn't

bear to admit in front of the other girls that I couldn't manage it.

So, when everyone else was sound asleep, I'd get up, sneak downstairs, and sew and sew for all I was worth by the light of an oil lamp. If it was winter, my hands would go numb and my nose would start to run. I'd work almost in a trance for hours on end, until finally I lost all feeling in my legs. Then, in the morning, thinking I'd got it more or less right, I'd take it along nervously to show Mrs. Kimiyama. And if she said, "Yes, I think this will do"—well, you can imagine how relieved I was.

But if you showed her your work and she didn't find it good enough, she'd just put her scissors into the seam and pull out all the stitches, however long it had taken to sew. That was awful. She really was very strict. But it worked, I suppose, because it made us try hard, and after three years of training we could honestly call ourselves good seamstresses.

The Midwife

Mrs. Sui Katayanagi (1915–)

When a woman gets pregnant nowadays, the first thing she does is go to a doctor for a thorough medical examination; she then usually goes back for regular checkups once a month throughout her pregnancy. But before the war, this sort of prenatal care was available only to the very rich.

Back then it was quite normal for an expectant mother not to visit a midwife until the eighth or ninth month of her term. In the worst cases—and these were very common—the woman wouldn't see one beforehand at all. When her contractions actually started she'd send one of her family around to me to say the baby was on its way so could I come quickly; I'd just have to drop everything and dash off to her house. When I got there I quite often found they didn't have a washbasin or soap ready and hadn't even bothered to boil up any water. So, at the same time as seeing to the mother, I had to order the other members of the family to go and fetch this and that, and they'd all be running around getting things. People who made the proper arrangements months in advance, as most families do nowadays, were few and far between.

I remember one house I went to in Tsuchiura to deliver a baby where they had no *tatami* at all and the woman was lying on an old straw mat spread out on the bare wood floor. They didn't even have a bucket or washtub I could use. "What do you normally do your washing in?" I asked, and the husband told me they used an old fish tub they'd been given. I asked if it leaked, and the husband replied it did a bit but not so much that you couldn't use it so he'd never bothered to mend it. I said, "Well, I suppose we'll just have to make do with that. Wash the tub out thoroughly with hot water. Then boil up fresh water and pour it in." While they were doing this, the baby was born and the poor thing had to have its first bath in a fish tub; we then had to wrap it up in rags because that was all they could find for it to wear.

There've always been poor people in this world and I suppose there always will be. But I don't think anyone today can have the faintest idea what sort of life they led back in those days. The whole world was in an awful economic depression, and working people spent most of their lives half-starved. There was nothing like social security, of course. The clothes of the women I attended were often little better than rags, and their mattresses were usually filthy dirty and covered in mold, lice, and fleas. You'd have thought they might at least have bothered to air the things once in a while, but quite often I'd find a woman lying on a mattress so damp it couldn't possibly have been aired for months. They sometimes wouldn't have anything in the house to use as diapers for the new baby, so I'd have to fold and stitch up an old towel, and that would be the poor little devil's first pair of diapers. Most of them were so hard up I couldn't charge them a penny for delivering their babies, not even to cover the cost of the supplies I'd used. Every time I helped out at births, I had to give away all sorts of things from soap to bandages, paid for out of my own pocket.

But the most frightening experience I had during my years as a midwife was when I went to attend a birth over in Tanaka. The baby was born safely, and both mother and child were doing well. We were all relieved everything had gone off all right and I was invited by the family to stay for a meal. It was the custom in the Tanaka area back then that everyone who'd assisted in the birth was given a drink. We'd all gather round to congratulate the new father and drink saké with him and, as long as there was enough food in the house, we were served a meal too. Even if the baby had been born at two in the morning, it was usual to give everyone a proper meal laid out on lacquer trays; sometimes you'd even get rice cakes. I finished my meal, made a final check that the mother's discharge was OK, and set off for home. Snow was falling and I remember, as I walked along the road into town, my body felt frozen right through.

Back at home, I was snuggled up in bed and just dozing off when suddenly there was a loud knock at the door. I got up and answered it, and standing outside in the snow, panting for breath, was the husband of the woman I'd just seen. He was as white as a sheet. "What's the matter?" I

asked, and he replied, trying to get his breath back, "It's my wife; her bleeding won't stop." "Oh, no!" I said, and without wasting a moment I got my things together and rushed out barefoot to the rickshaw station in Tajuku, where luckily I managed to get a ride without waiting. The driver took me back to Tanaka as fast as he could.

When I got there I found things were even worse than I'd feared: the woman's mattress was completely soaked in blood—it had trickled right down onto the floor. A number of neighbors were standing around the woman. "Now, don't panic," I told them, but I was shocked myself and I felt my whole body shaking. Eventually I managed to pull myself together and injected her with a styptic to stop the bleeding. I asked someone to go and fetch Dr. Ishijima from Tsuchiura Hospital.

Dr. Ishijima—a marvelous woman doctor—arrived very quickly clutching her bag. The first thing she did was to shout at everyone, "Will all of you, apart from immediate family, please get out." She then turned to the woman's husband and said, "Your wife's hemorrhaging badly. But with a bit of luck I should be able to save her life. Please make as little noise as you can." The doctor did various things to slow the bleeding and gave the woman several injections. And as we stood watching, the blood flow gradually got less and less and eventually stopped completely. I was absolutely delighted. It seemed like a miracle.

I asked the doctor later what had caused the hemorrhage and she told me it was malnutrition: the woman had been working day in and day out in the fields for years on end and eating nothing but rice and barley. This had weakened her, and when the baby was born the womb hadn't been able to contract properly. Luckily we managed to save her, but at the time it was a terrifying experience.

Incidentally, we used to weigh babies on an ordinary pair of scales in those days—the sort with weights—like a pound of potatoes. The midwife always carried a pair of scales around with her in her bag.

When I had to attend a birth out in the country, the baby would often be born before I got there, the mother, still dressed in her tatty old working clothes, having coped with it on her own and managed to cut off its umbilical cord without any help. "What did you cut it with?" I'd ask. As often as not, she'd tied silk thread tightly around it in two places, put a pair of scissors in boiling water for a while, and then cut the cord where she'd tied the thread. These women had incredible courage doing something like that; I mean, would anyone have the nerve for it nowadays, do you think?

I used to go back later to see that the mother was all right, but after a couple of visits she'd say, "Don't worry, I can manage on my own from now on." I'd warn her that until the baby's umbilical cord had fallen off completely, it had to be kept properly sterilized or it could get infected and the baby die. "No, no, it's a good strong baby. Don't you worry," she'd reply. So I had no choice but to stop visiting her, and I dare say the child grew up perfectly healthy.

Work for us midwives dropped off during the American occupation: the system was changed by General MacArthur, and, rather than rely on our services, everyone had their babies in hospitals. Fair enough, I suppose—we've all got to change with the times—but the fact that they still, invariably, have their children there suggests to me that pregnant women, like the rest of the Japanese now, are too soft to be able to look after themselves.

Women's Hairdressing

Mrs. Tamaki Asano (1918–)

Typically—though it depended a bit on your circumstances—when a girl reached the age of twelve or thirteen she had her hair done up in the *momo-ware* style, and from then on she kept her hair dressed in a traditional style for the rest of her life. So hairdressers always had plenty to do, which made it a useful job to have.

I started as a trainee in a hairdresser's shop in Tokyo as soon as I left my village elementary school. It was run by my aunt—she was a bit of a dragon, she wouldn't put up with any "slacking." I remember one example of how fussy she was: there was a bonsai tree in the salon and part of my job was looking after it. But I didn't just have to water the tree and put plant food on it, I actually had to brush every single leaf separately. My aunt would say, "Young lady, if you think you can miss out a leaf here or there, you'll never learn any trade properly," and she made me even clean the leaves that couldn't be seen by the customers. Back then the head of a salon was always very hard on her trainees—goodness knows whether it actually did us any good.

There must have been at least a hundred traditional hairstyles. Obviously I can't talk about them all, but I'll try and explain some of the ones shown in the pictures.

When they were children, girls wore their hair hanging loose in a style called *o-sage*, though sometimes the hair was plaited or tied up with a paper ribbon to make it look pretty. But the custom was that once a girl finished elementary school at twelve or thirteen she couldn't keep that style—she had to have it done in a *momo-ware*. In the countryside where I came from, a girl had to change her hairstyle on the very day she left school. She also replaced the simple sash around her kimono with a proper adult one.

The *momo-ware* is supposed to represent a bud—a girl about to bloom —so the chignon is very round and full. The style shown in the illustration is called a *miyako shidori*—it's a slight variation on the *momo-ware*, a bit fancier. In a true *momo-ware* the hair's tied with a paper ribbon and the *motoi*

Momo-ware   "Seventeen" *shimada*   Yuiwata

[paper cord] can't be seen. In the picture, the chignon's kept in place with silk floss and a dappled cloth of a pretty color.

Combs were used for decoration. There were several different types, flower-pattern or shellwork, for example; you can see another small piece of cloth just in front of the comb—this was known as a *chinkorogake*. Girls of fifteen or sixteen often wore a large red comb, and if you did it up nicely with a strip of colorful cloth it made them look really very sweet.

Ornamental pins were stuck into the hair on either side of the fringe; usually the pin on the left was much larger than the other one. They came in all sorts of designs, but a pattern of pine, bamboo, and plum blossom was popular; so was a fan pattern. Another type of ornamental pin had a design of wisteria blossom on it, but this was only worn by apprentice geisha and never by ordinary girls. The strands of hair next to the pins hung down slightly; they were known as "charm locks"—just another form of decoration really.

When a girl reached seventeen her parents would have her hair dressed in a special *shimada* style that was supposed to bring her happiness in the future. This was known as a "seventeen *shimada*," and here the shape of the chignon—the round "bud" of childhood—changed. An old woman once told me that at seventeen a girl's heart literally begins to divide in two, like her loyalties. When she's young, still wearing a *momoware*, a girl obeys her parents in everything and her heart's still pure, but once she comes of age her sense of duty begins to waver; so she also starts wearing her chignon split in two, one part behind the paper cord and the other in front. A colored band is used to wrap the base—without this it would just be an ordinary *shimada*—but the fringe and sides are much larger too; after all, she's now old enough to be a bride.

From the age of nineteen to twenty-one or -two, girls wore a hairstyle called a *yuiwata*. Here the chignon was much lower and flatter on the head than the seventeen *shimada*, and divided completely in two to suggest full maturity; this was also tied with a dappled band. In the illustra-

Kiritenjin   Maru-mage   Tsubushi shimada

tion it's a bit too tight—in fact it was usually wound fairly loosely around the chignon. And if you tied bits of gold or silver thread to both sides of the cloth the style was known as an *osome*.

Oh, of course, I forgot: between the seventeen *shimada* and the *yui-wata*, there was another style called *oshichigake*. This was almost identical to the seventeen *shimada*, except that you wound gold or silver paper ribbon all the way around the strip of cloth, and it was often worn on special occasions like New Year. It could look very pretty indeed.

After twenty-one, some girls wore variations of the standard *shimada*, others had it done in an *ichogaeshi*. *Kiritenjin* was also very popular: in this, the chignon was split into two bunches on either side of the head, you wound a paper ribbon in between, and a dappled cloth was tied on top of that. The chignon was fairly flat and low on the head, and the whole effect was simple but refined; the girl was now at an age when she might get married very soon, so she'd want a graceful style that wasn't too conspicuous. The *ichogaeshi* was basically much the same, but the hoop that divided the two sides of the chignon was larger and stuck up at the back—just for decoration, I suppose.

Once you married, you wore your hair in a *maru-mage* style for the rest of your life. No other sort of hairstyle was acceptable. If you look at the picture, you'll see why: it's a return to the single, round chignon, to show the woman's heart has become whole again—one with her husband's.

At the base of the chignon in the *maru-mage* you can see a small round bead. This was made of red coral. The picture doesn't show the cloth band very well, but tucked in above it was often another piece of jewelry called a *nakazashi*, made perhaps of tortoiseshell, to add a touch of elegance. White-spotted silk was often used for the band, but the color and material varied, and even black satin was possible.

The size of the chignon was fixed according to your age. Married women in their twenties had a large, full one called a *daitsukasa* or, if it was even bigger, a *daidaitsukasa*. But once a woman reached her thirties, the chignon was tied slightly smaller and was known as a *gokudaitsukasa*. After forty it was known as a "number one" or a "number two" and was very much smaller; and when you reached fifty or sixty the bun became tiny—rather sweet, sitting sort of perched on top of the head. When it was that small, you knew you were really getting on. The size of the chignon bead also got gradually smaller as you got older, and by the time a woman was seventy it was hardly bigger than a grain of rice. A red bead was always used, but the color of the cloth band again varied with age. In your twenties it was red, in your thirties pink, a slightly pinkish purple in your forties, and a deep purple color for your fifties. So, you see, anyone looking at a woman could nearly always tell how old she was, whether she was a spinster or married, and even what sort of work she did.

With geisha you could tell straight away—their styles were quite different from those of ordinary girls—though the apprentices were sometimes a bit hard to pick out unless you noticed their sidelocks, for instance, which were kept in place with stiff black paper, not grease. A *miyako oshidori* chignon was popular with apprentice geisha, using large, highly decorated pins, often with a wisteria pattern—I mentioned them before; they were most attractive.

After becoming a full geisha they wore what was basically a *shimada*, though, being geisha, there were all sorts of variations and extra ornaments. Veteran geisha—anyone over twenty-two or -three was called a veteran—had their hair dressed in a *tsubushi shimada*, where the front chignon was large and full, and the back one round and very small, raised off the scalp to some extent; putting it up like this was a frightful business.

But almost *all* these styles involved tugging the hair about and binding it up tightly, so inevitably the roots suffered. When a girl's hair was first dressed in a *shimada*, for instance, the roots usually gave off a small discharge and, even as I worked, the smell would be slightly unpleasant. It was also painful—girls would often be in tears—and it took about three months for the roots to settle down and the pain to go away. So it isn't surprising that women today won't keep their hair in a traditional style for any length of time. And it was only sensible back then, when the hair was being pulled and tugged about all year long, to give it a rest occasionally, which explains why geisha would wear a *tenjingake* for a few days—the paper cord tied very loosely, the chignon fairly flat on the head. Still, since they couldn't wait on any customers like that, they were soon back in the formal style—I felt sorry for them sometimes.

But I must stop, or I'd go on for days. I mean, there were special styles for New Year, when ears of rice or pine twigs were tied into the hair; and others only for the ladies who ran the geisha houses. . . . But you've heard enough.

GEISHA
AND
OFFICERS

Mrs. Miyazaki, as a young geisha

Errands

Mrs. Sui Nakazawa (1909–)

I didn't come to Tsuchiura till after I'd become a full geisha: I was born and brought up in Sawara. There isn't much contact now between Tsuchiura and Sawara, but fifty years ago steamers ran between the two towns, which were at opposite ends of the lake, and they were both prosperous communities, so we saw quite a lot of each other.

As soon as I finished my final year of primary school at the age of eleven, my family sent me away to become a *shitajikko* in a geisha house. A *shitajikko* was a girl who wasn't yet old enough to become an apprentice, but was made to run errands and taught the rudiments of being a geisha.

I was lucky even to finish my full six years of primary school: many girls were taken away from school at only eight or nine and sent into service or found work as baby-sitters. I don't think you can really blame anybody in particular for this; it's just that everyone like us was poor, and the world as a whole was much less advanced then. My father died when I was a baby, so my mother had to go out to work in order to bring us up. Every day I saw with my own eyes the sort of hardships she was going through for my sister and me, and I took it to heart. So it seemed only natural that I should be made to work too after leaving school, and I didn't feel particularly miserable when I was sent to the geisha house.

The point is that when a daughter was sold into a geisha house—unlike maids or baby-sitters—her parents were given a hefty sum of money: a hundred yen, which obviously went a long way toward paying off debts and helping them get by. It offered a way out, and that, in many cases, was reason enough.

Sawara in the old days, with the Ono flowing through the middle of it and crowded with boats, was a lively spot, and the largest tea house employed at least ten geisha; but in the place I worked at there were only three or four of them, plus a couple of apprentices and two *shitajikko* including myself. I had to wear a cotton kimono with a narrow sash and an apron on top.

Our geisha used to have their hair done every three or four days, so I was forever being made to run down to the hairdresser's. "The geisha would like to know if you can do her straight away," I'd have to ask, and the lady there, who'd be in the middle of doing someone else's hair, would look up and reply, "Could you ask her to wait a while?" I'd run back and pass on the message: "She says she can't do it just yet." The geisha would look sulky and sigh, "I'll just have to wait then, I suppose," and would go back to her picture book.

I'd sit there quietly beside her and before ten minutes had passed the geisha would say, "Go along and see if she's finished yet." I'd run down to the shop, and the hairdresser would get cross with me: "Didn't I just tell you I wasn't ready?" So I'd run back and pass on the message: "She says she still can't manage it." The geisha would then get cross herself and shout, "That woman's so slow"; but it was me she took it out on.

On winter evenings when I was sent out on errands five or six times in a row, I used to get frozen stiff; I remember longing to be back by the fire in the geisha house. But when I got back I wasn't allowed to rest even for a moment before I was sent off again. There were lots of times when I felt like crying my eyes out.

Occasionally, a geisha wouldn't have any clients and she'd sit around trying to kill time. She'd even stand in front of the household altar, with her hands together, and pray that a client would call for her soon. If she was then lucky enough to get a summons from one of the restaurants, she'd be all smiles; but if there was no sign of any custom, she'd get more and more depressed and would sit at the table staring off into space. She might ask me to rub down an ink stick for her. Once I'd got everything ready, she'd start frantically writing letters. When each letter was finished, she put it in a small red lacquered box and told me to take it along to someone. They were love letters.

Comedians quite often tell jokes about geisha getting their maids to take letters to several different clients, all saying exactly the same thing, like "I'm pining away because you never come to see me any more." But

Learning the shamisen

when I was a *shitajikko* this sort of thing did actually happen: I used to have to go and deliver identical letters to men all over town. I was still a child, of course, and innocent about relationships between men and women, so, when I got to the client's office, I often had no idea how I was supposed to hand it over and would hang around outside wondering what to do, sometimes on the verge of tears because one of the staff had told me off for doing so.

I seemed to be always running errands, day and night: "Go and buy me some socks"; "Go and ask someone from the haberdasher's to come and see me"; "Go and get a rickshaw to come and pick me up straight away," and so on—I never managed to get to bed till after midnight. And I always felt tired. It was awful being so bone-tired every day. I used to drop off still sitting up—it happened dozens of times—while I was waiting on one of the geisha. . . . They weren't very pleased.

But I did at least get a proper training in dancing, as well as playing the shamisen and drum. A woman came to the house regularly to teach me the drum, and for shamisen and dancing lessons I used to go out to different teachers' houses. But the strictest lessons were to do with the proper rules of etiquette for geisha: attitudes toward superiors, behavior in front of clients, the correct way of speaking. For example, it was impressed on us that geisha should never eat or drink when attending their customers. I was taught over and over again that the function of a geisha was not just to amuse the clients and give them a good time—a prostitute could do that. No, a geisha had to be an artist, and devote her life to it; this was drummed into us, till we were almost saying it in our sleep.

It took years of practice and hard work to become a fully-fledged geisha in those days; and because of this the atmosphere at geisha parties was quite different to what it is now. But when I think back on it, I do wonder whether the rigid training everyone got then was really a good thing or not. I mean, if the discipline is too strict you tend to lose the ability to express your own personality. If you're persistently told, "Don't do this, don't do that," and urged to suppress your own emotions, when you do want to do something on your own account you find that you haven't the courage any longer, and you can't even get through to anyone. The strain this produces, particularly on growing children, obviously can't be healthy.

But having said that, when I see the sort of sloppy manners and un-professional behavior shown by most geisha today, I'm always amazed. Perhaps you really do need strict training to be able to "entertain" clients properly, in the true sense of the word. It strikes me that it's always dif-ficult to find a good balance: in other words, training that's not so hard it smothers a person, but not so lax as to encourage sloppiness either.

Two Geisha

Mrs. Sui Nakazawa, geisha name "Ochiyo" (1909–)
Mrs. Tsuya Yamamura, geisha name "Umeka" (1915–)

Umeka: In the old days, the road running through Tsuchiura from the
town hall over Nioi Bridge and along to the offices of the Telephone Corporation marked the boundary between the red-light district where all the
brothels were and the geisha quarters.

The NCOs and lower ranks from the naval air squadron had their fun
in the red-light district. The largest brothels had as many as seven or eight
girls working in them, but in the smallest there were maybe only two or
three. Each brothel was built with an impressive entranceway and a dimly
lit corridor that ran off it through the center of the building right to the
back; and at the peak of the district's popularity, I suppose there must
have been a good seventy or eighty brothels there altogether.

None of the higher-ranking officers would've been seen dead near the
brothels: they were all entertained by geisha in the assignation houses on
the other side of the road. I don't think people realize today just how
sharp a difference there was between the lower ranks and the officers,
which included even the way they spent their off-duty hours. The fact is
they were kept strictly apart: the geisha district was patrolled by military
policemen who kept a close eye on the behavior of the troops, and a man
from the lower ranks would never have been admitted to one of the geisha
houses.

Ochiyo: Yes. It must've been the military's policy to fence them off like
that. The highest-ranking officers—the vice admirals and rear admirals—
would sweep up to the house in chauffeur-driven cars, and they'd always
sit at the head of the table, followed by captains, commanders, lieuten-
ants, right down to ensigns, all in strict order of seniority. It wasn't at all
unusual to have several famous admirals attending one of our parties.
The narrow road dividing the geisha quarters from the red-light district
sometimes seemed almost to separate heaven from hell.

Umeka: Not many people today know there was also a strict ranking
among geisha.

Ochiyo: No, they don't, do they? I suppose it's because they don't realize what a wide gap there was, in skill as a performer and so on, between an experienced geisha and a girl who'd only just moved up from the apprentice stage.

Umeka: I remember one party I went to fairly soon after I became a full geisha, when I was hanging back shyly only waiting on people at the lower end of the table. After a while, the senior officer sitting at the top caught my eye and beckoned me over; being young and not realizing I was doing anything wrong, I did as I was told and went straight up to join him. One of the more senior geisha, who was sitting near this officer, ticked me off in no uncertain terms: "It is *not* your place to be at this end of the table," she said. I had to go back, blushing and confused. Back then at a formal geisha party—except, perhaps, for the very smallest ones—none of the younger girls, however popular they might've been, were allowed to wait on customers at the top of the table.

Ochiyo: You know, the parties we had were far more colorful and sumptuous than they are today. The geisha all wore kimono with long black trains and, when food was served to the clients, a whole line of them would move down the long corridor of the restaurant with their black trains swishing along the floor as they walked, each geisha holding a lacquered food tray up in front of her at eye level. The customers were then served according to rank, beginning, of course, at the head of the table. I always took part in the procession, so never actually had a chance to watch it myself; but it seemed to go down well with the naval officers— they were always telling us what a grand sight it was.

There was a rather scholarly lieutenant—I forget his name—who once told me what this ceremony was called. *Seibi*, that's right: he said it was Chinese, and meant carrying food raised up in front of you, as if offering it up to the gods. The word apparently appears in some ancient Chinese chronicles, but in China the custom died out long ago. "Isn't it strange," he said, "that it should still be kept alive in present-day Japan? We've inherited so much of classical Chinese culture."

Umeka: I wonder who that could've been. It wasn't Lieutenant Koga, was it?—the man involved in the young officers' rebellion of 1932.
Ochiyo: No, not him. It wasn't anyone who came to geisha parties very often. All I remember is what he told me about the tray-carrying ceremony.
Umeka: I don't suppose you knew Admiral Yamamoto very well?
Ochiyo: The commander of the fleet? No, I was still too young to be allowed to sit near him. But do you remember Genda? I knew him pretty well. He weighed almost nothing, he was so small and thin. And sometimes when he got excited he'd suddenly put his hands on the lintel running around the top of the wall, jump up onto it, and before you knew what was happening, he'd shoot along it with his hands touching the ceiling, as easily as if he was just walking down the street.
Umeka: Who would ever have dreamed then that Lieutenant Genda would go on to plan the attack on Pearl Harbor?
Ochiyo: No, it's incredible, isn't it?
Umeka: But there was something a bit special about those naval officers, wasn't there? They had the pick of any girl they wanted, both geisha and ordinary town girls.
Ochiyo: Yes, they say that students at the top universities now are quite popular in that way, but it's nothing compared to the way girls used to go for naval officers. Apart from anything else, they looked so splendid. They were well built, and clever too. They were all young, but most of them were surprisingly mature and self-assured.

In the summer they wore white uniforms and carried short swords, with gleaming scabbards. And in winter they wore dark blue tunics, short capes over their shoulders, and caps. Groups of them used to march in full uniform through the town. All the young girls in Tsuchiura dreamed of falling in love with an officer, and in fact many of them did end up marrying one.
Umeka: I wonder why they found them so attractive. I suppose the thing

that made them different from ordinary men was the special sort of twinkle they seemed to have in their eyes. I imagine it came from having to fly planes every day and never knowing whether they'd come back alive or not.

Ochiyo: There was certainly something about them. None of them thought they'd survive the war when it came, though they never mentioned this outright, and I suppose we must have sensed it. It made them a bit frightening in a way.

Umeka: But, strangely enough, sometimes they could behave like spoiled brats. To us hard-working geisha they seemed—well, like naughty little boys who wouldn't do what they were told.

Ochiyo: Yes, it's funny, they could be like that, couldn't they? Most of the time they seemed solid and responsible, but just occasionally they'd suddenly start playing the fool. Some of them were so boisterous I often felt like giving them a good spanking. But on the whole, I suppose, they did try to keep things within reason—they never got completely out of hand.

Umeka: You see, they generally made a point of being extremely polite toward women, whether geisha or ordinary women in the town. You've got to respect them for that.

Ochiyo: Well . . . it was funny to see how differently the officers behaved in the daytime. I remember a captain who got very drunk one night and started pulling up the *tatami* mats in the tea house, saying he was digging for potatoes; he then piled the mats up, climbed on top, and started singing at the top of his voice. I happened to meet him in town the next day and he seemed altogether another person. He was walking along stiffly in his spotless white uniform with his back straight as a ramrod and a sword hanging at his side. Even when our eyes met, he walked straight past me with a totally blank expression on his face. Of course I understood it would hardly have done for an officer to start flirting and giggling with a geisha in the open like that, but the way he completely ignored me seemed rather horrid.

Umeka: It was a matter of "form," really. And it made things simpler in a way. I remember one of the trainee pilots from the flying school who became very fond of a young geisha. But after a few months he was told he was being posted away from Tsuchiura, and as the day of his departure got nearer, the two of them worked themselves up into a terrible state. I couldn't bear to see them so miserable at having to leave each other. For a while after he'd gone, the girl was in floods of tears all day and couldn't even do her share of work. The affair caused trouble for everyone.

Ochiyo: But some of the officers were very matter-of-fact about their affairs. When an officer was transferred to another post he might introduce his favorite geisha to one of his juniors and say to him, in a serious voice, "She's a wonderful girl, and I was very fond of her. I want you to look after her for me, so don't do anything you might regret"; it was almost as if he was bequeathing the geisha to his subordinate. And the junior officer would obey his instructions to the letter.

Umeka: Ground crew officers also came to the geisha parties, but the pilots somehow seemed a different breed. There was a certain charisma about the men who flew, which the ones who worked on the ground hadn't got. And army officers were nothing like as dignified as navy men.

Ochiyo: I remember once Prince Higashikuni, the elder brother of the present empress, visited Tsuchiura during army maneuvers and a party was held in his honor at the "Kagetsu" inn. The highest place at the table wasn't in fact taken by the prince but by the officer in command of the Tsuchiura area, and the prince sat at a place appropriate to his army rank, about a third of the way down the table. But his floor cushion was much fancier than the commander's: purple crepe, I think it was.

The prince was a very tall man, with distinguished features, and I remember being terribly impressed that, even from a distance, he had a real air of nobility about him. I thought I'd never have such a good chance again to see a member of the imperial family close up and so—being rather daring—I walked nonchalantly past him several times to get a good look at his face.

The more senior geisha were too overawed to go anywhere near him. So I decided to pluck up courage, and took a flask of saké up to the handsome officer sitting next to him, and asked whether the prince would like some. "Yes, he would. Leave the flask here; I'll serve him," the officer replied, and I retired to the back of the room. But I'm sure just once in his life the prince would've liked to have his drink poured by a geisha.

Umeka: Do you remember the 1932 affair?

Ochiyo: No, not really.

Umeka: Well, the night before it happened, I attended a party at a tea house called "Takeshiro." Lieutenant Koga, Lieutenant Nakamura—a trainee pilot from the flying school—and Lieutenant Obata were all there. Even now I can remember the scene very clearly. That night, Mitsuyo, the geisha who was Koga's lover, wasn't with us. The three officers behaved quite normally: Lieutenant Koga, a tall, heavily built man with a dark complexion, was as usual rather sullen, but he didn't give the slightest indication that he was planning to take part in a coup d'etat the following day. Lieutenant Nakamura was a handsome, fresh-faced young officer who always seemed very quiet and composed. The next day, when I heard these two had been involved in a military uprising and had murdered the prime minister, I was absolutely stunned. It *had* struck me that the party had finished rather earlier than usual, but nothing in the officers' behavior gave any hint of what must've been going through their minds. After that I began to feel there was something rather frightening and untrustworthy about military men.

Ochiyo: After the incident, Mitsuyo suddenly disappeared, didn't she?

Umeka: I suppose she must have been taken away somewhere.

Ochiyo: When the war began, the geisha district changed completely. In 1944 the government decided geisha were an extravagance, and from then on we were called just "hostesses." We were all miserable. Three or four "hostesses" were put in each assignment house, and we were treated little better than high-class maids. We weren't even allowed to play the shamisen any more.

Umeka: Yes, the relaxed atmosphere of the prewar years disappeared entirely. No sooner had a new batch of trainee pilot officers arrived than they were sent off on active service. Even at the parties we attended, the recruits would get so emotional that their instructors would have to shout at them, "Stop crying in front of the women." The officers all looked so young it often made me cry too. We knew the young pilots would fly to Chiran in Kyushu before going on their suicide missions, so we were always trying to persuade ourselves that it wasn't as if they were going straight from Tsuchiura to their deaths. It must have been even more upsetting for the people who lived in Chiran.

Ochiyo: They were so different from the officers before the war. I remember they wore dark blue tunics, and belts that crossed on their chests, with scarlet tassels on them; they also carried long sabers, but somehow they didn't look like proper officers at all.

Each of them was allowed to spend his last night here with a geisha. A lot of the girls were young too at that time, and just for a night they became young wives, to comfort them. I was already getting on a bit by then and just doing maid's work, so I only saw what was going on from behind the scenes; but in no way could you say those men had come to enjoy themselves. They all looked desperate. Lower-ranking officers and ordinary soldiers spent their last night in much the same fashion, in one of the brothels.

The next morning, before they set off, each man, in his immaculate uniform, would come and say goodbye to us: "This is the last visit for me in this life. I doubt I'll ever see any of you again. Goodbye." We'd all stand there, with tears streaming down our cheeks, quite unable to reply. We realized then what a really dreadful thing war was.

Umeka: And in the end we lost the war. GIs rode up in jeeps to places where we'd once entertained the navy. "Japan's done for," I often thought to myself in those days. Anyway, we've all got much older since then and, like it or not, we're now a very different country.

The Early Years of the Naval Air Squadron

Mr. Kunimichi Uchida (1899–)

I was posted to the naval air base in Ami near Tsuchiura in 1921. Before that I'd spent three years in the navy at Yokosuka, where I'd served on board the battleship *Fuji*, which had seen action in the Russo-Japanese War. The *Fuji* was in use as a training ship and we did all our sea training in her, traveling right around the coastline of Japan. Then a naval air squadron was started up in Yokosuka and began to recruit for trainees. I applied, was selected, and received some basic training there before being sent to Tsuchiura. About ten of my mates from Yokosuka came up to Tsuchiura at the same time.

I wonder if I can remember what the place was like then. . . . It was pretty isolated compared to Yokosuka. Right behind the station was the enormous lake; there was just a single main street through the town, and beyond were paddy fields as far as the eye could see. When I first arrived in Tsuchiura the road to Ami hadn't yet been built, and to get there you had to go through Nakajo, past Tajuku and Omachi, and finally turn left when you came to the crossroads at Shimotakatsu. And the lanes we followed were extremely narrow: most were only just wide enough for a single truck to pass along.

The air base was still under construction when we arrived, and the barracks weren't finished, so for a while we had to lodge in local farmhouses where we were given all our meals, and we walked to and from the base each day. Our headquarters was in Ami itself, near where the University Hospital is now. Mind you, it didn't look the least bit like an HQ: it was just a tiny, shabby wooden building.

We only had two planes. There was no hangar, so we had to park them under a makeshift canvas shelter to give them some protection. The airfield was in terrible shape, too—just a bumpy strip, cleared from wasteland and fields by a team of workmen, with us to help dig up tree roots and cart away barrowfuls of earth; there weren't any bulldozers then, of course.

I was attached to the squadron as an engine mechanic. Compared with modern aircraft, the machines we had to fly in those days were incredibly primitive: I reckon they were fighters the British had used during the First World War and then unloaded for a high price because they were too dodgy and old-fashioned to be worth keeping. The planes were known as "Avros." The engine—a Lone engine, it was called—was only about 110 horsepower; when you think that cars nowadays can produce 150 horsepower from an 1800 cc engine, you'll understand what sort of aircraft we were stuck with. And they were biplanes, of course. All three pilots, one an officer and two ordinary airmen, came from the squadron at Yokosuka. Before Colonel Sempill joined us in 1921 as an instructor, the pilots knew only the very basics of flying, so training day after day consisted almost entirely of practicing takeoffs and landings.

The Avro's propeller and engine were a single block, and the whole thing rotated; anywhere near it you got plastered with oil and grease—quite apart from the racket it made. To start it up, you had to turn the propeller by hand but you really had to put your back into it or it wouldn't shift. If your luck was in, it'd pick up on the second or third attempt, but occasionally you could try as many as twenty or thirty times and it still wouldn't fire—you'd end up dripping with sweat. Men even died starting the engines. Three or four men were killed on different occasions when the prop they were turning suddenly whipped into life and hit them. A few others had their arms broken as well. I saw one guy killed when he was helping me swing a propeller; it was a really nasty death—his whole body was left smashed and bleeding.

The planes were always crashing, too. Even after the colonel arrived, there were a number of crashes. If you listened from the ground you could tell straight away whether an engine was running properly or not; and if you thought it sounded a bit funny, as likely as not you'd soon see the plane stall and drop. But in those days they flew at such low altitudes and so slowly that, if they were lucky, they could ditch it and still get away with only a few cuts and bruises.

An "Avro"

As I said, the pilots were pretty inexperienced, and nine times out of ten they crashed their plane upside down. This meant trouble, and when we raced over to help, we'd often find the pilot covered in blood, screaming out in pain—"My legs, my legs," or something. Parachutes weren't used at all in those days, of course, so if the engine packed up while you were flying, that was it. I often wondered how on earth they could put up with the danger. Anyway, if the pilot was still alive, we'd drag him out of the wreckage and take him to the medical room on a stretcher—though the "medical room" in fact was just an office and there wasn't much equipment in it at all; so all the doctor could do was splint any broken limbs and disinfect the wounds. We watched many an injured pilot slowly fade away, his moans getting more and more feeble toward the end. An amazing number of the trainees died like this. As far as I remember, there were four fatal crashes while Colonel Sempill was with us, and after he went back to England and Japanese officers took over the instructing, the number of accidents shot up and there must have been more than twenty deaths.

The funerals, though, were a grand affair: the whole squadron turned out in the base's large assembly hall, and a priest from the Kanryoji temple nearby would chant passages from the sutras. They even built a memorial so people could pray for the souls of the dead pilots.

You know, planes were so unusual then that hundreds of sightseers came from Tsuchiura and miles around to watch. They used to sit on mats spread on the ground and spend the whole day gazing up into the skies, with a picnic and a few bottles of saké to help pass the time. So it must have been a nasty shock to see a plane crash right in front of them. . . .

Colonel Sempill was a tall and very handsome man—a member of the British aristocracy, I heard. He arrived in Tsuchiura with thirty other British pilots and a good many aircraft, including famous fighter planes like the "Spark." (Mitsubishi had just started manufacturing the first Japanese-made aircraft and the squadron was using those at the time.)

Officially Sempill was just an instructor sent to Japan by the British authorities, but he was more than that—he was a fine pilot in his own right. The most obvious difference was that he didn't show the slightest hint of fear when he was flying. Before the colonel arrived we'd never seen a loop-the-loop, but he did beautiful loops, spins, sideslips, and made it look as easy as whistling.

His landings were fantastically smooth. When one of our boys tried to land, it wasn't exactly elegant: the wheels would hit the ground with a bump, jolt back up into the air, and then bounce again further down the strip before finally landing. You got a lump in your throat just watching. They were certainly brave, to fly despite their lack of skill, and I admired them for that. But they really weren't much good, and they were always smashing the planes up.

The training had to stop when it rained or the wind was too strong. And you couldn't fly the day after a heavy rainfall either, even if the weather had cleared up: the runway turned into a mud bath, so if you tried to use it before it'd dried out properly, the fuselage of the planes became plastered with mud and you got all sorts of problems. The mechanics would have to wash them down, wipe the fuselage with rags, and scrape all the mud out of the engine. It was such a business you just had to hope there weren't any keen pilots who insisted on flying whatever the conditions.

When I think back on it, I really do wonder how on earth the men managed to fly such crumby old aircraft. The pilots must have realized they were laying their lives on the line every time they flew—they had terrific guts, all right. I suppose that's why the naval pilots were so popular with the girls in Tsuchiura. They were made a fuss of by all the geisha, and treated as if they were almost different beings from us mechanics.

Lord Sempill

Mrs. Shizu Okui (1896–1975)

In the early 1920s, the navy had very few officers who could handle an aircraft well enough themselves to be able to teach new trainees to fly. In Europe, on the other hand, aviation was already fairly advanced by that time, and air battles had played an important part in the First World War. So the Japanese government decided it couldn't afford to neglect the development of competent pilots any longer and asked the British whether they could send a number of flying instructors to help with their training program. The mission they put together consisted of thirty officers from the Royal Air Force and was led by Colonel Sempill, who brought his wife and children to Japan with him.*

Lord Sempill and his family were given a large house on top of the hill in Takatsu. I was employed as their interpreter, spending many enjoyable hours in the house with them. You see, there was almost nobody in Tsuchiura back then who could speak English so, since I'd learned a bit when I was at pharmaceutical college, the mayor had asked me if I'd help out. Whenever Lady Sempill wanted to go into Tsuchiura shopping, for example, she'd telephone and a few minutes later a motorcar would call for me at my house. Cars were extremely few and far between in those days, and I'd certainly never ridden in one before. It was a lovely feeling to be chauffeur-driven through the streets of Tsuchiura in a splendid limousine.

Lady Sempill was a very attractive lady, with bright blue eyes. She loved kimono, and in fact wore Japanese dress almost all the time, even to go out shopping. Her husband also occasionally appeared in Japanese clothes, though he usually wore his uniform. Unfortunately, foreigners were an extremely rare sight in Japan back then, so whenever Lady Sempill went into town, she'd immediately be surrounded by a crowd of people who trailed behind her wherever she went. This obviously seemed to upset her a bit.

The Sempills often invited me to tea or dinner at their house. I particularly remember the delicious biscuits they used to serve with afternoon tea—they really melted in your mouth—quite unlike anything we had in

The tram to the air base

Japan; it often struck me as strange that people could eat such very different kinds of food.

After Lord Sempill had been in Japan for several months, he began to pick up a few words of Japanese, sometimes with rather comic results. I remember once we were eating tangerines, and out of the blue he said to me, "*Mikan kimono achira sayonara*" [literally, "Tangerine kimono there goodbye"]. For a moment I had absolutely no idea what he was talking about, but it suddenly dawned on me that by "tangerine kimono" he meant the peel, and that he wanted me to "throw the peel away over there"! He often used to just string together any odd words he knew and come up with his own peculiar form of pidgin Japanese. He made some unfortunate mistakes, too: on a tram in Tokyo once he said to the conductor, "*Jinbocho de koroshite kudasai*" ["Please kill me at Jinbocho"], when what he'd meant to say was, "*Jinbocho de oroshite kudasai*" ["Please put me off at Jinbocho"]! He always claimed that Japanese was abominably difficult.

The colonel was a tall, splendid-looking man with handsome features. He came from a distinguished family whose history, I believe, dated back to the fourteenth century. I found him absolutely charming. But he could sometimes be rather haughty, his attitude being that the British were superior in every way to other nations, including the Americans and other Europeans. Japan didn't even come into the picture.

Still, you could hardly blame him: even modern Tsuchiura isn't very exciting, and in the old days it was a lot more backward that it is now; none of the roads was paved, almost all the houses were single-story wooden shacks, and the people were obviously poor. Britain and Japan were, in theory, equal partners in the Anglo-Japanese Alliance, but as far as national wealth and power were concerned Japan just couldn't be compared with Great Britain.

I remember, shortly before Lord Sempill was due to return home at the end of his mission, he asked me whether I would go back to England with him and his wife. He promised he'd look after me there and said he'd even pay for me to go to university. I wasn't sure what I should do, so asked the advice of a friend of mine, the American wife of Inazo Nitobe, the well-known statesman. She told me it was too good an opportunity to miss and thought I most definitely ought to take up the Sempills' offer. She even promised she'd see to it that I was appointed headmistress of the Quaker girls' school in Tokyo, after I got back to Japan. Eventually I made up my mind to accept, but my parents begged me again and again not to go. We were a family of eight and I was the main breadwinner, so if I'd gone abroad for a while my parents would have had a struggle to feed the other children. In the end I had to sacrifice my own ambitions for the sake of my family. You never know, though: if I'd gone to England I might now be the wife of some diplomat or prominent politician. That's life, I suppose.

* William Forbes-Sempill, 19th Baron Sempill (1893–1965), was a pilot in the First World War. After the war he headed technical missions to the U.S.A., Japan, and Greece and served on numerous Air Ministry advisory committees. He was awarded the third-class order of the rising sun by the Japanese government for his help with the Kasumigaura air squadron.

LIFE IN THE
COUNTRYSIDE

Rice planting

Sakura Village

Mrs. Michi Tsukamoto (1901–)

"Plain living," you could call it, but that wouldn't describe it: out in the country many houses didn't even have *tatami* matting and the whole family had to live on bare wooden floors with rough straw mats spread over them. The custom was that new mats, of fresh straw, were made at the end of December and put down in time to see the New Year in.

Most of the land around Sakura village belonged to various large land-owners, so during the harvest season, on the day the rice rent was due, the tenants would load sacks of rice onto either a handcart or a packhorse and take them down to the storehouse of the landlord's agent in the village. One of the landlord's clerks would be there to keep an eye on things.

When this heap was moved to the landlord's own storehouses, a lot of the tenants would volunteer to give a hand—not out of the kindness of their hearts, mind you, but for the extra pay they'd earn. The sacks were carried out of the agent's place, loaded onto handcarts, then pulled in a line, made up of dozens of tenants each with his own rig, winding down the road into Tsuchiura. The roads were very bumpy and potholed back then so it was impossible to carry more than four sacks per cart. With five or more on board, unless there was someone behind pushing as well, even the strongest man couldn't make the cart budge.

The men used to say that, by the time they got to Mushikake, they were so damn hungry they hadn't the strength left in them to pull their carts. So they used to break open one of the sacks, grab a handful of raw rice, and chew that to dull the empty feeling in their bellies; they could then just about find enough energy to pull their load the last few miles into Tsuchiura. When they arrived at the landlord's house they were given a decent meal and paid for their services, and it was only the thought of this bonus that kept them going.

Some of the landless peasants in those days were from families that had never owned any land, but quite a lot of them were people who'd originally had a field or two but then been forced to sell them. Banks

After the harvest

had a policy of never lending to the poor, you see, and though all farmers needed to borrow a bit of capital to buy seeds and fertilizer, the banks refused point-blank to deal with any of the "problem" cases. So smallholders would have no choice but to borrow money from either a wealthy farmer in their village or one of the rich merchants in Tsuchiura. They'd be lent the money against the small plot of land they owned. And what often happened was that the following year they couldn't repay the loan, so all their land was forfeited. There were any number of people who lost their property like this and were reduced to the level of common peasants.

The land in this area was very fertile so rents were high: twelve sacks of rice per acre. But you could only get about twenty-four sacks in all from an acre, and when half of this went in rent, you can imagine how tough it was to make a living. Most tenant farmers couldn't afford to buy fertilizer or anything.

And if a tenant couldn't pay his rice rent the land he farmed was, as they used to say, "given away" by the landlord, in other words leased to someone else. The original tenant would be forced to become a day laborer, he might even have to sell his daughter into a brothel or send his younger sons off to work as farmhands for some wealthy landowner and, by reducing the number of people he had to provide for, he'd somehow manage to find enough food to keep body and soul together.

Luckily we owned some land of our own, but my father died when I was only three and my mother had to run both the farm and house single-handed, working virtually day and night without a moment's rest. But she managed to get by somehow, employing farmhands on one-year contracts and, at the busiest times of the year, during the rice transplanting and in the silkworm season, getting a number of women from the Kashima area to come and help her out.

The soil around Kashima was much poorer than here, and the people there found it impossible to make ends meet unless they sent some of the family out to work. So every year several hundred young women from Kashima were packed off by their parents to work on farms in the Tsuchiura area. In our village there was even an agent for all this and if you told him how many girls you needed and when, he'd make all the arrangements for you.

Farmers never had time to go shopping back then, but there was a man with a horse and cart who traveled between Tsuchiura and the surrounding villages every day who'd fetch things from town for you. He'd buy anything you wanted: crockery, cloth, hardware. He used to lead his horse through the village early each morning, ringing a little bell; one of the villagers would hear him and shout, "He's here," and people would hurry out to place their order.

Not for fish, though: a dealer used to come around with a couple of large buckets attached to a yoke on his shoulders. But the villagers only ate sea fish on a handful of occasions a year, like New Year and during the various festivals. Sea fish could be dangerous: several people died from eating raw shark that had gone off. It took several days to bring a load up from the coast to our village, way inland, so on the whole it was considered pretty risky.

Which reminds me: I suppose some of my worst memories are of the time my eldest son was ill. He was born prematurely, and every day for months after his birth I had to tie him on my back and take him, with the cold wind whistling around my ears, all those miles down to the children's hospital in Tsuchiura. Only the very richest people in those days could afford to call the doctor out to visit them if they were sick. Most farming families left getting the doctor to come out till the patient was on the brink of death, so I had to take the child down to the clinic myself. I remember the way the wind used to push me about as I crossed Suijin Bridge at Mushikake. The toll at the bridge was one sen.

Country people used to pick plants like green gentian [a peptic], cranesbill [an anti-diarrheal], and lizard's-tail [used on swellings and boils]

Collecting herbs

when they went up into the mountains to collect firewood, to avoid, as much as possible, having to rely on the services of a doctor. These were stored and used as household medicines. The green gentian was hung from the eaves of the house to dry; cranesbill was said to work best if you picked it on the Day of the Ox during the last eighteen days of summer. We also kept a number of patent medicines from the northwest of Japan; they were special, and we never wasted them.

Let's see. There were also quite a few shops and craftsmen based in the village: a hardware store, a cooper, a basket maker, a tofu shop, a grocer's, a clog maker, a blacksmith, a carpenter, a barber; also a man who made spools for spinning silk thread, a man who respun cotton cloth, another who made silkworm egg cards, and a dyer of raw yarn.

Work clothes were made from cloth we wove ourselves; you'd get a dyer to dye the stuff for you, and then stitch it up on your own. If you were making a more formal kimono, you'd go and buy patterned material from the draper's. Cloth was so valuable in those days that when it got frayed it was either redyed or reversed and worn inside out, or even just patched up. Even clothes belonging to someone who'd died were divided up among the person's relatives, to be redyed and then worn again.

Talking about people dying, do you know what funerals were like back then? When someone died, every single person in the village did his bit to help prepare the funeral. First of all the deceased's family had to pound up a certain amount of rice. Neighbors came in to help with this and they were given a meal in return. While this was being done, others would go around telling the rest of the village the news. There weren't any telephones in those days, of course, so they'd have to traipse around for miles to make sure the outlying farms knew about it. Then they'd make the coffin. It was usually made of pine, but if the family didn't have any wood, an old clothes chest would be broken up and used instead. And then everyone in the village would lend a hand in putting it together. . . .

So there you have it. The fact is that, since the postwar land reforms, life for us farmers has been far, far better than it was before. A number of schools and colleges have been built near our village, for example. And the whole world, it seems to me, has changed beyond all recognition.

Mushikake: A Tale of Two Families

Mr. Shichirobei Tanaka (1907–)

In Mushikake there used to be just two family groups: the Tanakas and the Shibanumas. Each family had its own household god and a small shrine. The shrine in the village today was the one originally dedicated to the Tanakas' household god. The Shibanumas' stood slightly to the west of where the soy sauce factory now is.

When I was a child, the Tanaka shrine stood in large grounds and you could only reach it by crossing an earth-built bridge over the small stream that ran around it. There was no archway marking its approach, but there was an impressive statue of Jizo, the guardian deity, to the right of the entrance. The shrine had a front chapel and an inner hall and was dedicated to Inari, the god of the harvest. My friends and I often used to go there on rainy days to play: we'd lark about, playing tag up and down the corridors and shrieking at the top of our voices.

Some sixty or seventy years ago it was decided that, rather than have two individual family shrines, a single place should be used so the whole village could worship together as a community. The statues to Inari were all sold and the Tanaka shrine, rededicated to the god Ugayafukiaezu [the father of the legendary first emperor of Japan], became the village shrine of Mushikake.

As well as their own shrines, the Tanaka and Shibanuma families had separate cemeteries and Buddhist prayer halls. The Shibanuma prayer hall stood roughly where the *miso* shop in the center of Mushikake is today; the Tanaka one was on the outskirts of the village. Both were single-roomed buildings, about forty feet by twelve, with thatched roofs. Once a month the old people of the village gathered at their own halls and, after a few hours spent chanting Buddhist prayers, they'd sit down to a simple lunch of either vegetables in soy sauce or boiled potatoes. Maybe fourteen or fifteen people would attend each of the sessions.

After the war fewer and fewer people in the village were practicing Buddhists, and for some years no one went near the prayer halls at all. Many of the statues of Buddha toppled over, and around 1975 one was even found lying in a paddy field. Not long after that, both prayer halls and all the icons they contained were pulled down. I can still hear the mournful sound of the little handbells the old people used to ring as they followed the funeral procession when someone from the village died.

I was a member of the Shichirobei house of the Tanaka family. The Shichirobeis were in fact a branch of the Hachirobeis who had themselves, apparently, separated from the Kyubei house in the 1830s. The village headman came for generations from the Kyubei side. But in terms of social standing the highest-ranking Tanakas in Mushikake were the Ryuheis, though they'd fallen on hard times and been forced to sell their place and move into a smaller one. And the Kyubei family has now vanished from Mushikake without trace. But descendants of virtually all the other houses still live in the area.

The nearest village to Mushikake is Sanoko. The River Sakura runs between them and in the old days you had to take the ferry to go from one to the other. But I can't remember the ferry at all. All I do remember is that when I was a child, on the riverbank by the soy sauce factory, there were a few steps and the remains of a jetty, which must have been the landing stage for the ferry.

The riverbed was sandy and the water raced along, so it was perfectly clean and in the summer we often went swimming there. We always swam in the nude, not even wearing a loincloth. Farmers also used to bring their horses down to the river to wash them.

Suijin Bridge over the Sakura between Mushikake and Sanoko was built in 1906, when I was still a baby. At one end of it was a hut where the old tollman sat collecting money from people who crossed the bridge. Anyone from the two villages was allowed to cross free but for others the toll was one sen, two sen for bicycles, and three sen for carts. The tollhouse was about twelve feet square with a corrugated iron roof—large enough to sleep in; in fact, the little old man lived there permanently. The front of the hut could be opened up and the man usually sat inside, with

A prayer hall

the sliding doors along the front wide open, looking out. But when the weather was cold he'd shut the doors, leaving just a gap of a few inches in the middle, and would sit there huddled up to a brazier peering out toward the bridge.

I went to the tiny village primary school. We had only a single classroom, and there were no more than four or five pupils in each year. The teaching methods were a bit strange, too: the first and second years were taught together, as were the third and fourth, and the last two years as well. So from the very first day at school I found I was doing the same work as the second years. The reason for this odd system was that the school only had enough resources for three, rather than the usual six, classes. And it meant that the brightest kids could finish all the fourth-year work while they were still in their third year, but also that the slower ones got left behind completely and began to lose all interest.

The teachers were clearly prejudiced in favor of the richer kids. If there was ever a fight or anything, it was always the poor ones that got the blame. Mind you, back then everyone took that sort of discrimination for granted, so even if you got bawled out when it wasn't your fault, you just had to shrug your shoulders and forget about it. Anyway, we all came from the same village (everyone went home for lunch).

After finishing primary school, I went on to a higher elementary school in Tsuchiura. The children from Mushikake must have seemed real yokels in the other students' eyes, and we were always being teased and called "peasants." Even after several years at the school, we were treated as being lower down the scale than even the youngest town kids. In those days Tsuchiura seemed a very sophisticated place to country people, and as the way we talked and dressed was so different from the "townies" we realized we had no choice but to put up with their attitude. And we weren't as clever as them either, most of the lessons being a bit beyond us. The textbooks in country primary schools were different from those used in large town schools, so right from the start the Tsuchiura kids knew a lot of things we'd never been taught. To be honest, I whiled away my two years there not understanding a thing, and when I left I was still as clod-hopping as I'd been the day I started.

There was one big problem I had while at higher elementary school: children from Mushikake weren't really allowed to attend school in Tsuchiura unless they took lodgings in the town. So it was arranged that, if anyone asked, I should say I was staying with Mr. Marutani, the fer-tilizer merchant, in Nishimon. But one day a friend gave me a fright when he told me the teachers sometimes came around to check whether you really were living where you'd said. I was worried sick, but in the end I came up with a bright idea: I bought two satchels, one I took to school with me every day, and the other I left on a peg in Mr. Marutani's house so, if a teacher ever did turn up, he'd see my satchel and assume I was ac-tually living there.

When I was in the first year, I used to walk into Tsuchiura every day wearing either clogs or straw sandals. But the following year rubber shoes went on sale in Tsuchiura and as a special treat my parents agreed to buy me a pair. Still, whenever it rained or snowed the shoes leaked and made my feet feel so soggy I used to take them off and walk most of the way barefoot.

But that was all long ago. Nowadays, Mushikake's ringed by bypasses and expressways and a good many outsiders have come to live in the village. In fact only a handful of the present inhabitants are from the two original families, the Tanakas and the Shibanumas.

The Shrine of the New Moon

Mrs. Tomo Hanari (1889–)

We had a Shinto shrine in Kise, dedicated to the new moon; the small pond in front of it was also called the New Moon Pond. On the third day of each month [the day when, by the lunar calendar, the new moon appeared] people—and particularly anyone who wanted to get rid of warts or boils—would go along to pray there. It was usual on such occasions to make an offering of tofu, but rather than waste the tofu by leaving it on the altar to rot, the shrine used to sell it off to the villagers for half the normal price.

There was also a small Buddhist prayer hall in the grounds where, again on the third of every month, the old folk in the village used to gather and spend a few peaceful hours chanting prayers to the accompaniment of a small drum.

And twice a year, on February 3 and August 3, a grand festival was held at the shrine. The approach would be lit by hundreds of lanterns, and the sound of drums echoed among the trees for hours on end; performances of masked dancing and plays were put on. The locals, in their brightest clothes, came out into the streets carrying paper lanterns, and people from other villages, some miles away, poured down into Kise. Young girls dressed up in their best kimono and put on makeup. And the lads of the village would hang around trying to catch the eye of the better-looking girls. They were fun, these festivals—a splash of color in our country lives.

The school I went to was run by the Gonshoji temple in Konda—I didn't actually start there till I was nine. From where we lived to Konda was about two and a half miles, and on sunny days my friends and I used to dawdle our way home, spinning it out as long as we could, playing as we went and picking flowers at the side of the road.

When it rained, I would take a lacquered paper umbrella with me. I'd usually carry my clogs and trudge barefoot through the mud till I reached the stream by the temple, where I washed my feet before passing through the temple gate. I wasn't the only one there, either: farmers used to lead

Work clothes

their horses down to the stream to drink, so the banks were always littered with dung and bits of straw.

Classes were held in the main hall of the temple, with desks laid out in rows on the *tatami* floor. The teacher—not a priest in this case—was a Mr. Toyoshima, who I remember always wore Western clothes. Funnily enough, the only other thing I can remember about him is that his lunch box was made of porcelain, not the usual lacquered wood. His wife—they also came from Kise—often asked me to take it to school for him when he was on night duty.

It's only odds and ends like this that seem to have stuck in my memory, but I suppose I must have been quite keen at school. You see, I remember the prizes I won: whenever anyone got really high marks in an exam, they'd be given a certificate of merit, and an inkstone case or a couple of new notebooks. I used to be so pleased when I got one—you can't imagine—thrilled! Better than any birthday present.

Country Food

Mr. Orinosuke Ihara (1904–)

In our village a meal of a mixture of rice and barley, with six parts barley to four parts rice, would've been considered above average. And as side dishes, to flavor the rice, we ate things like dried plums, vegetables or fish preserved in *miso*, and pickled radish. Fresh river fish we almost never had up in the mountains where I lived, unless you count the tiny ones we found in mountain streams; this in spite of the fact that the Tsuchiura area as a whole seemed to have plenty. We never saw any fresh sea fish, either, from one year to the next.

But at New Year most families bought one salted salmon, though only after an awful fuss. Toward the end of December fish sellers used to come up to the village with large baskets on their backs (if they were women) or buckets hanging from a yoke (if they were men). They knew roughly which families bought from them each year, so they'd go along and show the whole household what they had to offer. "This salmon's nice and big," they'd say, "but it's a bit on the pricey side. Here's a smaller one—I can let you have that fairly cheap," and so on. The whole family would crowd around to have a look, and together they'd eventually decide which one they wanted.

The salmon was then hung from a lintel in the kitchen till the first of January. And every day till then, when I walked past and saw the thing hanging there, I'd get more and more impatient. When the fish was finally served up, not a thing was wasted: the head was boiled with soybeans for several hours and eaten, and even the bones were edible if you cooked them long enough in the same way. In the end we ate the whole fish—tail, bones, and all. We used to say that even the fish must've felt its life had meant something, it being polished off so thoroughly.

Now, what else did we eat? Oh yes, almost every family in the village made their own *miso* pickles. The ones with money used *miso* that was as old as any of the buildings in the village, and they'd preserve giant radish, carrots, burdock, or aubergines in it, leaving them to ferment in barrels in a dark storeroom for up to four or five years. A barrel would only be opened when a special guest came to visit. You can't imagine how good pickles made like this tasted. But unfortunately only a few of us could leave the vegetables that long; most people couldn't afford the soybeans to make enough *miso* for them to pickle anything for even as long as twelve months. There were even some who could only buy tiny quantities of *miso*—they obviously weren't going to put any of it aside. So the fact that a family could afford to eat pickles more than four or five years old was sure proof that they had a fair amount of cash.

The poorer people almost never ate eggs, either. Nowadays they're as cheap and plentiful as anything, but when I was young farming families didn't think of eggs as something to be eaten, though all of us kept five or six chickens. Every egg the chickens laid was sold. Back then it was very difficult for subsistence farmers to raise any cash: selling part of the rice crop or making charcoal could bring in some money, but only on a pretty irregular basis. It wasn't enough for us to cover all our daily needs, like salt, sugar, paper, candles, oil, and sometimes towels, none of which we could make ourselves. It just wasn't possible to be self-sufficient in everything. So the quickest and simplest way of getting cash to buy these things was to sell eggs.

Every day someone came to our village to buy up eggs—most of the dealers were old men and women, but there were also one or two young men in their twenties and thirties. One egg sold for about the price of a box of matches; a box of matches would last a whole month so, you see, each egg was worth a fair amount to us.

If they were so profitable, you might wonder why we didn't keep fifty or a hundred birds instead of only five or six. The reason was that they were fed on scraps of food and leftovers, and this wasn't enough to support more than a dozen or so at most. If you'd kept more chickens than that, you would have had to give them some of the rice meant for your own family, and you'd have ended up with nothing for yourselves to eat.

Anyway, because of this, country people in those days didn't use eggs

at all in their cooking. It wouldn't be exaggerating to say that, at primary
school, not a single kid had a lunch box with anything made of egg in it. In
fact, some of the girls at school had theirs full of barley and nothing else,
with no extras at all. The poor girl would be so embarrassed about this
she'd cover the lunch box with her arms or stand a textbook in front of it
as a screen, so nobody could see what she was eating. And if, as happened
occasionally, one of the children brought some boiled fish to school for
lunch, someone would notice and say, "Look what he's eating—it's carp,
isn't it?" and the rest of the class would crowd around, green with envy.

However, if you were laid up in bed and completely lost your appetite,
someone would suggest giving you an egg to help you get your strength
back; you'd be fed a meal of rice gruel with an egg on top. So lots of
children actually thought it was just something you had when you were ill,
like medicine.

I remember the excitement of having a guest from a long way off come
to visit. "We've got a guest coming, so we must have proper rice without
barley," my father would say: guests and pure white rice always went
together. We children loved the "silver rice," as we used to call it, and
we'd hang around by the stove, playing and getting in everyone's way,
while it was being cooked. My mother also made delicious side dishes
when the occasion called for it.

And we'd eat till we were fit to burst, then sit there unable to move,
groaning quietly in satisfaction. In fact, rice without barley tasted so good
one didn't really need anything else. It was nice with just a little salt
sprinkled on top, or mixed with soy sauce—I could eat three or four
bowlfuls of it like that. People had good appetites in those days, you
know: out in the country most adults ate at least three large bowls of rice
a meal.

But the situation nowadays is hard to credit: they're worried about too
much rice being produced. They're rich, they're comfortable, but they
still complain—about the quality of fish, the price of meat or whatever.

We ate what was available and just got on with it when there was nothing else in the house; but now that life's become much easier, it seems people are never satisfied, never grateful.

A Village Prone to Floods

Mr. Hiroshi Hisamatsu (1906–)

It's now more than sixty years since I came to live in Tsuchiura. Compared to the north of the prefecture, where I was born, Tsuchiura is a much nicer place to live. Apart from anything else, floods happen so much less often here. That's not to say there have never been any floods in Tsuchiura, but in my village of Kamidogiuchi every year without exception there was some flooding, and at least once every two or three years the place was inundated.

The village was about five hundred yards downstream from where the Sato and Kuji rivers joined. It was a small community of only about forty families. Because it was so near the two rivers, which were narrow and twisting, the level of water only had to rise a few inches to overflow.

When the water first began to rise, the lads from the village Young Men's Association would take a large drum and climb onto the part of the riverbank that looked like giving way first. They'd then sound the flood warning, with single beats of the drum. As the water rose higher they'd give the danger signal, which was a short beat followed by a long one. And when the river was so swollen it was about to burst its banks they'd sound the final signal, warning the villagers to take shelter: this was three short beats of the drum, and one long beat. As soon as this was done, they'd run for it, dragging the drum with them.

When they heard the danger signal, everyone began to collect up shoes and things strewn about the entrance of their house and bring them inside into the safety of the main part of the building, which was raised two or three feet off the ground. All they could do then was wait. They'd hear the final warning—*tat, tat, tat, bom*—and soon a torrent of water would pour down into the village.

Almost immediately the whole place, with all the paddy fields around it, was underwater. But it was quite rare for any of the houses to be flooded out. The floodwater was very fast-flowing and hit the village in one great surge, but it usually ran straight through, under the raised floors of the houses, and continued on down the hill. Within about an hour or, at the very worst, two or three hours all the water would have passed on. So floods in Kamidogiuchi were very different from those that used to leave Tsuchiura knee-deep for months.

But the debris left behind was appalling. For example, if the floods came in August or September just before the rice harvest, the ripe plants would be completely flattened and the paddy fields reduced to sand and rubble. And things like cucumbers and watermelons would also be so damaged they weren't fit for sale. In the area around where I lived the land would only support one rice crop a year, which meant that once the harvest had been ruined nothing could be done to make up the loss.

So you see, with conditions like this, the farmers in our district weren't any better off than simple peasants, and they managed only by the skin of their teeth to scrape a living from the land. Around there you never saw the sort of magnificent farmhouses, with grand entrance gates and high ceilings, that some of the wealthy farmers in the Tsuchiura area owned. If we'd only cared to think about it, we'd have realized we were stupid to go on living in a place like that. But when it came down to it there wasn't anywhere else we could go; we were pretty well tied to that land.

There was one advantage to it, though: we were only three miles from the coast, and fish sellers used to visit fairly often. (We may have had a tough job making a living, but these people used to walk on from our village through Ota and all the way to Urizura and Omiya to sell their stuff, a round trip of more than fifty miles—just think about it for a second.) Anyway, whenever a big catch came in and they couldn't offload it all, they used to let us have some for almost nothing, rather than see it go to waste. Even if we weren't in when they arrived, they'd walk straight into the house, draw water from the well, and leave a fish soaking in cold water for us. Then they'd go out into the fields, find a member of the household and call out, "I've left some fish in a bowl of water. Hope you enjoy it." All sorts of other salesmen came around with carts as well:

drapers, medicine sellers, people peddling daily household goods like soap and toothpaste.

So we had that to look forward to. And when we were small, depending on the season, we were allowed out to play whenever we wanted. There was a craze for spinning tops: I seem to remember I once bought an ordinary wooden one and took it along to the village blacksmith to get him to hammer an iron ring around it for me. The heavier and stronger the top was, the more likely it was to win in spinning contests, so I got him to make me a ring at least half an inch thick. He never seemed to mind doing this—we used to take our tops to the forge during his short midday break. Once the ring had been fastened on, we'd leave it to soak in salty water for two or three nights. This made the metal rim eat deep into the wood, pulling it even tighter and making it go that much better.

But it was only during the winter months that children from farming families were free to muck about like this: from the beginning of spring until the autumn, almost every minute of our time was spent working in the fields. In the plowing season, for example, we had to be up before four each day and out with a horse to till the fields.

Here's how it was done: a bamboo pole about nine feet long was tied to the horse's lead rein and the kid then led the horse, pulling the plow, with the pole. The reason for the pole was that there weren't any horses in Kamidogiuchi—they had to be borrowed from neighboring villages when they were needed—and to a kid of seven or eight who wasn't used to them, they must have seemed enormous. So to keep as far away from the things as possible, they used this long pole attached to the rein.

From half past four in the morning, I'd have to walk around and around my family's paddy fields, plowing. By the time the six o'clock siren sounded I would hardly be able to move another step; but it was still a while before I got my breakfast so I'd just do my best to carry on, trudging on and on around my patch. There'd be friends of mine in neighboring fields doing the same thing, yet none of us could spare the time to talk.

Back then it was taken for granted that the more finely the soil was broken up the better it was for the rice plants, and we were even taught this at primary school. So the work wasn't something you could get out of the way in an afternoon: it had to be kept up for at least ten days or so. I suppose I must've walked a good twenty or thirty miles daily in those paddy fields during that time.

The first time the soil was plowed it was only turned over fairly roughly. But in the second plowing the earth had to be churned up really thoroughly, and I'd be up to my knees in mud as I led the horse. All this exercise should in theory have made us kids physically strong, but in fact the work was so tough it went beyond that and had the opposite effect and we'd end up losing quite a lot of weight.

Around three in the afternoon I'd stop work and take the horse back home. My parents then took care of it, washing the mud off in a nearby stream and wiping it down—I can still remember the look on its face when its coat was being rubbed clean with a scrubbing brush: pure satisfaction. In the evening the horse was given a proper bath. For this we used a "horse tub," a large tub strong enough to bear its weight when it stood in it, without the bottom breaking. This we half filled with hot water, and the horse's legs were given a good wash. The right level of water was about four or five inches above its hooves. And if the horse was in a bad mood that day, we'd give it a lump of sugar to keep it quiet.

It was also the children's job to make up the horse's feed. They seemed to like soybean husks best, mixed with barley and water that rice had been rinsed in. They're greedy beasts, you know: as the old saying goes, "Cows drink and horses eat."

In May we were also made to help with pest control, and when that was done we had to weed the paddy fields. We even had to work on Sundays and festival days. But, being children, we used to find some way or other to slip away from our parents and go off to play. We often went fishing for bullheads. The water in the streams around there was so clear

you could actually see the fish swimming around, so we used to try and hook a few. We'd dangle a line, with a worm on the end, just in front of the bullhead's nose and sometimes, as we watched, it would suddenly rise to take the bait. Great fun, it was. If we caught enough of them we'd grill them or make a soup with noodles; they weren't bad at all.

From the beginning of June on, we all used to go swimming in the River Kuji. Boys went either stark-naked or wore loincloths, and the girls usually wore waistcloths. We also went down to the sea from time to time; it was five miles to the beach at Mizukihama. Each of us would carry a pack wrapped around our waist containing a couple of pounds of rice, enough for two meals, and we'd move slowly through the blistering heat of the summer's day down to the sands. The coast there was lovely: the beach was wide, and there were lots of bright-colored shells scattered about it. On the way home we'd walk along the coast to Kujihama, where we could watch the fishing boats going out; then we sometimes went to see the factory where they dried bonito. By the time we got back to our village it'd already be dark.

So I can't complain: I may have been brought up in poverty, but there were a lot of happy times as well.

The Charcoal Burner

Mr. Yaichiro Okano (1893–1984)

In the spring and summer I used to tour all the farms in the Yamano-sho area buying up silkworm cocoons, and then take them down to "Toyoshima's" cocoon market in Tsuchiura to sell them. But the winter was the off season for cocoons, so instead I spent the winter months each year making charcoal. I'd buy some trees from a farmer with land in the mountains, build my kilns, make the charcoal, and sell it to a firewood dealer in Tsuchiura.

The best forest land, at least as far as we were concerned, contained a good number of sawtooth oak trees about seven years old. Timber that age was only about two foot six across, so it'd burn quite easily and turn into charcoal with the bark still on. But with trees anything much over that, the bark peeled off when they burned, so the finished charcoal logs weren't really up to scratch and they sold for a much lower price.

But since every charcoal burner wanted to buy the logging rights to the best land, the farmer who owned that part of the mountain would be pestered by men trying to do a deal with him. Naturally, the owners sold off their trees only to the highest bidder so, you see, you had to have a fair amount of capital to be able to work in our line of business.

Once you'd managed to buy up the timber on a certain plot of land, you then had to build your kilns. Kilns varied in size. The largest type was called a "five-eight": as the name suggests, this was five feet wide by eight feet long. The earth on the roof was about five inches thick, and nine or ten inches thick along the sides. To make it as hard and tightly packed as possible, the earth was beaten down with a wooden board.

When you'd done the building, you put the oak wood, cut to lengths of one foot nine, upright inside the kiln. You then laid small twigs on top of the logs to make sure the heat from the fire reached right to the back of the kiln.

The fire was lit just inside the entrance, so it was very difficult to tell whether the logs at the back were at the right temperature or not. But you could usually roughly judge by smelling the smoke from the chimney:

when the heat was about right, the smoke had a sharp tang to it. This didn't come from the burning wood itself, but from the sap that dribbled out onto the floor of the kiln, turned into steam, and then emerged from the chimney, mixing with the usual smell of wood on the way out. But if a yellowish smoke started coming out it meant the wood was burning too fast and the inside of the kiln was too hot; if you didn't do something to correct this, the bark would peel away and the charcoal logs would be pretty nearly useless. Ideally you should just have little puffs of white smoke coming from the chimney.

I used to build four kilns at a time. The reason I needed four was that it took four days to turn oak wood into charcoal, so by having four kilns on the go at the same time, I could produce one load of charcoal every day. My charcoal was good quality, so the wholesalers in town bought as much as I could make, and I was kept pretty busy.

Cutting down the trees, bundling them, and bringing them along to the kilns was the job of the "cutter." I usually employed the son of a local farmer to do this. In the winter all farming families had a lot more hands available than they had work to do, so anyone wanting to take on casual workers could always find men there very easily.

One bundle was the amount of firewood that could be tied together with a four-foot length of rope. The cutters were paid three sen for each bundle they collected. A good worker—and it would be hard to find one nowadays!—could collect thirty or thirty-five a day, so in only nine or ten hours he could earn as much as a whole yen. [By way of comparison, one yen in 1917 would have bought just over five and a half pounds of rice.] Back then the average wage for farm laborers was only about one yen for three days' work, so a job that earned you the same amount in a third of the time was really well paid.

I suppose some might think it odd that a man could only put thirty bundles together in a day. But you should try shifting a pile of wood as large as our ones and see how heavy it is. Two of these enormous loads were humped together on the cutter's back and, even for someone used to hard physical labor, carrying a thing like that up steep mountain paths was real backbreaking work. The whole job took from dawn to almost dusk.

You could get something like thirty bundles of oak into one kiln, and from that you could produce ten or eleven sacks of charcoal. Getting the charcoal out of the kiln, though, was particularly difficult: after you put the fire out, you had to wait a day and a night before you could even touch the stuff. Even then the temperature inside was pretty hot and it was impossible to get all the logs out in a single go. You'd end up covered in sweat, and you'd have to rest dozens of times and go outside to let your body cool down a bit. But if you had a cold or anything, a few hours spent getting charcoal out of a kiln soon cured it!

The charcoal was then put in sacks and taken down the mountain by packhorse. One horse could carry ten sacks, each weighing thirty-five pounds. Until I was about twenty-five, seventy-pound sacks were common; a packhorse could only carry four of these at a time. Once the charcoal had reached the bottom of the mountain, I'd arrange for a farmer, with a horse he wasn't using that day, to take the sacks into Tsuchiura for me. The man might have to make as many as three trips into Tsuchiura and back in a single day.

In recent years the number of places where charcoal's produced has got less and less. Back in the old days every mountain had its charcoal burners. When I was at work in the hills, I often used to gaze across at the other slopes, and on all of them you could see smoke rising into the air from clearings in the woods where charcoal was being burned. It was a really pretty sight: wisps of white smoke curling up among the trees.

The Carter's Revolver

Mr. Washichi Takimoto (1901–1984)

I was born in the tiny hamlet of Nagaya, part of Nakagawa village. The area around Nagaya in those days was nothing but farmland.

In the neighboring hamlet of Iwai there was a large general store called "Arakan," which sold a variety of goods, from daily provisions to salt, sugar, pickles, and even drapery. All the stuff sold in the shop had to be brought from Koshigaya in Saitama Prefecture, on the other side of the River Tone—a round trip of nearly forty miles.

My father was a carter and most of his work came from transporting things for "Arakan." My parents had lots of sons, so he'd been able to give up working in the fields and start up as a carter instead. For some reason the shop insisted that all business should be done in cash, which meant the carters who went to Koshigaya to buy up stock were given large sums of money to take care of. But my father's family had owned land in the area for generations, so the people at "Arakan" trusted him completely and were quite happy about giving him work.

He had to be up and out of the house very early in the morning, before any of the rest of us were awake, and he didn't get back till late at night. Nowadays it doesn't take any time at all to get from Iwai to Koshigaya by car, but in the old days neither the Edo nor the Tone had bridges over them so it was a long and difficult journey.

The Tone had to be crossed by "horse ferry." This was a flat-bottomed boat, larger even than a *takase* river barge, made so it could carry several horses and carts; it was at least ten times bigger than the usual passenger ferries. My father would cross the river to a place called Koyama and from there move on to Noda, eventually arriving at the Edo, which he crossed by another horse ferry to Kanesugi. And from there he'd plod on with his horse and cart until he finally got to Koshigaya.

When he first started as a carter, there were very few men in the neighborhood who did any carting work. "Arakan" had a policy of only buying good-quality stock and selling it at a low price, so they made large profits and my father's role in this was much appreciated by the owner of the shop. On one occasion even, at a banquet during the God of Wealth Festival in October, when many of the shop's best customers and all the assistants and clerks were present, he was given the place of honor at the table, and the owner said he was "as valuable to 'Arakan' as the protection of the God of Wealth."

But as the shop's business grew and the amount of goods bought increased, Father had to carry larger and larger sums of money to Koshigaya with him. This began to scare him: he thought he might be attacked as he walked along one of those remote country roads, and robbed of either the cash or the stuff he'd just bought. Eventually he went to see the boss and told him he wanted to pack it in.

The boss looked shocked. "I could never find another carter I can trust like you. What can I do to make you change your mind?" he said and he refused to accept his resignation. In the end he made my father an offer: "You say the work's become too dangerous, so if I was to give you a revolver to carry when you went out, would that help?" He handed him this heavy, solid-looking gun. Nowadays, apart from guns smuggled into Japan, it's almost impossible to get hold of firearms, but before the war anyone was allowed to keep them provided he had a license from the police. Since the owner of the shop had gone so far as to give him a revolver to persuade him to stay on, Father allowed himself to be talked into not giving up. So he went on working as a carter for quite a few more years.

From that time on I used to watch him leave each morning with a pistol hanging from his belt. I even used the gun myself once too. There were lots of sparrows around in those days, particularly during the rice harvest, and rather than the handful of nice little birds you might see now, thousands of them used to swarm in from all directions. Putting up a scarecrow was the only way to chase these thieving birds away: proper bird-scares only came in later.

Seeing all these sparrows in his fields, my father told me to take the revolver and go and frighten them off. I was only about eight or nine—the

youngest of seven children. If a parent today sent a boy that age out on his own with a gun, he'd be thought plain irresponsible, but in the old days people got a lot less worked up about such things. So with the gun in my right hand I went down to the paddy fields. As I left, Father warned me: "Don't shoot into the air because you won't know where the bullet's going to land. Shoot into the ground."

When I got to the fields I calmly walked over to where the flock of sparrows was and fired. But the thing had a kick like a mule! "I'm not going to do that again," I thought, rubbing my arm, and went home without firing another shot.

My father always carried the gun when he went out with the horse and cart, yet he never imagined for a moment he'd actually have to use it. But just once he did fire the gun in self-defense. On the day this happened, he wasn't working for "Arakan," he was just taking our own homegrown tea to Koga. We produced about half or three-quarters of a ton of tea a year, and Father was taking the year's crop—it had been particularly good—to sell in the market there.

From our hamlet it was about seven or eight miles to Koga. That morning, on the way in, a man my father had never set eyes on before started up a conversation with him. He could hardly ignore him so he replied civilly, but the man wasn't a local and had a rather evil-looking face, so Father decided he'd better be on his guard. The two of them talked as they made their way toward Koga. But as soon as they arrived the man suddenly disappeared. During the day Father sold all his tea and, with the money he'd earned stuffed safely in his pocket, he set out for home leading the horse and cart, now empty.

It was already dusk. As he urged the horse on, he began to have a funny feeling that someone was following him. He looked back over his shoulder but couldn't see anyone. He continued on into the most heavily wooded part of the mountains. The forest has since been cut down, but in the old days it was so dark along that road it could be frightening even in the daytime. Father finally emerged from the forest onto Kukuido Marsh. All of a sudden, he saw the shadow of a man standing in a field of mulberry bushes ahead of him; he seemed to be keeping a watch on the road. My father quickly drew his gun and fired in his direction.

The man, however, didn't move; he didn't fall down either. Father found this rather strange and thought about firing another shot. But he dropped this idea and instead, plucking up courage, decided to approach. Slowly and nervously he walked toward the shadow. When he got to within about fifteen feet, though, he suddenly realized that what he'd seen wasn't a man at all: it was a tree stump, sticking out from the mulberry bushes like a dark figure in the moonlight. Father was a bit shaken at first but he pulled himself together and set off again, winding through the fields, a lantern in his hand, chuckling to himself. . . .

After the first few years of this century, carting became a fairly profitable trade and lots of men took it up. And one of the best sources of work for carters was the Tobacco Corporation: during the tobacco harvest, the area around the Government Monopoly Office in Iwai would literally be buried under mounds of tobacco leaves, all of which eventually had to be sent on to Tokyo. They were taken there by boat down the Tone, but the boats left from a spot three or four miles from Iwai, so the Monopoly Office had to employ carters to carry the tobacco down to the landing stage. If the harvest had been good there would be a line of carts, loaded high with bales, stretching back two miles or more, making their way down to the river. They left a trail of horse dung all along the road, and the local farmers would get up at the crack of dawn to come and pick it up, using it later as manure.

The horse and cart has now died out completely, of course. So have the horse ferries. But, after all, everything I've been telling you about happened more than seventy years ago. How could it help but change, over such a long stretch of time?

Smothered at Birth

Mrs. Fumi Suzuki (1898–)

My mother once told me that I only just avoided being killed the day I was born. "Thinning out" babies was pretty common in the old days. It was thought bad luck to have twins, for example, so you got rid of one before your neighbors found out. Deformed babies were also bumped off. And if you wanted a boy but the newborn was a girl, you'd make it "a day visitor," as they used to say.

In my case, I wasn't deformed, I was downright ugly. My parents and grandparents were very shocked apparently. "We'll never be able to find her a husband—not with those looks," they said. My mother told me that when she first saw my face, she thought, "What a waste of time, giving birth to a thing like that."

"I mean, you're still ugly now," she went on, "but when you were born you had thick arms and legs, an enormous head, and a short, stubby neck. If you'd been a boy, you'd have made a fine worker. But when I saw you were a girl, I was terribly disappointed. Anyway, we decided we'd better ask the midwife to get rid of you."

There were two midwives in our village: one was married to an old shoemaker, the other to a retired pawnbroker. Our village was quite small but, being on the main highway, it had a number of shops, including a pawnbroker's and seven or eight brothels. Neither of the midwives had any qualifications, of course.

Killing off a newborn baby was a simple enough business. You just moistened a piece of paper with spittle and put it over the baby's nose and mouth; in no time at all it would stop breathing. In my case, the midwife wrapped me tightly in rags as well. Everyone felt relieved to have got the problem out of the way, and went and sat around the fire chatting over a cup of green tea. Mother was asleep on her mattress. She told me that she woke after a while, and saw the bundle of rags moving. She could hear the baby crying. It really gave her a start, she said.

Everyone gathered around to look, and, when they unwound the rags, they saw that the baby was still alive. It began bawling its head off. "What

the hell do we do now?" they all thought; they eventually decided that the kid must have been fated to survive and that to try and kill it again would bring bad luck on the house. So they let me live.

Luck's a funny thing, you know, and as it happened I managed to find a man, married him at the age of twenty, and came to live in Tsuchiura. The day before the wedding, my elder brother said to me, "He must be a very good man if he's prepared to marry an ugly, fat old thing like you. However hard your life is, you stick it out. If you come running back here, we won't so much as give you the time of day." But Mother at least was still concerned about me, and once a month she used to walk the four or five miles into town to bring me vegetables, rice, firewood—all sorts of things. And not just for the first couple of years after I got married: she brought me stuff regularly for more than twenty years, right up until she died. Even during the war, when most people in town were on the verge of starvation, we never went short at all. It's now more than sixty years since I came to Tsuchiura. I reckon I've got a good few years left in me yet, though.

My little sister was a real beauty just like my mother, and very clever, too. But one day, when she was ten, she came down with food poisoning and by the next morning she was dead. It seemed quite unbelievable that a kid who'd been running around playing happily one day could be dead the next. The day after the funeral I went out into the fields and you could still see her footprints in the mud. I told my mother, and when she saw them she began crying her eyes out. She covered them up with pebbles and leaves; and whenever she came across them afterward, she'd uncover the footprints and stand there staring at them. It made me feel miserable as well.

A couple of years later another of my sisters died, this time from diphtheria. For about a month she'd not been able to eat a thing, but when Mother asked if there was anything special she'd like she said, could she have some sweet potatoes. Mother and I went out into the fields, but it was only June and the potatoes were still tiny. Still, we dug some up and cooked them, and my kid sister said they tasted lovely. She died the same night. For a few weeks after that, every time my mother saw a potato she'd burst into tears. It really did upset me to see her so unhappy.

Birth and Death

Mrs. Tai Terakado (1899–)

I was born in a small village called Kihara, on the shore of Lake Ka-sumigaura about seven miles from Tsuchiura. My mother was a very strong, dark-skinned woman. She had eight children altogether—I was the fourth. My father had once worked as a clerk in the village office, but before I was born he'd packed up the job and just used to loaf around at home all day. He was a very good chess player—there was no one in the village who could beat him. He even used to give lessons. He loathed working, though. Most days he'd complain of having a headache, and while Mother was out in the fields working herself to the bone to provide something for us to eat, he'd just sit by the fire with pickled plums pressed against his temples; he said they helped his headaches. My mother was strong as a mule, but in the end she died of overwork. She was only forty-one when she died. I was twelve.

I remember clearly one incident that happened when I was about four. It was an autumn evening and I was playing in the fields with some friends, when I saw Mother coming back down the road from the moun-tains, where she'd been chopping wood. She was carrying an enormous bundle of branches on her back. She quite often brought me quinces or persimmons she'd picked in the woods, so I ran up to meet her, hoping she might have something for me. She was, in fact, carrying a large round object wrapped up in her apron. "Have you got something nice for me?" I asked; and just then I heard a squeal inside the apron. Mother laughed and said, "Yes, I've brought you back a little baby sister." Afterward I realized she must have given birth to the baby alone up in the mountains, cut its umbilical cord with her billhook, and then carried it the five or six miles back home. She didn't want to leave all the firewood she'd collected up there, in case someone came along and pinched it, so she'd lugged it all the way back as well.

When we got into the house, Mother left the baby on a straw mat in front of the kitchen stove. You know, she didn't even wrap it up to keep it warm. And then she set about boiling up a pan of water to wash out her afterbirth. The baby was bawling its head off and I went to see if it was all right, but Mother said, "Leave it alone. If it's a weak thing it's going to die anyway, so let it get on with it."

I had four younger brothers and sisters: two of them were born up in the hills, and the other two on the floor in our kitchen. When Mother felt her contractions coming on, she'd start getting things ready for the birth, and though the neighbors always offered to help she insisted on doing it all on her own. I remember waking up late one night and hearing something crying in the kitchen. When I went to look, there was a newborn baby lying on a mat in front of the stove, completely naked though it was the middle of December. I seem to remember a couple of babies died soon after they were born but I'm not absolutely certain.

As you can imagine, all this didn't do much for my mother's health. What finally broke her was something that happened during the great floods of 1910. One of the local landowners asked for some help removing sacks of rice from his flooded barn and all the men from the village went to lend a hand. Father said he wasn't feeling well so my mother had to take his place, though she was eight or nine months gone. She spent several hours up to her neck in water, heaving huge sacks of rice about. In fact the local policeman saw her and told her off. "A pregnant woman like you shouldn't be doing this sort of work," he said. "You'll kill yourself. Go home!" But Mother just smiled and carried on.

The baby was born just a few days later; after the birth Mother felt weak and couldn't go back to work. Her body gradually began to swell up until it was two or three times its normal size, and water oozed out from all over her—her clothes and bedding were soaked. Within three weeks she was dead. By the end she was so swollen that we even began to worry whether she'd fit into the coffin. But right up till the last moment, she never once complained about the pain.

During the three weeks Mother was ill in bed, my brother and sister also died. It's still a puzzle, the way my sister went: it was so peculiar. She

was outside playing and, when the doctor came to see Mother, she rushed back in and screamed at my father, "Give me some money, I want some money." Well, this made him angry, and he told her: "Your mother's dying—you know that, don't you? How can you ask for money at a time like this?" My sister then suddenly collapsed onto the floor. She managed to get up once but fell down again with her head toward the north. Father rushed over and tried to revive her but, though her eyes did open for a moment or two, within a few seconds she was dead. Afterward everybody said it was because she'd collapsed facing north, the unlucky direction. But I just couldn't figure it out.

My little brother, though, had been sickly from the day he was born. Most of the time he just sat by the fire with my father. He was a strange child: he was only nine, but he used to worry about things like whether we had enough to get by on that month or how much rice we had in store. We got a faith healer to look at him, and she said he'd been born with the mind of an eighty-year-old and probably wouldn't live long. Anyway, when Mother was first confined to bed, he got sick too, and he died about a week before her. Every day as he lay there in bed, he'd tell me, "Don't forget to give Father his saké." Father liked a drink, you see, and the two of them were very close. When we told Mother he'd died, floods of tears poured down her swollen face and from then on she seemed to lose any will to live.

It took four men to lift her coffin. Incidentally, it used to be the custom at funerals in our village for the family to scatter coins about in front of their house and in the temple. If the dead person had been wealthy, people came from miles away for a chance at the money. A poor family like ours, though, couldn't afford to spread very much around.

The little village graveyard had been used for generations and you only had to dig down a few inches before you began to turn up old bones: shoulder blades, ribs, skulls—all sorts. Some of the villagers were so poor they didn't have their own family grave, and when a relative died they'd bury him in the corner of someone else's plot; only afterward would they go and explain what they'd done to the people whose grave they'd "borrowed." Since this sort of thing had been going on for generations, nobody knew any longer whose bones were whose. Another problem was that the land was very soggy, and as fast as you could dig a grave it would fill up with water. When someone was buried it was usual, in most villages, to pass the coffin down to a man waiting at the bottom of the hole, but in our case this was impossible, and instead the coffin had to be lowered with ropes. The hole was then filled in with earth, which was piled into a mound, but if you went back a few days later you'd find that the grave had caved in because of all the water.

The new baby lived for two or three weeks after Mother died. The trouble was, we couldn't find a wet nurse and cow's milk was impossible to get in those days, so I had to help my father make up a thin rice gruel and feed it with this. I carried the little baby around with me on my back every day. I remember it made me rather smelly: we couldn't afford to change its diaper more than once a day, so by the evening its pee began to trickle down my back and my clothes got soaked. It didn't really bother me, though.

One day, a fortnight or so after my mother's death, I was up in the hills playing with some friends. Suddenly one of them said, "Look, the baby's hands are all swollen." I touched the baby, which was still strapped to my back, and screamed—it was stone cold. My friends began to panic and jump up and down, shouting "It's dead, it's dead." It felt awful having something dead tied to me, so I ripped off my jacket and dropped the baby, before joining the others as they ran back down the hill as fast as their legs would take them, shrieking. But after a few hours, I began to feel guilty and returned. It was lying face down at the foot of a pine tree. I held it in my arms for a few minutes and then wrapped it in my coat and ran whimpering all the way home with it.

My father looked at it sadly for a while, then said, "There was nothing we could do for the poor thing, I suppose, what with its mother going first and everything." I don't remember what sort of funeral the baby had.

When I was a bit older, I went off to work as a maid for a rich farmer who lived up in the hills a couple of miles from us. His wife was a thoroughly nice woman and well liked by all the other farmers in the area. In fact she'd helped out most of the villagers at one time or another: she often lent money to people without telling her husband, for example, and wouldn't complain if they failed to repay it. So everyone was upset when she came down with a terrible illness, three or four years after I'd started there.

She must have been about forty-one at the time. In those days it was considered a great disgrace to have a baby after the age of forty—they were usually either aborted or killed at birth. A middle-aged woman only had to look tired or slack off from work and tongues would start wagging.

Anyway, my mistress got pregnant. I think she wanted to keep the baby really but her mother-in-law, who was a horrible old bag, used to come along almost every day and bait her about it: "It's disgusting a woman your age having a baby—you want to get rid of it just as soon as you can," she'd say.

The old woman reckoned the best way of dealing with unwanted children was by *usugoro* ["mortar killing"]. This isn't, I'm afraid, a very nice subject, but I'd better tell you all the same. Back then the usual method was to stick a piece of paper over their nose and mouth or, if that failed, to press on their chest with your knee. In *usugoro* the woman went alone into one of the buildings outside and had the baby lying on a straw mat. She wrapped the thing in two straw sack lids, tied it up with rope, and laid it on the mat. She then rolled a heavy wooden mortar over it. When the baby was dead, she took it outside and buried it herself. And the following day, she was expected to be up at the crack of dawn as usual, doing the housework and then helping in the fields. It's incredible, isn't it?—enough to drive a woman mad, I would have thought.

Oh, she was a nasty bit of work, that mother-in-law—I was scared stiff of her. You know, she loved snakes. She often used to go up into the mountains on her own and catch grass snakes and vipers, which she cut up and pickled in *miso*. Whenever anyone came to visit her she'd offer them some. She claimed it gave you energy. Of course, she didn't say it was snake, because nobody would've eaten it—she called it "mountain eel." Grilled, it smelled quite good, so lots of people accepted it without realizing what it really was. And she made me try some, too, when I had to go to her house. Can you imagine having to listen to her grisly stories and eat that stuff as well? . . .

Anyway, my mistress said she couldn't face destroying a newborn baby so she went into Tsuchiura to have an abortion instead. Something must have gone wrong with the operation, though, because a few days later, when she was at a party in a neighbor's house, she suddenly complained of a terrible pain and collapsed on the floor. Everyone was worried, of course, and after she got home she began bleeding heavily—it just wouldn't stop. Two or three local farmers, people she'd shown some kindness to in the past, ran all the way into Tsuchiura and got a doctor to come out. The doctor arrived late that evening and, when he'd examined her, he said that part of the afterbirth was still stuck inside her womb. He sterilized various bits of equipment and set about getting it out, but medical treatment was still pretty primitive then so I suppose there was very little he could do. The bleeding continued and got heavier every day.

It was my job to wash the mistress's bedding, and after a few days I noticed little white insects in her discharge. Each day there were more of them and they got bigger and bigger. We eventually realized what they were—maggots. As she lay on her mattress, you could see dozens of them squirming around between her thighs. When I had to wash the sheets, they made me feel quite sick.

The local farmers did everything they could to help: a couple of them took a rickshaw into Tsuchiura every day to fetch the doctor, and many of the wives went around from one temple to another praying for her. But she got steadily worse and developed such a fever that her face was almost too hot to touch. They even tried calling out a different doctor from Tsuchiura, but he gave her one look, said there was nothing he could do, and went straight back into town without treating her at all.

In the end, they had to call the first doctor back. When I showed him the maggots he said, "We'll have to try and get a specialist up from Tokyo. He won't come right out to the farm, but we might persuade him to come as far as Tsuchiura." The villagers were desperate to help and said they'd carry the woman anywhere; in case it was needed in a hurry, they made a stretcher out of an old door and some bedding.

But the next morning, just as day was breaking, she passed away. Everyone cried and cried, men and women alike, and some fell sobbing on the floor. Only the old mother-in-law was unaffected. "Well, we've all got to die one day," she said. But at least for a month or two afterward she did give up that "mountain eel."

The funeral was everything one could have wanted: a dozen or more priests chanted sutras; hundreds of people came from other villages to pay their last respects; and a good deal of money was tossed around. Shortly afterward, I went off to work in Hokkaido in the very north of Japan so I don't know what became of the family. I did hear, though, that the farmer became more and more bad-tempered after his wife's death and that the villagers began to keep their distance.

CRAFTS
AND
CRAFTSMEN

A clog mender

The Reed Thatcher

Mr. Kumanosuke Yoshida (1903–1981)

My family has been in the thatching business for generations: my grandfather was a reed thatcher and so was my dad. And now my son's in the trade as well. It's so many years ago now, I can't exactly remember when I first learned how it was done, but I suppose it must have been just after I left primary school. Farms in those days consisted of as many as six or seven separate buildings: the main house, the quarters for the old people in the family, stables, a manure shed, a bathhouse, and a privy. Each of these buildings would have been thatched, so there was obviously plenty of work to get on with.

Of course, before you could thatch a roof, you had to go and get the reeds for it. In those days you could find all the reeds you needed on Ukishima Moor—in fact, you still can, though there's nothing like as many as when I was in the trade. As far as I remember, I used to ride to Ukishima by bicycle, even though it was more than twenty miles away and the roads were terrible.

Once I'd got to Ukishima I'd talk to the dealer there and then buy what I needed. To thatch a normal-sized house, you'd have to reckon on buying enough reeds to cover 1,200 square yards. The best kind were two or three feet long—anything longer or shorter was no use to us—and they came in sheaves about three or four inches across. You needed several thousands of these to thatch an average roof, and for a big house it was sometimes as many as ten or twenty thousand.

The next step was to ship the stuff back across the lake on large flat-bottomed barges, built so that people could live on board them; back then most of the houseboats on Lake Kasumigaura paid their way by shifting goods around the lake. We used two boats lashed together, this being safer than just one, which with all our cargo piled on deck might have capsized in a strong wind. You know, I must have crossed that lake dozens of times, sitting on top of a pile of reeds, gazing at the mountains around Tsukuba and admiring the view; it's nothing like as pretty nowadays.

There wasn't a harbor where I lived, so we had to moor some way off

Mr. Yoshida

the shore and transfer the reeds to a smaller boat. Then, once the cargo had been landed, we took it all out to the work site by cart; but only after the sheaves, which were difficult to handle, had been tied together into bigger bundles, roughly twenty in each. You needed a fair number of carts to carry that many reeds, so the man whose house you were going to thatch would ask his relatives or the village cooperative to lend him some for the day. I also had my own cart and that often got used too.

The job of knocking the old roof off could be done by anyone—you didn't need a skilled thatcher for that—and most of the neighbors would turn out to help with it. So you'd have farmers clambering all over the roof, ripping out old thatch and making an almighty mess, bits of straw, rubbish, and dust getting everywhere; which, of course, they had to clear up later—the women didn't help: they had their own work to do, cooking or whatever. Anyway, they all got a meal at the end of the morning.

But in my case it wasn't food that mattered so much as drink. I like my drink; I started when I was thirteen or fourteen and always had a drop with my lunch. Unless I was given a glass or two with the midday meal I just couldn't do the work properly; and if the man who wanted his roof thatched had any brains about him he'd give me a little something to get me going. It was priming I needed, you see. Later on, I even used to have a glass before leaving for work in the morning.

So, after "lunch," I'd start making the base of the roof. Bamboo was used for this. The rafters were made of bamboo about an inch thick, and ran right along the roof at intervals of about two foot six. At right-angles to these, you had to attach thinner, vertical struts every fifteen inches or so, from the crown of the roof right down to the eaves. On top of this you added what was known as *yuzuri* bamboo. This was bamboo cut into thin strips with the nodes left on, and it was put on facing downward. The nodes stuck out, you see, so when you put the straw on top, it wouldn't fall off. The *yuzuri* bamboo was tied to the rafters at intervals of six inches. When this was done, you'd thatch the whole roof with rice straw. You'd

then spread an extra one-inch layer of straw over that, and the base of the roof was finished. Once the base was done, water couldn't seep through. So as long as this was in place, even if it rained the next day, people could still live in the house and stay dry. Whatever you did, you had to get the base finished. That would be one day's work.

The more experienced farmers could manage the base themselves, and they'd only need a thatcher when it came to doing the eaves. In those days the eaves of a house were built in a very different way, and with very different materials, to today. In fact, the modern method only came in quite recently.

First you spread straw out over the eaves. On top of that you put blackened reeds from the old roof; then a layer of eulalia stalks with their white sap cores removed; and thin strips of cedar bark. The next layer was called the *mizu-giri*: for this one could use either ditch reed or eulalia, depending on the time of year. These materials were added in the same order for several layers—sometimes as many as eleven or twelve—depending on what the owner of the house had asked for.

Once the eaves were done, the whole roof—most of which was still straw-based—was thatched with cogongrass, from the edge of the eaves right up to the ridge coping. And you had to get it right to make it really waterproof, packing the thatch in from behind with a special bamboo tool; but I won't try to explain this, it's a bit too technical.

In the old days, you didn't teach a lad something just by explaining it to him; you showed him how to do it and if he didn't remember you just belted him. That was my method, anyway. We reckoned it took ten years to become an experienced thatcher. If the thatching was done by a skilled man the roof could last fifty years, but if it was a botched job done by some clumsy half-wit, you'd often get rain leaking in after only three or four years. I'm not trying to boast, but I think I always did my work properly. When I was teaching my son the trade, if he ever made a mess of it I'd just go and knock down all the thatch he'd put up, however long the work had taken him. That was the best way of making him realize he had to do it right every time. You didn't need complicated explanations to teach a boy a lesson like that.

I wonder if he drinks at work . . . like father, like son. I've been a hard drinker all my life and it probably hasn't done my health any good but, for all that, I've lived a good long time. I usually get through a whole three-pint bottle of saké a day, and I drink pretty well solidly from the time I get up till I go to bed. And if I ever go out anywhere, I'll usually have something there as well. I suppose I've just got a taste for the stuff.

The Tiler

Mr. Koichi Sunada (1904–)

When I was young, very few people had bicycles, so however far we had to go to do a job, we were forced to walk. If the work was in Tsukuba or Yasato, for instance, it meant an early start and, when the job was finished, a long trudge home in the evening.

Of course if you were going somewhere on the lake—Edosaki, for example—you could catch the steamer from Kawaguchi; but it was a fairly rough trip. The inside of the boat was completely bare apart from some matting on the floor and a single light bulb hanging from the ceiling. And in winter it was so cold you'd find yourself shivering like anything—even if you curled up into a ball to keep warm, you couldn't stop. So I'd go ashore at Kihara on the lighter and walk the five miles to Edosaki; the boat did in fact eventually stop there, but it put in at so many places in between, it was much quicker to walk. On the way back as well, I'd walk as far as Kihara and then catch the boat home from there. But sometimes when the wind was up, the steamer couldn't get in near enough to pick up any passengers and I'd have to go the long way around to Tsuchiura on foot. Still, one tended to accept things like that in those days—there wasn't much point in fretting.

Anyway, let me tell you a bit about my job. The tiles in this area were made mainly in the Nihari district. I bought them directly from the pottery, maybe two hundred and fifty at a time, then had them loaded on a wagon and delivered in advance. But they honestly weren't much good: comparing them, for example, with Sanshu tiles would be like comparing something a child had made with an expert's work. You see, the skill of different manufacturers varied a hell of a lot. With our local tiles, even if the plasterer filled in the gaps after they'd been laid, they just wouldn't lock together neatly and there was always a danger that water would seep through. If you used high-quality Sanshu tiles, however, you didn't even need any plasterwork; and they kept their color for generations, while ours turned black as the years went by.

The first step in tiling a roof, after the carpenter had got things ready, was to lay strips of cedar bark all over it. This was a form of insulation: when it rained, the tiles would gradually get damp underneath, particularly if they were local ones, and the damp could spread through the layer of earth that held them in place. Without the bark, the roof might leak.

Next you plastered earth on top of the bark; you had to use the stickiest sort you could find. But, having said that, clay wasn't any good, it had to be loam. Clay tended to freeze solid when the weather turned really cold. What we called loam was the sort of mud found either on the bottom of rivers or in paddy fields. So, when I was asked to tile someone's roof, I'd first go to the area and wander around looking at the rice paddies. If I thought the soil was good enough, I'd chat to the owner of the land, fix a price, and eventually buy about a quarter of an acre's worth of soil. I'd then cart it off to the house and work it over till it was ready to use.

The earth was mixed by treading it barefoot. When you did this in the middle of the winter, of course, you'd get absolutely frozen and your nose would start to stream. All you could do was build a fire and hop over to it when you couldn't stand it any longer. But the job had to be done barefoot: rubber soles always got clogged up. Fortunately, most tilers—the ones who'd been around a while—could usually find a young apprentice or one of the casual laborers to do it for them.

Once the earth had been properly mixed, you rolled it up into large balls and lobbed them onto the roof. We used to reckon you needed about one ball of earth, something like a cannon ball, per tile.

In any batch of tiles, we always found some that were well made, some average, and some fairly shoddy: ones that had been baked near the fire were hard and a nice glossy color, but those baked at the top of the kiln were often a bit brittle. If we'd been able to use only the good tiles for roofing, it would've been simple work. The trouble was, if you told your employer that some of them weren't fit to use, you'd have ruined the reputation of the pottery. So you had to make the best of it by cleverly combining the good ones with the bad. That was the real test of how good a tiler you were.

But sometimes I'd find they were so bad that, no matter how well I did the roof, there'd be no way I could stop it leaking. This was, as often as not, because the man whose house I was working on had a limited budget and hadn't been able to let me buy a decent batch. And sure enough, not long after I'd finished the job, just as I was beginning to worry about the heavy May rains or the rainy season, I'd get a visit from the owner: "The roof's leaking," he'd say. "Can you come and look at it, please?" I'd been expecting this all along so I'd just calmly reply, "Ah, I see. Well, I'm sorry about that. I'll take a look at it as soon as I can."

But I only said this to keep the customer quiet; I had to bide my time. You see, if I had gone straight away, I'd have been forced to mend the thing and, with tiles like those, it would've meant repairing the whole surface of the roof; what's more, I'm quite sure he would have blamed *me* for using "inferior tiles."

So I'd put him off for as long as possible, and strangely enough, as the days passed and it kept on raining, the roof would eventually stop leaking. I didn't have to do anything—it would stop all by itself. In fact, this was what I'd been waiting for. Why? Because once the rain had seeped in behind the tiles, the gap between the bottom of the tiles and the earth would stay damp for a while and mold would start forming there. This would slowly spread over the whole roof and work as a sort of extra skin. All the tiler had to do was wait till the mold had grown. When you worked with low-quality stock, you knew from the start that this would happen.

Tiles back then were only made of earth, which was first mixed by the same old barefoot method, then dried in the sun, and baked at a relatively low heat, so every single one was a slightly different shape—all warped a bit, of course, but each warped differently. The true test of a tiler's skill—and we each had our own idea of how best to line them up—was to be

able to lay a load of warped tiles in such a way that the roof itself was still trim and waterproof.

Frankly, that's what made it interesting. Tile-making techniques have improved no end, and a batch of, say, a hundred will be almost identical nowadays; they're also much harder than they were in my time, so there's little or no risk of any leaking. Which is fine, in its way. But the skill's gone out of it when all you've got to do is slot the tiles together. Easier, certainly, but a bit too routine for me.

The *Tatami* Mat Maker

Mr. Seitaro Yamaguchi (1901–)

With my son now started in the business, my family's been making *tatami* mats for five generations, which must make it one of the oldest in Tsuchiura. My father was in the trade, and when I left higher elementary school after my second year, at the age of sixteen, I went straight to work as an apprentice with a firm in Nihonbashi in the center of Tokyo. It was a large place with five craftsmen and they did a hell of a lot of work.

The first job all the young lads had after joining the workshop was unpicking empty straw bags. The straw was used as padding for the mats. Each of us was given a certain number to do each day—say, fifty of them. When they arrived from the rice shop they still had their straw lids attached and rope wound around them, so we had to undo these first. And we couldn't just rip the sacks apart either: each strand—woven with the tips alternately thick and thin—had to be unraveled, then lined up identically. From fifty sacks you could only get enough straw to pad two mats.

The reason we used rice sacks, though, was that farmers made them from only the best straw, carefully cleaned and with the sheaths removed; and they looked after them even when they weren't needed. A lot of rice stores, in fact, had agreements with *tatami* makers to supply them with old sacks, and there were even people who worked as sack wholesalers.

After a few months of unpicking these things, we were gradually allowed to lend a hand with the padding itself. Without showing how it's done, it's a bit difficult to explain, but I'll try. First you spread out a layer of straw lengthwise over the back matting, adding cut straw about two inches long to a level depth of two inches. On top of this went a row of bunched straw crosswise from one end of the mat to the other, with another row above placed at right-angles. Next you spread out thin, diagonal layers, making sure each meshed with the other and that the whole thing was flat. And a final layer went lengthwise on top. You had to build it up in this laborious way or with time the *tatami* would start to warp and eventually cave in. They used to say that even an arrow or a sword couldn't penetrate a well-made mat.

Anyway, by this stage the padding would be more than a foot thick, and by stitching it all together it had to be squashed down to a width of one and seven-eighth inches (though nowadays it's more usually an inch and a half). It had to be exact because doorsills always used to be precisely two inches off the ground, and the top matting that was stretched over the padding was an eighth of an inch thick.

So to stitch up the straw to a sixth of its original thickness, the craftsman had to squat on top of it, thread a length of twine through to the back of the padding, pull it through to the front again, and tug hard with both hands, while pressing the straw down with his feet; there weren't any machines to do any of it in those days. With each mat needing several hundred stitches, he could only produce a couple of good paddings in a day: you see, it took about an hour to lay the straw and another two or three hours to sew it up. It made all the difference, though, if the job was well done. A finely sewn padding was absolutely flat whatever angle you looked at it from, while the rougher ones—which took half the time to do—could be a bit uneven. And it took five years to become expert at this work.

When I was an apprentice, the customers in the big Tokyo department stores like Mitsukoshi and Shirokiya used to leave their clogs or sandals at the entrance; a doorman then took care of the things. There was a very long strip of matting laid out on the floor just inside, and it was the job of the *tatami* maker who supplied the store to put it down every day. It must have been a good eighty yards long, I suppose. So someone—one of us, obviously—had to go along in the morning and lay it out, then clean it again in the evening. That wasn't all, either: whenever anyone bought something big at the store, we used to deliver it for them by horse and cart. We even had what we called our "bicycle squad" for getting a load of smaller parcels to the customer as quickly as possible, piled high on the luggage rack. How's that for service!

We also delivered the *tatami* we made to various parts of the city by handcart. But anyone who's wandered around Tokyo for a few hours will know it isn't flat. That was the toughest thing: getting the handcart up the hills. Funnily enough, at the bottom of most steep slopes and humpbacked bridges there always used to be a "hill pusher," who for five sen would give the cart a shove from behind. And with eight or more mats on my cart I could have done with some help. The problem was the five sen: my firm would never have given me the money, and it wasn't only one hill I had to get over, it was more like a dozen on some trips. The cost would've come to more than a day's pay for a skilled worker. So I hadn't much choice but to struggle up the hills on my own.

We even used to go out as far as Shinjuku, Shibuya, and Ikebukuro. In my time there was nothing but fields around there—I remember seeing rows of carts carrying night soil in what are now the busiest shopping districts in Tokyo. It was pitch-dark after sunset and so quiet you almost expected a ghost to appear. In fact, all the areas to the north and west of Tokyo were more rural even than Tsuchiura. And just look at them now!

There's another little detail I remember: I went to fit *tatami* mats in a room in the clock tower of Tokyo Station. The station was still under construction then, and outside it, in Marunouchi [now the financial heart of Tokyo], grass six or seven feet high grew everywhere. You know, when I arrived with the mats there was nobody around, just a ladder leaning against a wall that stretched high above me. And when I finally managed to drag the mats up into the tower, all I found was this tiny room, six feet by three, which was absolutely empty apart from the clock itself. . . .

Now that rice is harvested and threshed by machine, the straw gets hacked to bits, and the days of high-quality straw are pretty well over. For the best mats we needed as many as eighty bundles, each eight inches across, but it's become almost impossible to find that sort of quantity. It's hard to find the time for it all, either, I suppose.

The Dyer

Mr. Hiroshi Sano (1919–)

My father did his apprenticeship in a large dyeing shop called "Minatoya" and moved into his own shop, which is still standing, in 1895, the year of the first Japanese Constitution. He was born in January 1868, so when he set up on his own he'd have been only twenty-seven.

At that time, we had a fair number of other dyers in this area. There was Chosaemon Hakata's firm, for instance, known as the "Big Dyer's," which mainly did yarn work. Farmers would bring in a batch, get it done there, and then weave it themselves. It had the advantage of taking up very little space, and work didn't have to stop when it rained, so business was pretty good for them; whereas for people like myself who dyed cloth, there wasn't much one could do if the weather was wet or windy. In fact that's where we get the saying "Tomorrow for a dyer": we were always making excuses for not having something ready in time, and telling customers we'd definitely have it done by tomorrow.

I didn't go out to work as an apprentice; I was taught the trade by my father. We had sixteen indigo vats in our shop and next to them, sunk in the ground, a row of large pots in which fires were lit. We burned charcoal in these to keep the indigo warm; as the pots gradually got hotter the heat would spread to the ground around them, so you could keep the temperature of the dyestuff fairly constant. There were always fires burning inside our house and the air was smoky—our ceiling was pitch-black from the soot.

The biggest problem for dyers was making a good indigo. Nowadays there are plenty of chemical dyes on the market that are simple enough even for non-professionals to handle; the color's also easy to control. But before these became available, the stuff had to be made by boiling down the leaves of indigo plants. The way this was done depended on how dark a dye you wanted, but even a trained hand couldn't tell just by looking at the liquid what shade it would turn out to be. It was a tricky business. Apprentices used to practice it again and again, and unless you could handle it reasonably well you'd never really make the grade.

Workman wearing a *hanten*

During most of my time as a qualified dyer we used a German chemical we called *piya* to make up our indigo. To each pound of *piya* you added three pints of lime and a pound of zinc powder and mixed them in warm water. Each dyeing vat held up to sixty gallons. When you wanted a dark blue—for *hanten* jackets, perhaps—you doubled these quantities, blended them, and left them for about a week. This liquid was then mixed with boiling water in one sixty-gallon vat. A second vat was then made up with half the strength of the first. You then prepared one more vat, with the indigo only half as strong again.

The next step was to get the *go* ready. To make *go* you first cooled five pounds of soybeans, mashed them with a stone mill, dissolved the mash in two gallons of water, and finally squeezed out the liquid. You then prepared pine soot and glue. The first was made by burning pinewood with a high proportion of resin, removing the soot from it, and stiffening it with paste. This was then put into a mixing bowl with boiling glue and stirred thoroughly. But they didn't combine at all easily, and you had to stir like mad for at least an hour before the stuff would blend to the right consistency, something like jelly. After dissolving this in water till it looked like black India ink, it was poured into the soybean liquid you'd already made. The result was known as *go* and, before you could dye the *hanten* coats in indigo, they had to be dipped in this mixture. Indigo alone wouldn't have produced a good consistent color, so it was best to dye them black first.

The cloth was then hung up outside to dry, which didn't take long—the soybean solution helped speed things up. The process up to this point was called the "first *go*." When this was done, you took the soybean lees and mixed them thoroughly with two gallons of water, then wrung this out, producing the "second *go*." You then prepared another liquid by adding a pint of lye to six pints of water and allowing the lye to settle. After about an hour the water would look as clean and clear as a mirror. With the lye well settled at the bottom, the water was poured into the "second *go*," but it had to be done very carefully: even a small amount of the sediment would have ruined the coats you were dyeing.

You now covered both sides of the cloth with the second *go*. There was just one more undercoat left to put on: a light brown dye called *tankawa* that would give the dark blue a slightly reddish tint. The ingredients—mainly mangrove bark—were boiled down, diluted, and applied to the cloth, and the black of the two *go* dyeings took on a pleasant, brownish color. The underdyeing was now finished.

We usually waited three days before using the indigo. Of course, if it was a rush job it could be done the same day, but in this method—known as *iresome*—the color faded easily. Normally, after three days we gave the cloth a soaking in water so that the indigo would penetrate right into the cotton, hung it up on a rope, and beat it till it was merely damp before putting it in the dyeing vats. You could get two rolls, nineteen yards long, into each. Two rolls were the equivalent of four *hanten*, without sleeves.

The cloth was first placed in the medium indigo. When you pulled it out again it was yellow, but after waving it in the air for a minute or two the color turned light blue. You then hung it on a length of rope for a short time, while the next piece was being dipped.

The next stage was a dousing in the darkest indigo, which left the rolls a deep blue color. This was followed by the thinnest dye. By dipping the cloth into the three vats one after the other like this, the color was gradually built up and resulted in a good deep tone that would last. The process was called *undengaeshi*.

After a final dip in the medium-strength vat, the material was strung out on bamboo poles to air; about ten minutes outside caused just the right amount of color change, so it was then brought in and left in water overnight. This soaking was to get all the starch and glue out it. In the morning the rolls were given an "acid bath"—sulphuric acid was used to get rid of any stuff like lye or pine soot that might have stuck to them. A teacup of dilute sulphuric acid was mixed with water in a tub and the cloth was thoroughly rinsed in it. All sorts of muck were removed like this and it came out a beautiful bright indigo color.

Now we were almost finished, but not quite: it all had to be washed again in water, three times, to make sure none of the acid—which would have spoiled it—remained on the fabric. And when we'd stretched it on tenters to dry, the job was done.

How much did we make out of it? Well, from six rolls of cloth you could get ten complete *hanten*. Up until 1935 *hanten* sold for one yen fifty each. A roll of cotton cost fifty-five sen at that time, so six rolls were three yen thirty, making it thirty-three sen per article. We could reckon on getting one yen seventeen sen for each coat we dyed, but when you take fuel costs, dyestuffs, and other expenses into account, you can hardly say we were raking it in. And however fast a dyer worked, he couldn't do more than five *hanten* a day; even that was pushing things. Every yen earned in this trade had to be worked for.

You know, it was the weather that gave us the most trouble. With three different stages involved in the underdyeing, for example, the cloth had to be dried three times. But you just couldn't get good results if the sequence was interrupted. You see, unless the *tankawa* bit was done the same day, the dye would roll off the surface, not soak right through. And if it started raining when you were doing the indigo dyeing, things were even worse: you could easily ruin the lot. So we were always worrying about the weather.

The winter wasn't much fun, either. When the cloth was left to soak overnight, by morning the tub would be covered with ice. You'd have to lift the ice out before you could wring the stuff out, and your hands would get so numb you'd hardly be able to move them. When I couldn't even feel them any more, I used to go and knock them against the edge of the well to get the blood circulating again. And they'd soon get all cracked and rough doing this. Then, when you had to put your hands into the sulphuric acid during the cleaning stage, it'd sting so much the pain would

actually bring tears to your eyes. But they used to say that if you ever cried
out from the pain, you'd never become a proper dyer, so you just had to
grin and bear it. And to think I've been doing this sort of work all these
years!

Anyway, most of it's now done by machine in enormous factories, and
the dyers' shops have all closed down; there's hardly anywhere you'll find
an old-fashioned dyer still operating. All that's left in my place are a few indigo vats I've kept as souvenirs.

Paulownia Wood

Mr. Hisashi Sakamoto (1904–1981)

The "Shichibei Terrace," one of the rows of housing built all over the town by Shichibei Kikuta, a rich landowner from Manabe, stood just by Zenikame Bridge. It was a large wooden block and my father rented seven of the tenements in it and made *geta* there. We always had at least twenty craftsmen working for us and sometimes as many as thirty.

Almost everyone wore clogs back then, so business was good—we even sent our stock by rail as far away as Osaka and Kyushu—and we needed the staff; in fact we also had three maids to do the cooking and laundry, since most of the men were single and lived in.

They were a hard-working bunch, willing to carry on through the day without a break, and young enough to play around as well, even get in fights occasionally. Summers were so hot they'd strip down to their loincloths; they used to join the kids in the river sometimes to cool off for a bit, splash about, dive in off the bridge. I was eighteen when we moved the shop to its present site, still on the Sakura, and even then the men used to wash in the river at the end of the day, before going in to supper.

My job was to buy up paulownia wood for the shop to turn into clogs. Some of the timber was from the Tsuchiura area, but most years I'd go off on trips further north, to Aizu, Nanbu, and Akita as well: being colder up there, the quality of the wood was naturally a lot better than our local stuff. I've heard the amount of paulownia grown in Aizu has gone down a good bit recently and they've even started bringing in wood from outside and selling it as Aizu timber. But in my time there was always plenty of it around as long as you had the money to buy it. Business was all done in cash, of course.

Aizu is mountainous and its forests were hard to get at, whereas the paulownia in these parts grew on flat land. Also, the forests were mixed— cedar, paulownia, all sorts—and that too made the search difficult. I used to go up there with the man who owned the land and tramp around, and when I'd decided which trees I wanted, I'd haggle over the price for a while, then pay for them on the spot. I might buy just one tree from each

Assorted clogs

grove of his, or several from one patch if the trunks were more than two or three feet wide—a size you're now unlikely to find anywhere much in Japan.

This was done in the summer, though they weren't cut down till the winter months. One reason was that it was much easier to get a big tree down from the mountains when you could use a snow sledge. Also, the snow helped cushion its fall and usually kept the trunk and branches from snapping off. So we'd deliberately wait till the snow was thick on the ground before felling the trees.

I used to go along then, too. Past Aizu, deeper in the mountains around Okutadami, was some of the best wood of all; the snag was, getting there wasn't exactly easy. Even when I'd made it, a blizzard might hold things up for days, and I'd be stuck in an inn with the lumberjacks, drinking and chatting to pass the time. They were good men, though—honest and hard-working; they'd do anything you asked, just the way you wanted it.

And it was hard work, I assure you. To fell a tree we first had to dig out a great big hole. When the snow was five or even ten feet deep, if you only cut the trunk off at the point where it showed, you'd end up with the best part still buried. So the men had to scoop out an area about the size of a small room. This took them a good two or three hours.

When they'd finished, they'd light a fire at the bottom and warm themselves up, with a little help from a type of liquor we used to drink called *kasutori shochu*, made from saké lees—it really was the best thing I've ever drunk. Particularly in the freezing cold, it'd warm you right through. With a dose of this to perk them up, they could then make a start on the tree itself.

A good thick trunk took a while to saw through—northern paulownia's not as soft as some. After an hour or two they'd have got one tree down, and we'd walk on a bit further into the mountains; they'd dig another hole, and work on another tree—you can see why we could only get a couple of them done in a day. But at least the snow helped when it came to getting the timber off the mountain. This was the "sledder's" job. His rig was just a large board fastened to a pair of skis, but he fairly shot down the steepest slopes through the woods, till he arrived with his load at the freight depot.

I sometimes even went as far north as Akita. It was a hard trip, and I couldn't expect to be home in less than a couple of weeks. But the shop did pretty well for itself, and we could afford to make things of the highest quality, so I didn't mind the distance if it meant finding the best materials.

What's more, I wasn't only on the lookout for whole trees: I also bought ready-made *geta* bases. These were blocks of paulownia cut to size, which the craftsmen could get straight to work on. Buying this sort of thing was mainly a matter of personal contact, between me and the trader, so we'd usually go up together to a hot spring—Higashiyama or somewhere—and have a bath and a few drinks before we got down to business. I suppose to some we may have looked like a couple of friends on holiday, but the bargaining was serious and could get pretty heated. Still, we both realized we'd be doing business for quite a while to come, so neither of us tried any dirty tricks; and when that part of it was over, we spent the rest of the evening drinking. . . .

I haven't been back to Aizu since the war. I'd like to go sometime, but it might all have changed. Nobody much wears *geta* any more, and maybe the forests have gone as well. I'm afraid of being disappointed. . . .

The Master Joiner

Mr. Kaoru Umehara (1913–)

It's getting on for forty years now since I moved to Ami, but I was actually born in Isohama, further up the coast. I know it hasn't much to do with Tsuchiura, but if it's all right with you I'd like to say a bit about life in a fishing town, and then talk about my work.

My family ran a noodle shop for three generations, right in the heart of the red-light district of Isohama, which covered a wide area along the seafront and contained, I suppose, more than thirty brothels; there was also a geisha area in the town, but that was in another section. Our customers were mostly street girls and men who'd come to look for some entertainment—the house was surrounded by brothels. In those days, most of the girls were from farming families who'd sold them into prostitution. Each brothel employed about four or five of them, and the clients were mainly fishermen.

The way those fishermen lived was so different from anything you'd see today that you may think I'm exaggerating; you'll just have to take my word for it. For one thing, they used to go around completely naked in the summer—they didn't even wear a loincloth. They also had this habit of pulling back their foreskin and winding straw around the tip; honestly, it was like something in a film about Bushmen! . . . On board their boats or pulling in the dragnets from the beach, that's all they had on. The women used to help them with the nets, and though the younger girls had a waistcloth wrapped around them and some might wear an undershirt, the older women had nothing on either.

So it's obvious things were pretty basic there, and only very few houses, for example, had thatched or tiled roofs. Houses thatched even with tree bark covered with stones, and anywhere with proper matting on the floor, would've been considered better than average. It was usual to find a whole family having to sleep in a single room on a rough straw mat. And as soon as one of the men had any money in his pocket, he'd usually blow it all in a few hours on food, drink, women, and gambling. You see, the attitude then was that there was only a plank of wood in a small boat

233

between you and oblivion; life was short, so you made the most of it while you could.

The children didn't do a stroke of schoolwork, either, and spent the whole day playing on the shore. The sea in front of my house was shallow out to some distance; I often used to stand and watch as the catch of bonito was unloaded there. The harbor was fairly shallow, too, and large boats couldn't come right in, so lighters had to ply back and forth to unload them. In those days bonito were so common you could see whole shoals of them swimming about, and catches were often very big. When they saw the boats coming in, the kids would swim out to them and beg to be allowed on board—the fishermen knew them all, of course, so they couldn't really say no. And after they'd nosed around for a while making a nuisance of themselves, eventually the men would give them a fish to take home and tell them to "bugger off." I remember seeing them dive off, each with a fish tied to his back with a piece of straw rope. But, even with all this bonito around, you couldn't expect to make much from a catch, you know; you couldn't keep it on ice—it had to be sold, in a limited area; so the families were poor.

I left home when I was sixteen. My father wanted me to follow him into the family business and was always getting me to help out in the shop; but I had my own ideas. I'd always loved fiddling around making things, I may even have had some talent for woodwork, and from a very early age I'd decided I wanted to be a joiner. So it became more and more difficult to stay at home.

I first went to work in a large furniture-making firm, just off Nankin-machi in Yokohama. There were about ten craftsmen and three maids employed at the place. As far as I'm concerned, though, there's not one good thing to be said for that firm: from the day I joined, the only work I was ever given to do was deliveries. I started my apprenticeship there in 1929 or 1930, and although there were already one or two cars around by then, goods were still all transported by handcart or horse-

drawn wagon; when you went out into the street, there was always a solid line of carts being pulled along at walking pace—and I was soon one of them, hauling furniture.

Because I was keen to be taught the trade, I used to hurry back but there wasn't much point: I'd only be sent out on another delivery. Even when I did have a few minutes to spare in the workshop, I was only allowed to watch the joiners at work, and was never given a chance to have a go myself. I remember once, when I'd come back exhausted after a day of the usual routine, I flopped down onto the floor to watch one of the men making something; and without my having said a word, he suddenly gave me a hard slap with his ruler. "You think you can sit and watch, do you?" the man said. So I stood up, and got hit hard again. "You're not going to stand there and watch me working either," he shouted. "Squat down!" He was really mean about it. Now, it doesn't take much to set me off so I shouted back, "Right, that's it. I'm leaving. I'll never be a proper joiner here, not if I stay a hundred years," and I just walked out. I was eventually taken on by another joinery firm in Kawasaki; nobody particularly used their influence to get me the job—the firm just seemed to like the look of me. They gave me some simple work to do as a trial, and having seen how well I managed that, the boss told me, "OK, you seem quite good," and he gave me the job on the spot.

The first thing I learned was how to cut up wood. The idea was to saw exactly the amount needed from the rough timber, without even an eighth of an inch to spare; it was also important to bring out the best in the grain. Trees being living things, each has its own particular hardness, shape, and pattern. Unless you understand the qualities of the piece you're dealing with before starting, you'll mess it up each time. Of course, unless you're God Almighty, you can't avoid wasting a fraction of an inch here and there, but as long as you approach the work with the aim of not wasting a single scrap, you find that you soon begin to improve.

I was next taught how to make shutters. My boss said, "Look, I don't

mind showing you—but only once, so you'd better remember." I thanked
him, and was determined to remember straight off everything he taught
me. After listening to every word he said, concentrating as hard as possible, that evening in my clumsy handwriting I wrote it all down in my
notebook, and even when I was wrapped up in bed ready for sleep, I ran
over the details again and again: "That's done this way . . . the front is
made like this . . . you've got to be careful here"; I was probably making
shutters in my dreams. The next day, without needing another lesson, I
found I was able to put it all together on my own. This being the first time
I'd made anything by myself, I was obviously a bit short on technique, but
I'd watched the men in Yokohama (when they let me) and remembered
my boss's instructions, so I managed it fairly well; and I was soon moved
on to making sliding doors, front doors, and fine lattice doors.

One comes up against all sorts of problems, it's inevitable, but the real
key to success is using good-quality tools and, particularly, getting to
know the character of each of them. Each of a hundred saws, for instance,
will have its own slightly different features: the way the teeth have been
set and rasped, the space between them, the way the blade flexes, etc.
And you have to recognize within seconds of touching the wood just how
the thing handles. But, having said that, I've got to admit that even after
all these years I can only turn out a few sliding doors—to take one example—that I'm really satisfied with. It's hard to believe, but it's almost impossible to make a set of four with absolutely no defects.

Let me try and explain just one of the problems—the traditional frame
(they're simpler nowadays). For this you had to cut several dozen lengths
of wood. In all, there might be three hundred joints when these were fitted together, and each had to click in perfectly when pushed into place.
Too tight, and the wood buckled; too loose, and the frame rattled. And
almost always you'd find three or four that were somehow just too tight.
A little tap with a mallet would usually tuck them in, but the wood there
might warp later on. It only took a tiny error and you missed the mark.

Making a sliding door

Still, there are some men who deserve to be called true craftsmen. One of my uncles, for instance, made furniture in Tokyo, and I remember seeing a lattice door he'd done; it was stunning. The wood was covered entirely with a thin layer of bamboo bark, and the frame itself was made up of several hundred struts assembled perfectly, not even a whisper out of true. We didn't have any synthetic adhesives back then, so he'd stuck the bamboo bark on with "grain lacquer," made by mixing wheat flour with lacquer, which bonded well; paste would have come away if anything had knocked a joint. The way he'd combined the two materials in a graceful network of struts, without damaging anything, was superb. There can be very few men alive now skilled enough to produce work like that.

Joiners handle timber in a very different way to carpenters. A carpenter will ink a line where he wants to cut the wood, but in my trade you wouldn't get anywhere with lines as thick as that. Instead, we used to score them with a very sharp knife called a *keshiki*. And if you'd drawn the line so that the inside edge of the blade was the correct measurement, you absolutely had to saw the wood along that edge; you could ruin the job by cutting along the wrong side of it. That's how difficult the work was. The saw used for this sort of precision job was a *dotsuki*, used only by joiners, and with thirty-five teeth per inch. There was a trick we sometimes played to demonstrate just how fine a standard of work this tool could produce. In those days people slept with their heads on wooden box pillows; the idea was to sneak into a room where someone was sleeping and saw the pillow in half lengthwise without waking him up. I've done the trick myself on several occasions.

Anyway, after I'd worked as an apprentice in the joinery firm for about four years, I started to have second thoughts. "If I stay here, I'll only ever learn fittings," I told myself, "but I'd also like to make chests of drawers and various sorts of cabinets"; so I resigned, returned to my hometown, and went to work for a cabinetmaker.

That's where I "graduated." I could bore you stiff about it all if I

Mr. Umehara

wanted to, so I'll stick to a few details. Take chests of drawers. These days, only the front is made of paulownia, and even that is only offcuts of the wood glued on; in my time, though, the whole thing was paulownia. The trees are generally small and, on the rare occasions when you did get a big one, if you tried cutting it into large slabs as you would with zelkova or pine, the chest always warped in the end. So, after its bark was stripped off, it was cut into pieces almost an inch thick and these were then stuck together. By carefully matching the grain, we could make a drawer six inches deep look like a single piece of wood, though in fact it was six or seven layers combined. We used a rice paste to do this, but as it was rather weak we'd knock in a number of dowels too. These were made of deutzia and were boiled first to prevent them rotting; you needed over a thousand for one chest of drawers, varying in length from one to about three and a half inches.

Professionals used to say that "unless you can plane seven-eighths board down to seven-eighths of an inch, you can never call yourself a cabinetmaker." Think about it: it sounds like nonsense, doesn't it? And of course, if the board had actually been exactly that thickness, you couldn't have done it. But the wood delivered from the lumberyard, though called seven-eighths board, was really just a fraction over this. And the test of a skilled worker was not whether he could plane off this extra fraction on just a couple of these pieces but fifty or sixty of them.

It was a beautiful piece of furniture, a chest of drawers made entirely of seven-eighths paulownia. Not that you'll find many of them around. For one thing, the inside of most chests is disappointing: if you look closely at the bottom of a drawer, searching for the join, you'll notice that although the part at the front is the full measurement, from about three or four inches back the wood is only half an inch thick. This wasn't done to cheat the customer, just to keep the cost down. And even the real thing could vary in standard depending on the quality of the wood used. There's no end to it.

But there's another tip that's worth passing on to anyone looking for a good piece: try taking out all the drawers, turning them upside down, and putting them in again from the back. If they still slide in smoothly, then it's well made. You see, paulownia dents fairly easily; with over a thousand dowels to knock in, it only needs a heavy touch with the mallet here and there for the whole thing to be just a bit out of true.

Still, one can spend a lifetime in the trade and never learn to do things quite to one's satisfaction. It's an old-fashioned approach, I know: they want quantity not quality these days, they value appearance more than genuine skill. But there are still a good many people left who can recognize fine workmanship when they see it, so the old techniques will probably somehow survive.

AT SCHOOL
AND
AT PLAY

A summer festival

Streams and Ponds

Mr. Isei Hirose (1895–)

Tsuchiura Second High School was built on the site of a group of houses that belonged to some of Lord Tsuchiya's retainers. Ours was one of those knocked down to make way for the school—we lived there until I was about five, I suppose. My father was a samurai in the Tsuchiyas' service, and had spent some time as governor of an area of Tsuchiya land in what's now Yamagata Prefecture. But after the Meiji Restoration the samurai lost their stipends so, in order to make a living, he and his former master decided to set up a company, and in 1871 they founded the Mitsuwa Trading Company. Mitsuwa wasn't just a bank in those days; it also traded in rice, beans, and general wholesale goods.

Our house was surrounded by a moat and backed by open fields of rice and lotus plants; you could see over the fields as far as Nishimon. There were nine children in our family, but I was the only boy. Whenever we went outside to play we'd take a twelve-foot ladder with us, carrying it on our shoulders: the area was such a network of streams and paddies that you couldn't get anywhere without one, and at the first piece of water we'd lay it across, file over it, and move on till we found the next obstacle.

We used to dam the smaller streams and ditches sometimes, then empty the channel to get at the fish trapped inside—we did quite well out of it, I remember. Nor have I forgotten the thrill of trying to grab a fish, squirming in the mud, with bare hands. Water chestnuts also grew in the streams; we used to pick loads of them, bake them in a pan, and eat them. They tasted a bit like lotus root.

The girls came out to play as well, of course, tucking up their kimono and padding around barefoot. It was delicious walking through the paddy fields with the mud oozing through your toes. And in March we went digging for loaches, scooping them out when we found their holes. Our clothes got filthy.

Though we hadn't any proper tackle, we fished in the rivers, too: for rods we used bamboo poles picked in the hills and, for fishing lines, hairs from a horse's tail. There were horses everywhere then, so we'd sneak up behind one and tug out a few strands. "What the hell are you up to!" farmers used to shout if they caught us at it, and we'd clear off in a hurry. But if we wanted to go fishing we needed lines, so we'd scout around elsewhere. Black or brown hair was no problem, but it was the paler kind we prized—we reckoned no fish could see it—and this sometimes meant going miles out of our way to find a gray horse.

Hooks we bought at Mr. Iseki's shop in Tajuku. Back then about the only shop in Tatsuta, where I lived, was a baked potato seller, so if you wanted anything else you had to go into town. You could get ten potatoes for a sen—Toyama was the man who sold them, he had a barbershop by Nishimon Bridge as well. And it was always me who was sent off to buy an armful of them; my sisters hadn't the nerve.

Just before I started primary school, we moved to the poorer part of Tajuku, a maze of little back streets on very low-lying ground. I remember the site of our new house had to be raised before it could be built on, and since it was difficult to move earth any great distance in those days, we dug out part of our own land. As a result, three large ponds, one nearly a third of an acre and the others about a quarter of that size, appeared in our garden—the house itself ended up about ten feet higher than the sur-rounding land. This, in one sense at least, was the height of luxury. In the floods of 1902 only our house in the whole neighborhood was left high and dry above the water, and many of our neighbors came and sheltered with us. It was bad, that time: Lake Kasumigaura rose above the lock gates blocking it off from the Kawaguchi, and boats and even houses from the other side of the railway were washed into the river.

You know, floods were so common that all the larger places kept a small boat hanging from the ceiling of the entrance hall ready to use in an emergency. Our family had two of them. But most of the time they were left unused, so we often took one onto the Kawaguchi and rowed down under the plank bridge and out into the lake for a swim or some fishing.

Catching dragonflies

In the summer I used to dig up earthworms with some friends, then fish for baby mullet in the middle of the lake; it wasn't exactly "sporting"—we sometimes hauled in twenty or thirty in an hour. And when we got tired of this we'd all dive in off the boat, or search for shellfish in the sand.

Carp were kept in the ponds in our garden, and we used to swim there as well, chasing the poor things toward the bank, trapping them and even picking them up in our hands. They were fed on silkworm grubs; but these were too big for some of the smaller fish, so we bought pond snails instead and crushed them up. There was a man who came around every day without fail, selling snails he'd caught in the rice fields—he did quite a good trade in them: people bought them either for themselves or to feed their fish with.

Apart from scaring them occasionally, we took good care of our carp, though we never managed to sell any—when we had any to sell, that is. You see, they were always being stolen in the middle of the night. Some bastard used to come along with a small dragnet and swipe the lot. We got wise to this and hammered in stakes to stop him using nets, but he managed to think up other ways of fishing them out and we never did quite put an end to it.

Soldiers used to fish in the ponds too. In the period just before the Russo-Japanese War at the beginning of this century, the army was always on maneuvers in this area. Thousands of soldiers did their battle training near Tsukuba and Yatabe, and they were billeted in people's houses. Ours was large so we had to put up as many as thirty soldiers, or ten officers. We'd stick a little notice up outside the front door, something like "X Company. Thirty men under Captain Y." We were all very patriotic in those days—thought we were doing our bit for Japan—so we didn't particularly mind the extra work: providing soup and side dishes to go with the ration of rice they brought with them, and trying to find enough mattresses to go around.

On their days off the soldiers spent their time cheerfully dangling lines in our ponds. But even my father turned a blind eye to it; after all, we could hardly have told them off, and it was much better to lose a carp to one of "our loyal troops" than to some local poacher.

From our house you could see as far as Tsukuba and beyond, and even catch glimpses of the wild geese over Shimoda. It's hard to imagine how peaceful this countryside used to be, when you look at that view today.

Shorts

Mrs. Sawa Imaizumi (1917–)

I come from a fishing family; in my day everyone in Kawaguchi was either a farmer or a fisherman on Lake Kasumigaura.

Since my parents were always out on the boat, I was pretty much brought up by my grandmother. It's funny, isn't it: now *I'm* a grandmother and it's me who looks after the grandchildren! But that's not the only thing that's been turned upside down. When I was a kid, Kawaguchi was just a single street of houses, with rice fields behind them—it was so quiet and deserted that in summer you could hear dozens of frogs croaking in the ditches.

We were a bit like tadpoles ourselves: most of our summer days were spent diving in the river off the wharf by "Hidakaya's" and swimming up and down for hours; naked, of course—no one, boys or girls, ever wore a stitch of clothing in the water. But when I was in my first year at primary school I found out there was something called "shorts." I can't remember whether I saw a picture in a book or someone told me about them, but anyway I went straight to my grandmother and asked her to make me some. She said she'd never in her whole life even seen a pair of shorts, so how could she make any. But I kept pestering her: "I want to be able to ride a bicycle, but if I wear a skirt, the wind'll keep blowing it up as I'm riding along. So please, please. . . ."

I was quite a tomboy in those days, and desperate to try riding a bike—in the end I think I was the first girl in the area to have one. And I'm not the sort of person to give up easily, so once I'd asked her I kept on at her till eventually she gave in. She got someone to explain what to do, cut the pattern out of pieces of newspaper, and finally stitched the things together out of some sort of cloth—muslin, as far as I remember.

I was over the moon, and from then on wore the shorts every day. None of the other little girls in the neighborhood had anything like them and they were all jealous. Particularly when I was swimming in the river the shorts—they were white—really stood out. All my friends said they wanted them as well, and badgered their mothers to do something with a bit of toweling or whatever; and within ten days the girls were wearing shorts of their own, and swimming proudly up and down showing them off.

In our new outfits, we'd even jump in off Taiko Bridge and cling to one of the gravel boats going downstream; then swim back, twisting through the beds of prickly lilies.

Dangerous Games

Mr. Seinosuke Otake (1896–)
Mr. Isei Hirose (1895–)

Seinosuke Otake: We used to get up to all kinds of tricks when we were boys, didn't we?
Isei Hirose: We certainly did. Do you remember making gunpowder? You were pretty good at it.
Seinosuke: I know, but it was daft—we should've known better. We mixed saltpeter, sulphur, and those charcoal sticks you put in hand warmers, and then ground them up. All you needed then was a little bamboo pipe and you had a firework. The best were ones that shot a parachute into the air: we'd pour in some powder; push the parachute, made of thick paper attached to a weight, down inside; make a fuse by rolling gunpowder up inside a long paper spill and fixing this to the bamboo; then light it. A small flame shot along the fuse, the firework exploded with a bang, and the parachute rose into the air. We used to have competitions to see who could get theirs to go highest.
Isei: Some of the kids used tubes a foot or even two feet long and crammed in as much gunpowder as possible, to boost the parachute even higher. God knows why nobody got hurt.
Seinosuke: I think I made a shotgun too, didn't I?
Isei: Yes, so did I. That was asking for trouble.
Seinosuke: To start with I just had a hollow bamboo pipe that I put gunpowder in, to fire a tiny bullet like a blowdart; but eventually I made a tin barrel that went inside the tube.
Isei: And proper shot—for birds.
Seinosuke: That's right. The guns were pretty accurate, what's more. I rather fancied myself as a marksman.
Isei: Do you remember we also made a brass case to store the powder in?
Seinosuke: We used to go and pick up empty cartridges the soldiers had thrown away during exercises. But they were a bit narrow at the end and it was difficult to get the shot in. So what we did was cut the top off, pack the powder in, then plug the cartridge with little balls of paper, put the shot on top of that, and finally plug the whole thing up with more paper.

Swordplay

Our homemade powder wasn't very powerful, though, so in the end we went and bought proper commercial gunpowder.

Isei: Yes, there was a man near Sakura village who sold the stuff. He used to let us have some on the quiet for ten or fifteen sen. It was nice, smooth powder—and we were so keen to get hold of it that walking all the way to Sakura didn't matter. You got about five ounces for ten sen.

Seinosuke: From the outside his place looked like an ordinary farmhouse, I remember.

Isei: I wonder why he sold gunpowder, then. Sometimes as many as fifteen of us kids would troop off together to buy it.

Seinosuke: You could get shot from the hardwareman, numbered according to size.

Isei: When I made the barrel for my gun, I remember I had a hell of a job getting the metal pipe inside the bamboo tube. And the butt was just an ordinary block of wood.

Seinosuke: There was nothing wrong with the trigger, though—I thought it was rather ingenious. It was attached to a spring with a tiny firecracker on the end; you pulled the trigger back into a notch cut in the bamboo, and when it was released—a little flick is all it took—the spring shot forward, the cracker hit the cartridge and went off, the gunpowder ignited, and the charge burst out of the barrel.

I used to keep the fact that I had a gun secret from my parents, but I hate to think what would've happened if it had gone off accidentally and— I don't know—the house had caught fire or something.

Isei: You hid it, did you? I used to make guns and things in the house and my family even watched me doing it, but nobody ever said anything. This was just after the war with Russia, so people probably thought it was a good sign to see boys playing with guns.

Seinosuke: I got burned quite badly once. I was walking along with a lot of firecrackers in my pocket. I stuck my hand in suddenly without thinking; and my fingernails must have rubbed against them because they all

Teasing a snake

started going off. It hurt like hell afterward, but I couldn't tell my parents so I went to the doctor secretly—it was old Dr. Tanabe in Uchinishi; he'd been Lord Tsuchiya's doctor at one time, I think.

Isei: But I bet it didn't make you give it up?

Seinosuke: No, of course not. In fact there was a teacher at school who took us out sometimes to shoot birds in the woods on Mt. Oiwata; I used to bring my homemade rifle along. Our teachers didn't make a fuss about things the way they do nowadays. I doubt whether the parents would even have held the teacher responsible if there'd been an accident or anything.

Isei: By the way, do you remember playing *namari buttsuke*?*

Seinosuke: Yes—all the time. We even used to color the tiles with pictures of samurai or Sumo wrestlers on them. We put a lot of work into it.

Isei: And we played *sekihitsu otoshi*** too, didn't we?

Seinosuke: We did, we did. We'd do anything to win, even oil and polish the sticks.

Isei: And do you remember using cyanide to catch fish and insects?

Seinosuke: Oh yes. After all, it was me who got the stuff. My father was a good friend of the local chemist, and the fellow helping him in the shop used to say, "All right, then, if you know what you're doing," and he'd give me a bit. I kept it in a poison jar—very effective, it was, with insects and things. It seems incredible now, but I just used to hang the jar, full of poison, on the wall at home.

Isei: What we did with fish was wrap the powder in a piece of cloth, tie it on the end of a stick, and dip it in the river; and in no time at all, fish would float up to the surface. You could bring them around by putting them in clean well water. Surprisingly enough, we even ate the things later; it didn't seem to do us any harm. Another way of doping them was with a mixture of crushed prickly-ash and tea berries.

Seinosuke: But if a policeman had ever caught us, we'd have been in a real spot, so were always careful, and ran for it when anyone came our way.

Isei: Yes, we were careful—and lucky. They were dangerous, some of games we played. But we're still here, eighty years later, to tell the story.

* A game played with square lead tiles about the thickness of cardboard. They were often decorated with pictures of animals and well-known samurai. Each boy brought along his own tiles and laid them in a line on the floor. The first player flung one of his collection against one on the floor, and if he managed to make the tile flip over he won it. But if it remained face-up, play passed on to the next person.

** This involved the slate sticks that were used at school for writing with. The stick was cut in half and the two pieces rubbed against a stone to flatten out the bottom part, making them semi-cylindrical. The tip was then cut into a downward-pointing wedge and the flat surface rubbed in oil to make it slide easily. The game was played on a writing slate, which had a low rim around it. One player slid his stick across the slate, aiming its tip at its opponent's side, and tried to knock it off the board. If he succeeded he kept it; if he failed the other player had his turn. Slate sticks were expensive, so some children couldn't afford to play.

The Strike at the Girls' School

Mrs. Kin Kikuchi (1904–1983)

I taught flower arranging at Tsuchiura Second High School for twenty years. I particularly remember one occasion when I went along to be introduced to a new headmaster. We chatted about various things, and after a while he asked me which year I'd graduated from the school in. "1926," I replied. "1926?" he said. "So you must have been here when *that* happened," and he drew back, looking rather stunned. . . .

Though it all took place more than fifty years ago, I've never been able to forget it—it still seems as clear as anything. It was when I was in my second year. In February 1925 the pupils, led mainly by the boarders, went on strike to try and get Mr. X., the headmaster, sacked.

It seems that the deputy head, a Mr. Y., didn't get on at all with him, and the teachers split into two groups—those supporting the headmaster and those in favor of his deputy. For some reason, this Mr. Y. was very popular with the boarders. I'm not sure whether he put them up to it or whether they acted on their own, but anyway the boarders got together and began to press for the headmaster's dismissal. I wasn't a boarder and didn't actually like Mr. Y. much: he seemed to me a bit weak and effeminate. But the boarders had a good deal of influence, and rumors started flying around that anyone who didn't join in the strike would get beaten up, so the day girls had no choice but to take part, though we didn't really know what we were going on strike about.

I'll never forget what happened one morning during an English class with Mrs. Terada. She was a very enthusiastic teacher and her English was fluent. She came in, gave us a cheery "Good morning," and then said in English, "Please open your books." We all did as we were told. At that point a commotion started at the back of the room, and when I looked around to see what was going on, I saw rows of girls sitting there, grim-faced, exchanging glances. Then suddenly one of them slammed her book shut. All around her, other girls started closing their books, the sound gradually spreading right around the room and, before long, they were standing up and leaving. The teacher had absolutely no idea what the

High-school girls

disturbance was all about and just stood there looking astonished.

When we got out of the classroom, we ran over to the Memorial Hall on the far side of the school. The senior girls had shut themselves inside it, so we all sat squashed together on the steps, in a state of great excitement. Then fifty more girls from West House came running up. I was in East House—there must have been about fifty in each; another thirty girls, who were doing practical courses, had the sense not to get involved.

The whole school was in turmoil. Mrs. Abe, who gave needlework classes, walked up and down in front of us, tears streaming down her cheeks, completely overcome. In a strangled voice she managed to say, "I really do understand . . . why you're doing this. But . . . just for today . . . won't you calm down a bit and come back into class?" It had never occurred to me that teachers could break down like this. Privately, I began to regret what we'd done, and I felt awful about making Mrs. Abe cry.

The teacher in charge of our class was Mr. Ishiyama. He was a short, rather stocky man but very nice, and he lived quite near me in Omachi. In the mornings, when I went past his house on the way to school, his wife would often run out to say her husband had forgotten his lunch box, and would I mind giving it to him. And now this same Mr. Ishiyama was also standing there, with tears in his eyes, saying: "Why are you doing this? If there was something wrong, couldn't you just have come and discussed it with me?" I couldn't bear it.

Meanwhile, the leader of the seniors, a fiery, headstrong girl called K., had gone into the headmaster's study and was making a speech. (She went on to university in Tokyo afterward, and got involved in some complicated love affair which ended with her trying to commit suicide with a man.) Anyway, apparently she stood on his desk, lecturing him at the top of her voice. It must have been an extraordinary sight: K., dressed in the usual schoolgirl's uniform of the time—a kimono, with a long, pleated skirt—and carrying a white fan, standing on a desk shouting at the headmaster.

But the drama ended fairly quickly: the School Board brought things under control without too much trouble, and were determined to stop any news of it leaking out. Soon afterward both the headmaster and his deputy were demoted; but not a single pupil was expelled.

The person I felt most sorry for was Mr. Ishiyama. He was so upset about the incident that two or three days after it ended, he had a stroke and died without regaining consciousness. This shocked us to the core, and many of the girls burst into tears when they heard about it. A number of us—including me—had just blindly followed the others, but, with his death, we suddenly realized just what we'd done. By then, of course, it was too late to be sorry.

Songs and Schooldays

Mrs. Mineko Toyama (1903–)

There weren't any exercise books in my day—I went to the Girls' Primary School near Tsuchiura Hospital—so we all had slates. When our slate sticks got worn down to a stump, we'd wedge them in long tin tubes, and kept on using them till there was literally nothing left. And if you ever lost it, you not only got into trouble but it wasn't replaced: there were none to spare, quite simply, so from then on you'd just have to watch the others writing.

For calligraphy practice, we used to bring newspaper to school to write on; since my family was one of the few that subscribed to a paper, I brought as much as I could and shared it out. But one never wasted paper if one could help it—it was too useful—so if the weather was good we'd go outside, smooth over the sandpit, and practice writing our Chinese characters in the sand. The teacher would write the character for "big" and we'd copy it, singing it out loud as we traced the shape with a finger. Then "mountain," copied and recited in the same way. If the sand was too dry we'd sprinkle the pit with a watering can; the strokes were much neater then.

I remember the windows in our classroom were sliding paper screens, not glass—handmade paper with a brownish tinge, and slogans stuck in prominent places on them, saying "Feeling Secure Is the Greatest Enemy," or "After a Victory, Fasten Your Chin Strap Even Tighter!" They were everywhere then, these slogans, just after the war with Russia.

Singing lessons were held in a different room, and to get there we had to walk along a wooden veranda that was soggy underfoot whenever it rained; the buildings as a whole were shabby and run-down.

Our music teacher was Mr. Otani, the only person in the school who wore Western clothes. I always had the impression he was very old, so probably born well before the 1870s when we started opening up to the West. But he played the organ beautifully; his age made no difference there. Incidentally, we didn't use the "Do, Re, Mi" system but one that went "Hi, Fu, Mi, Yo, I, Mu, Na"—counting from one to seven.

"Raindrops" was something we often used to sing:

> One drop, two drops, in the rushing stream.
> Rainy days, windy days, keeping on and on.
> We must be the same, yes, we must be the same.
> We must not be lazy, keeping on and on.

At the end of the nineteenth century, government policy was based on building a "rich country with a strong army," and Confucian ideas dating back to the feudal period were still very important; as a result, many of the songs at school were terribly patriotic and "improving." The "Pickled Plum Song" is a good example; I wonder if I can remember it all.

> It's February, it's March, and the plum tree blossoms,
>> Spring is in the air and the nightingale sings,
>> But the days pass away like a dream.
> It's May, it's June, and the plum begins to ripen.
>> Before long it falls, shaken from the branches,
>> Falls and lies there on the ground.
> They take me to town, to be weighed and sold.
>> They put me to pickle in briny water,
>> So my flesh grows as salt as the sea.
> It's July, it's August, and for three days and nights
>> They leave me to dry in the open air.
>> I don't mind, I'm serving my country.
> My skin may be wrinkled, but my spirit stays young:
>> I go and make friends with all the children,
>> I join them in all their games.
> And now in time of war I know that I am needed.

Just next to our school were the ruins of the old castle, and troops often used to assemble there before taking part in exercises—in fact thousands of them poured into the Tsuchiura area when the army held

256

maneuvers. One of the imperial princes also came sometimes as an observer; one would see him riding out of the castle surrounded by high-ranking officers, and we went to watch when his horse was being fed and washed at a spring in the grounds there. The only other horses we ever saw in the streets of the town were carthorses—work-worn things that were a far cry from these officers' gleaming beasts.

Most of the troops and officers were billeted in local houses, though generals stayed at an inn, and we always had five or six men to put up. There was a "routine" to life when we had an officer staying; it must have impressed me as a child. I remember the way the orderly would rush out as soon as the man—a captain, perhaps—got in. The officer would call out to my mother to say he was back, flop down on the step in the hall, and his orderly would kneel there undoing his boots as quickly as he could. His tunic, once unbuttoned, was whisked away and hung on a coat hanger, his trousers neatly folded in a corner. If the captain wanted a bath, the orderly would stoke the fire and, when the water was at just the right temperature, he'd call out, "Your bath is ready, sir"; he even had to scrub the man's back for him. And when the officer emerged, the orderly would dress him in a fresh set of clothes, and take the dirty stuff down to the pantry and scrub that too till it was spotless.

All this made my mother feel sorry for him, but though she offered to help with the washing, he almost always refused: "No, no, don't worry, I'm used to it," he'd say. On the few occasions when she did do the laundry for him, she found the coarse uniforms that needed cleaning so ingrained with dirt that they had to be boiled twice before it all came out. As for mending things, which was also the orderly's job, we soon found that he was far handier with a needle and thread than any of the women in the house, including our best maids.

So you can see how regimented things were in this country then, and why we children were made to sing the "Pickled Plum Song" in our shrill little voices. Fortunately, not all the songs were patriotic; there was "A

Pattern of Flowers," for instance:

> At New Year the yellow adonis blooms,
>   The flower of long life and joy.
> And then plum blossom scents the air,
>   While warblers sing in every village.
> In March at the time of the Dolls Festival,
>   The red of peach trees covers the hills.
> In April the pear and cherry flower;
>   Their delicate beauty takes the eye.
> The fields before long are covered in green,
>   Wisteria clusters float in the wind.
> Sweet-scented iris lines the lake banks,
>   And morning glory entangles the hedge.
> Standing clear of the meadow's mud,
>   White lotus buds are drenched in dew.
> On summer evenings, as we view the moon,
>   The evening primrose shyly opens.
> At the bush clover's foot when October comes
>   Grow bellflowers, day lilies, and valerian.
> In autumn the fragrant chrysanthemum blows,
>   Lasting symbol of our imperial line.
> At the year's end, though the wind is keen,
>   The loquat tree flowers in the grove.

雁雁渡れ
大きな雁は先に
小さい雁は後に
仲よく渡れ
一、二、三、

定価3,500円
in Japan